Mother & Daughter Jewish Cooking

Mother
& Daughter
Jewish

ROBSON BOOKS

Cooking

Two Generations of Jewish Women share
Traditional and Contemporary Recipes

EVELYN ROSE AND JUDI ROSE

*For Myer, Marc, Jamie, David, Alan, Nanna, and Poppy
With thanks and love*

First published in Great Britain in 2001 by Robson Books, 10 Blenheim Court,
Brewery Road, London N7 9NT

A member of the Chrysalis Group plc

First published in the USA by William Morrow, and imprint of HarperCollins, New York

British Library Cataloguing in Publication Data
A catalogue record for this title is available from the British Library

ISBN 1 86105 383 5

Book design by Susan McClellan

Typeset by SX Composing DTP Ltd, Rayleigh, Essex
Printed and bound in Spain by Book Print, S.L.

CONTENTS

ACKOWLEDGEMENTS

THIS BOOK REFLECTS THE LIVES AND LIFESTYLES OF MANY PEOPLE WHO HAVE generously given of their time and experience, and we are deeply grateful for their unstinting help and support.

Several people have been particularly closely involved: our editor, Lorna Russell; our copy-editor, Rosalind Beckman; and Evelyn's assistant, Diane Ward. We have also had tremendous support and encouragement from our immediate family — Evelyn's children and grandchildren, Judi's brothers and their families.

However, the book could not have seen the light of day, written as it was simultaneously on two continents with an ocean in between, without the computer skills of Judi's husband, Marc Gerstein, and Evelyn's husband, Myer Rose.

FOREWORDS

THE ONLY TIME I REMEMBER SEEING MY LITHUANIAN GREAT-GRANDMOTHER, Pesha Mendelsohn, she seemed to my childish eyes a tiny figure, lying in an iron frame bed in the Home for Aged Jews in Manchester. I don't remember speaking to her—she spoke mostly Yiddish and I was a second-generation English-speaking seven-year-old—but from that day onwards, she has remained a source of fascination to me, even though I have had to rely on the memories of my mother and grandmother.

What I loved best was to hear how Pesha made the cream cheese to sell in my great-grandparents' little dairy in the heart of the Jewish immigrant district.

A hundred years ago, in the days before pasteurisation, when milk soured easily, she would set a large bowl of it on top of the coal-fired kitchen range. When it had separated into curds and whey, she would hang it to drain on the washing line in a snowy-white pillowcase until it was time to take it down, stir in the *smetana* (soured cream) which she had skimmed off the curds, and season it ready for sale.

Pesha's daughter and granddaughter carried on the tradition by making wonderful *kaes kuchen* (cheesecake), and I have tried to do the same—albeit with bought cream cheese and reduced-fat soured cream.

This book is an attempt to preserve the food legacy handed down by all our mothers, grandmothers and great-grandmothers, but to modify it to suit the life we live now, and to introduce other dishes that are imbued with the same spirit yet are looking towards the future.

—Evelyn Rose

MY CULINARY INFLUENCES BEGAN EARLY.

While he was still in the womb, Frank Lloyd's mother read him books on architecture. In preparation for *my* arrival, my mother feasted on a sinfully rich chocolate cake named after the Queen of Sheba, a creamy tuna and pasta concoction gleaned in Seattle during World War II, and spicy homemade pickles made from a recipe handed down by my great-grandfather. To this day these are three of my favourite foods.

My culinary education began as soon as I was tall enough to see over the kitchen units. And each summer, with me in tow, my parents roamed Europe and the Mediterranean, seeking out new tastes and new culinary temptations, boldly going where no Jewish family from Manchester had gone before.

No matter where we stayed, my mother would track down the Jewish connection. Be it a hill town in Provence, the medieval heart of Sarajevo or a suburb of Istanbul—somehow she would unearth the local characters and persuade them to share their cherished family recipes.

As I entered adolescence, my horizons broadened. In Paris I ate *tagine* and couscous with Jewish French-Tunisians; in Florence, as a penniless student, peasant soups heady with garlic and sun-dried tomatoes. In Hong Kong, my taste buds thrilled to fragrant, fiery stir-fries, the onset of a love affair with the chilli pepper that blossomed during a stay in Texas.

And this culinary synthesis continues. At eleven months, my baby son, Jamie, slurped his way through a bowl of chilli-spiked chicken soup without batting an eyelid. When not yet two, he savours cheese soufflé as much as chopped liver.

Like the rest of his generation, Jamie will have the best of both worlds. Pesha Mendelsohn—and all the food lovers whose genes he carries—would, I'm sure, be delighted.

—Judi Rose

INTRODUCTION

LEGEND HAS IT THAT THE ART OF JEWISH COOKERY WAS BORN on the day recorded in Genesis when the matriarch Rebecca, by skilful use of herbs and spices, persuaded her husband Isaac that the savoury casserole she had made using the insipid meat from a young kid was really succulent venison. This culinary ruse ensured that her favourite son, Jacob, would become the founding father of the Jewish people.

Had the story of Israel begun not in the land of Canaan but on the steppes of Russia, Rebecca's seductive stew might have been flavoured with dried mushrooms or juniper, rather than the fragrant herbs of the Mediterranean.

Jewish cooks have always drawn their inspiration from the culture and cuisine around them, adapting local ingredients and recipes to Jewish laws and customs. Long before there was a name for it, Jews had invented 'fusion cuisine'.

While we may think of bagels as quintessentially Jewish, they are probably a descendant of the *pain échaud* or boiled bread of medieval France. Chopped liver, another triumph of Jewish cooking, most likely began life as a poor man's version of the fine goose-liver pâté made in

1

Alsace in western France. (By a strange irony, much of the goose liver used in Alsace pâtés these days is imported from kibbutzim in Israel!)

Whatever their origins, the endurance of these 'Jewish' dishes, and their ability to survive the forced transplanting of Jewish communities into new cultures and climates, has earned them a unique place in Jewish hearts and kitchens from Birmingham to Bombay.

This book continues that tradition. We have brought together many of the most enduring dishes from Jewish communities around· the world, recipes that recapture the nostalgic flavours of childhood for one generation and, for their children, bring to life a heritage they long to discover.

But although it is fascinating to look back, we believe it is just as important to look forward. So we offer you this two-generation cookbook. Evelyn's recipes are a passport to the delicious dishes of the past, tailored to today's health-conscious—and often hectic—lifestyle. Alongside these, Judi offers dishes that draw on the world of international cuisines and ingredients that are part of the way we live now, yet are very much in the spirit of the culinary synthesis that has always defined Jewish cooking past and present.

Thanks to the creativity of Jewish women throughout the centuries, Jewish food stands out as one of the most vibrant and varied cuisines in today's global village. And it continues to adapt and evolve. Judi's generation can hardly imagine a time without a food processor or access to ingredients from every corner of the globe. The next generation will be as likely to glean recipes from the Internet as from a cook book. But what will continue unchanged, we hope, is the love of food and traditions that have been passed from mothers to daughters—and now sons—across the generations.

In this book we are seeking the best of both worlds—the remembrance of tastes past and the thrill of the new. What matters in this updating of the classics and the culling of new ideas from communities around us is that we adapt and integrate them in the spirit of Jewish history, making them our own as our ancestors have always done. In doing so we continue a tradition that began more than five thousand years ago. We feel sure that Rebecca, as she seasoned the casserole that changed history, would have approved.

2

How to Use the Recipes

- Spoon measures are level unless otherwise indicated.

- Butter is lightly salted unless unsalted is specified.

- Eggs are large.

- Sugar is granulated unless caster, icing, or a variety of brown sugar is specified.

Speciality Ingredients

- **Black pepper** refers to black peppercorns freshly ground in a pepper mill and is measured in 'grinds', that is, turns of the mill.

- **Fines herbes** — a mixture of dried herbs, usually tarragon, chives, parsley and chervil.

- **Herbes de Provence** — a mixture of dried French herbs, including thyme, rosemary, bay leaf, basil and savory.

- **Morello (sour) cherries** — imported from Eastern Europe, available in jars.

- **Sea salt** — recommended in all recipes where salt is called for. In our opinion, regular salt or kosher (rock) salt imparts an unpleasant 'chemical' taste to food.

- **Soy sauce** — our recipes use Chinese-style light or dark soy sauce, not Japanese soy, which has a very different taste.

- **Worcestershire sauce** — for Kashrut reasons Worcestershire sauce must be anchovy-free when used with meat.

3

Equipment

Baking tin sizes are given for guidance only. Other tins of approximately the same size can be used, provided they are the same depth or deeper than specified.

Oven temperatures are given for guidance only, as different ovens vary in the distribution of heat and the time taken to complete the cooking of a particular food.

We recommend using pots and pans with a non-stick or stainless steel interior whenever possible.

Food Storage Times

The recommended storage times given in the recipes are based on certain assumptions:

In the freezer, all foods, whether cooked or raw, are stored in airtight containers, freezer storage bags or aluminium foil packages to prevent 'freezer burn'. The exceptions are soft or fragile foods that are 'open frozen' until firm and must then be packaged in the same way.

The recommended storage time is based on the maximum period after which deterioration of flavour or texture may take place. If foods are frozen for longer than recommended, they may not be dangerous to eat but will be past their prime.

In the refrigerator, all cooked and prepared foods are stored in airtight containers or covered with clingfilm or aluminium foil to avoid dehydration and the transference of flavours and smells from one food to another. All raw fruits and vegetables are stored in plastic bags or containers, according to variety.

Recommended storage times are based on the maximum period during which the food is pleasant and safe to eat.

4

In The Beginning:
Satisfying
Soups

'Then Jacob gave Esau . . .
a pottage of lentils'

—Genesis 25:34

THERE ARE FEW MORE COMFORTING THINGS TO COME HOME TO than a bowl of steaming chicken soup 'just like Mama used to make', that amber nectar which refreshes both body and soul. We'd go so far as to say that soups are perhaps the greatest and most enduring contribution Jewish cooks have made to international cuisine, be it for flavour, nutrition, or economy.

Jewish cooks have had a long time to practise soup making—about five thousand years! Ever since that fateful occasion when Jacob persuaded his brother Esau to part with his birthright for a tasty 'mess of pottage', soup has been a vibrant part of Jewish heritage.

Jacob's recipe hasn't survived the intervening millennia but archaeological evidence suggests it was probably made with lentils—still a key ingredient in Jewish soups, like the creamily thickened *Heimishe* Winter Soup with Lentils, Barley and Beans.

Soup is also a wonderful way to connect with the long line of Jewish women who, over the centuries, have devoted their lives to the well-being of their families. When we make a pot of Great-Grandma

5

Mendelsohn's vegetable soup (alas, we never knew her), we almost feel we're there with her in some Lithuanian *shtetl,* enjoying the warmth of the first sunshine of spring—and making a simple but elegant soup with the first tender young vegetables.

We believe that soups also have an important role in today's diet. We have friends who always have a pot of soup ready to be heated up on top of the stove or in the microwave for the unexpected guest. We call this 'everlasting soup', a direct descendant of the medieval 'cauldron soups' which were topped up daily with water, vegetables and any meat or bones available—so you never, ever got to the bottom of the cauldron!

The rich flavour of hearty soups is developed during a long, slow cooking, after which the soup is left to mature, preferably overnight. The next day, the additional depth and complexity in flavour is almost magical.

Many traditional Jewish soups are particularly nutritious, thanks to their high proportion of dietary fibre and vegetable protein—and often the absence of any kind of fat. While it's true that earlier generations of Jewish cooks prized fatty soup-meat or a plump stewing chicken as the basis for a soup, today's versions are made with lean meat. The soup is chilled overnight, so any fat still lurking in the pot solidifies and can easily be scraped off the surface. Technology helps too—a plastic fat separator has become an indispensable part of our chicken soup making.

Apart from a few chilled soups, now much prized in the Mediterranean heat of Israel, those recipes that have survived the years originated mainly in the cold climes of Eastern Europe. Drink a bowl of our Hearty Hungarian Goulash Soup and you've invested in your very own personalised central heating!

While today's generation of Jewish cooks and gourmets love those hearty, nurturing soups of their childhood, many also find themselves yearning for tastes from farther afield that now form part of modern urban living—the light, citrusy palate of Thai food, the recently discovered treasures of rustic Mediterranean cooking, the elegant *cuisine soignée* that marks the best in French home cooking.

So a traditional chicken soup can form the basis for a wonderful Oriental Chicken Soup with Crispy Crescents that combines the best of both cuisines; *Heimishe* Winter Soup with Lentils, Barley and Beans inspires a version of Tuscan Bean Soup with a Parsley Pesto; and alongside our beloved borscht, you'll find new classics like Cream of Watercress Soup or A Spring Vegetable Soup from Paris — the archetypal *potage du jour* made with whatever is in the refrigerator and a true successor to Grandma's *Milchike* Soup with Springtime Vegetables.

BEST OF BOTH WORLDS CHICKEN SOUP

Evelyn

THIS HAS ALL THE FLAVOUR OF traditional chicken soup but a fraction of the calories. The secret of a superb 'brew', as we call it, is to refrigerate or freeze the cooled liquid for several hours, during which time a metamorphosis takes place and, lo and behold, the chicken stock is miraculously changed into golden chicken soup! Remove every particle of fat from the surface and you've got a slim-line soup but with all its wonderful depth of flavour.

Makes 8 servings

Keeps 3 days under refrigeration.

Freezes up to 2 months.

½ **large young fowl, all visible fat removed**

2 **roast chicken carcasses**

3.5 **litre (6 pints) water**

2 **teaspoons sea salt**

pinch of white pepper

2 **large onions, peeled and halved**

3 **large carrots, peeled and halved lengthwise**

3 **stalks celery, leaves and top 5 cm (2 in) of stalk only**

1 **sprig parsley**

1 **very ripe tomato**

For the next day

2 **large carrots, peeled and diced**

1 **fat leek, 7.5 cm (3 in) of the white part, finely shredded**

For the garnish

Grandma Rose's Matzah Balls (page 10)

Lokshen **(noodles) (page 73)**

Put the chicken in a large, heavy saucepan with the broken-up carcasses, water, and the sea salt and pepper. Cover and bring to the boil. Remove any froth with a large, wet metal spoon. Add the onions and carrots to the pan with the celery, parsley and tomato. Bring back to the boil, then reduce the heat so that the

8

liquid is barely bubbling. Cover and continue to simmer for a further 3 hours, either on top of the stove or in the oven at 150°C (300°F/Gas 2).

Lift out the chicken and use for another purpose such as a chicken salad or chicken pie. Lift out and discard the chicken carcasses. Strain the soup into a large bowl or freezer container and discard the vegetables, which will now have given their all to the soup. When cool, cover and freeze overnight.

The next day, remove any congealed fat and return the soup to the pan.

To serve, add the diced carrots and shredded leek. Bring to the boil, then lower the heat and simmer for 15 minutes or until the vegetables are bite-tender. Garnish with matzah balls and/or *lokshen* (cooked noodles).

BABIES ARE WEANED ON IT, wedding guests celebrate with it, mourners are consoled with it—no wonder chicken soup, or 'Jewish penicillin' as it is affectionately known, is one of the most famous soups in the world.

Its genesis lies in the villages of the Russian Pale of Settlement, where for centuries poultry was the cheapest form of meat. From the weekly bird, with its fat and giblets, the clever housewife could prepare an entire Sabbath meal, starting with chopped liver and *gribenes* (crackling) and going on to soup and matzah balls (*knaidlach*), stuffed *helzel* (neck), and the bird itself, made tasty with fried onions. The flavour of all these dishes depended on the fact that a mature fowl was used rather than a young chicken.

An older bird still makes the best soup but as it is not so popular today because of its high fat content and coarse, if tasty flesh, the old method of making the soup by simmering a fowl until it had given its all and then using it as the main course has been modified.

In our interpretation, roast carcasses and half a young fowl are used to make a slim-line version. In earlier, less diet-conscious days, chicken soup reached its apotheosis when, crowned with golden beads of fat, this *goldene yoikh* was brought forth in triumph at Jewish wedding feasts. Today it is still served at weddings, though without its golden crown. And is still a memorable dish to come home to on a winter's night.

9

GRANDMA ROSE'S MATZAH BALLS

Knaidlach

Evelyn

THIS RECIPE makes tender but firm *knaidlach*, which seem to suit most people—certainly there are never any left in the soup plate! The ground almonds greatly enhance the flavour.

Makes 6–8 servings
Keeps 2 days under refrigeration.
Freezes up to 1 month.

2 large eggs
2 slightly rounded tablespoons rendered chicken fat
   or soft margarine
about 75 ml (3 fl oz) warm chicken soup or water
1 teaspoon sea salt
¼ teaspoon white pepper
¼ teaspoon ground ginger (optional)
50 g (2 oz) ground almonds
50 g (2 oz) matzah meal

Whisk the eggs until fluffy, then stir in the soft fat, the warm soup or water, the seasonings, ground ginger (if using), ground almonds and matzah meal and mix thoroughly. The mixture should look moist and thick but should be not quite firm enough to form into balls. If too soft, add a little more meal; if too firm, add water 1 teaspoon at a time until you have the right consistency. Chill for at least 1 hour but overnight will do no harm. The mixture will then firm up.

Half-fill a large saucepan with 3½ litres (6 pints) of water and bring to the boil, then add 2 teaspoons of sea salt. Take pieces of the chilled mixture the size of large walnuts and roll between wetted palms into balls. Drop these balls into the boiling water, reduce the heat until the water is simmering, cover and simmer for 30 minutes without removing the lid. Strain from the water with a slotted spoon and lower into the simmering soup. You can cook the matzah balls in chicken soup

10

rather than in water. They will absorb some of the soup but with it also its delicious flavours.

Allow two matzah balls for each serving. Place in soup bowls and ladle over the soup.

~ 'SOUP DUMPLINGS'—the usual translation of *knaidlach* (also known according to the birthplace of a particular recipe as *halkes*, matzah balls and matzah *kleis*)—does poor justice to these masterpieces of traditional Jewish cuisine.

Like so many 'folk' dishes, there are no written recipes for them—they are passed down by example from one generation to another. When, for example, I asked my mother how much matzah meal went into *knaidlach*, I was invariably told 'as much as it takes', or 'enough to make a nice mixture'! I just had to learn by looking and then try to express 'as much as it takes' in visual terms. But it was worth it. Yet that's not the end of the story—one family's perfect *knaidlach* are another family's cannonballs!

~ **A time-saving tip**: The *knaidlach* can be prepared in advance and frozen until needed. Open-freeze the cooked and drained *knaidlach* on baking sheets until solid—about 2 hours—then put them into plastic bags. To use, defrost for 1 hour at room temperature, then reheat in the simmering soup.

11

ORIENTAL CHICKEN SOUP
WITH CRISPY CRESCENTS

Judi

A POT OF CHICKEN STOCK becomes fragrant and exotic with the addition of classic Szechuan flavourings—ginger, chilli and roasted sesame oil. The crispy crescents make wonderful appetisers in their own right.

Makes 4–6 servings

Soup **keeps** 3 days under refrigeration. **Freezes** up to 1 month.
Uncooked crescents **keep** 24 hours under refrigeration,
freeze up to 1 month.

12 to 14 circles 9–10 cm (3½–4 in) diameter cut out from
    very thinly rolled-out puff pastry

For the filling
    1 tablespoon sunflower oil
    3 spring onions, white part and 5 cm (2 in) of the green,
      finely chopped
    2 cloves garlic, minced
    75 g (3 oz) white closed cup mushrooms, cut in 1 cm (½ in) dice
    ½ teaspoon sea salt
    75 g (3 oz) cooked chicken or firm tofu, cut in 1 cm (½ in) dice
    1 small green chilli pepper, finely chopped (optional)
    1 teaspoon soy sauce
    1 cm (½ in) piece of fresh ginger, peeled and finely grated
    10 grinds black pepper
    1 tablespoon Chinese rice wine (Shaoxing), medium sherry,
      or chicken stock (page 15)
    1 teaspoon sugar
    pinch of chilli powder or crushed red pepper flakes (optional)
For frying
    3 tablespoons peanut or vegetable oil

12

For the soup

> 1.5 litres (2 pints) chicken stock (page 15)
>
> 3 spring onions
>
> pinch of chilli powder or crushed red pepper flakes
> (optional)
>
> 2.5 cm (1 in) slice fresh ginger root, peeled and sliced paper-thin
> (grate if too tough to slice)
>
> 2 tablespoons Chinese rice wine (Shaoxing) or medium sherry
> (as in ingredients on page 12)
>
> 2 teaspoons rice wine vinegar (substitute 1 teaspoon
> white wine vinegar if not available)
>
> 10 grinds black pepper
>
> 1 teaspoon sugar
>
> 1 teaspoon soy sauce
>
> 75 g (3 oz) dried rice noodles, egg noodles, or vermicelli

For the garnish

> 1 small fresh red chilli, sliced as finely as possible (optional)
>
> thinly sliced spring onions
>
> ½ teaspoon dark (roasted) sesame oil (optional)

To make the filling, heat the oil in a medium frying pan over high heat until very hot but not smoking, about 1 minute. Add the spring onions and cook, stirring, for 30 seconds, then add the garlic, followed immediately by the mushrooms, sprinkling with the sea salt. Continue to cook, stirring, over medium heat for 3–4 minutes, until the mushrooms have browned slightly.

Remove from the heat and add all the remaining filling ingredients, mixing gently. Taste and adjust the seasoning if necessary. Transfer to a bowl and allow to cool to room temperature.

Have ready a baking tray lined with a sheet of greaseproof paper. To fill the crescents, place a heaping teaspoon of the cooled filling in the centre of each pastry circle. Brush the edges lightly with water and seal firmly into a half-moon shape. Place the filled crescents on the greaseproof paper. At this stage, the crescents may be chilled or frozen until needed.

To fry the crescents, put the oil in a large frying pan or wok to fill to a depth of at least 1 cm (½ in). Have ready plenty of paper towels for draining. Heat the oil over high heat until very hot but not smoking, about 2 minutes. Add enough

13

crescents to fill the pan in a single layer without crowding, then fry over moderate heat until crisp and golden brown, 1–2 minutes. If necessary, reduce the heat further to prevent the crescents from browning too quickly. Turn over and fry the other side until brown. The oil should remain hot enough to sizzle whenever a fresh batch of crescents is added. As each batch is cooked, remove and drain on paper towels.

The crescents can be kept at room temperature for up to 1 hour at this stage, then reheated and crisped up for a few minutes under the grill just before serving.

To make the soup, put the stock in a large saucepan. Slice the spring onions as thinly as possible, separating the white part from the green and reserving the green part. Add all the soup ingredients except the noodles and the green part of the spring onions to the stock. Heat gently until steaming, then add the uncooked noodles. Do not allow the soup to boil or it will become cloudy. Half-cover the pot and keep on a very low heat until ready to serve.

To serve, slice the chilli (if using) as thinly as possible. Pour the soup into shallow serving bowls, sprinkle each serving with a few rings of chilli and spring onion, and a drop of sesame oil, if desired. Pass the crescents in a basket.

14

WHILE THERE'S NOTHING quite like a bowl of traditional Jewish chicken soup, soups based on chicken broth feature in a multitude of world cuisines from Hungary to Hawaii. The Orient is no exception, with numerous versions of the 'amber nectar', fragrant with ingredients like ginger, chilli, lemon grass and garlic. Incorporating local ingredients has been the key to the creation and evolution of Jewish food over the centuries — to Jewish cooks in Cochin or Karachi, spicing up chicken stock with soy or ginger was the most natural thing in the world.

If you're the sort of cook who likes to improvise, this dish offers great scope. Add quick-cooking vegetables like bean sprouts or frozen peas and some cooked noodles or rice to the steaming soup a few minutes before serving. Or omit the soy and add paper-thin slivers of fresh lemon grass for a Thai-style version.

TRADITIONAL BEETROOT BORSCHT

Evelyn

Borscht, with its glorious ruby colour, is a soup that delights the eye as well as the palate. By chopping all the vegetables in the food processor, the flavour can be extracted from them very quickly, producing a very fresh-tasting soup. The processor also helps to distribute the beaten eggs that are used to thicken the soup so there's little chance of them curdling.

Makes 6–8 servings
Cooked beet juice **keeps** up to 4 days under refrigeration;
the complete soup, for up to 2 days. **Freezes** up to 2 months.

900 g (2 lb) of old beetroots, peeled, or 3 bunches of young beetroots,
    trimmed and cut in 2.5 cm (1 in) cubes
1 medium carrot, peeled and cut in 2.5 cm (1 in) cubes
1 medium onion, peeled and cut in 2.5 cm (1 in) cubes
1.4 l (2½ pints) vegetable stock (for dairy borscht) or meat or chicken
    stock (for meat borscht)
1 teaspoon sea salt
15 grinds black pepper
2 tablespoons sugar

To thicken
    3 tablespoons lemon juice
    3 large eggs

For the garnish
    125 g (6 oz) or three 225 g (8 oz) potatoes, halved and boiled until tender

Have ready a large saucepan. Process the vegetables in the food processor in two batches until very finely chopped. Put in the saucepan with the stock, sea salt, pepper and sugar. Bring to the boil, cover and simmer for 20 minutes, until the vegetables are soft and the liquid is a rich, dark red.

Pour the contents of the saucepan through a coarse strainer into a bowl, pressing down firmly to extract all the juice, then discard the vegetables. Return the strained juice to the saucepan and leave over low heat.

16

Put the lemon juice and the whole eggs into the food processor and process for 5 seconds, until well mixed. With the motor running, pour two ladlesful of the hot beetroot juice through the feed tube and process for a further 3 seconds, then add to the beetroot juice in the pot and heat gently, whisking constantly until the soup is steaming and has thickened slightly. Do not let it boil or it will curdle. When the egg has 'taken' and thickened the soup, the bubbles on the surface will disappear. Taste and adjust the seasoning so that there is a gentle blend of sweet and sour.

The soup reheats well but remember not to let it boil or it will curdle. Garnish each serving with pieces of boiled potato.

Variation

BORSCHT ON THE ROCKS

225 g (8 oz) soured cream
ice cubes

Make the soup with vegetable stock. Chill thoroughly. Just before serving, whisk in the soured cream. Fill wineglasses a third full with ice cubes and fill up with the chilled borscht.

MY MOTHER USED TO MAKE two kinds of borscht. One, cabbage borscht, is a kind of Jewish *pot-au-feu,* with meat (usually brisket) cooked in the soup, resulting in a happy exchange of flavours. But the borscht I remember with particular pleasure is beetroot borscht, garnished with a small boiled potato. My mother had to grate the beetroots by hand, using a *rebeizen* or small handheld grater. Praise be, then, for the advent of the food processor, which takes seconds to do the same job!

CREAM OF WATERCRESS SOUP WITH A TOASTED WALNUT GARNISH

Judi

THIS EXQUISITE PALE GREEN summer soup is satisfying and sophisticated. It's thickened with potatoes, not flour, giving the soup a velvety texture, while the toasted nuts add a surprising and delicious finishing touch. Try to use walnut halves or whole nuts rather than the cheaper walnut pieces, which come from the bottom of the sack and are often dusty. It can be served hot or chilled but in either case the flavour is best if the soup is made at least 12 hours before you plan to serve it. For a touch of French elegance, replace the soured cream with crème fraîche.

Makes 6–8 servings

Keeps 2 days under refrigeration. Purée **freezes** up to 2 months.

250 g (9 oz) watercress
60 g (1½ oz) butter
1 medium onion, finely chopped
1 fat leek, 7.5 cm (3 in) of the white part thinly sliced
1 large baking potato about 225 g (8 oz), peeled and thinly sliced
1.2 litres (2 pints) vegetable stock (or 3 vegetable stock cubes dissolved in 1.2 l (2 pints) boiling water)
1 bay leaf
1½ teaspoons sea salt
10 grinds black pepper
pinch of cinnamon
pinch of nutmeg
300 ml (10 fl oz) milk

For the garnish
3 tablespoons soured cream or crème fraîche
3 tablespoons finely chopped walnuts or whole pine kernels

18

Wash and thoroughly dry the watercress. Wrap about one-third of it in clingfilm and refrigerate. Coarsely chop the rest, stems as well as leaves, and reserve.

Melt the butter in a medium saucepan, add the onion and leek, then cover and cook over low heat until soft and golden, about 6 minutes. Add the potato, stock, bay leaf and seasonings, bring to the boil, then cover and simmer for 20 minutes, until the potato slices are tender. Add the chopped watercress, bring back to the boil and simmer, uncovered, for 2 minutes (this preserves the colour).

Remove the bay leaf, then purée in a blender or food processor until absolutely smooth. Return the purée to the rinsed saucepan and bring slowly to simmering point. Stir in the milk, remove from the heat and leave covered until cool. Refrigerate for at least 12 hours.

Toss the pine kernels in a small, heavy-based frying pan over a medium heat, shaking all the time, until they smell 'toasty', 1–2 minutes. Allow to cool, then chop finely (they should still have some 'bite' in them). Cut 8 small sprigs from the remaining bunch of watercress and coarsely chop the rest.

If serving the soup chilled, stir the chopped watercress into the cold soup. To serve hot, reheat the soup over moderate heat until simmering, stirring, then turn off the heat and stir in the chopped watercress. Taste and add extra salt and pepper if necessary.

Garnish each serving with a swirl of soured cream or crème fraîche, a sprig of watercress and a scattering of the chopped nuts.

TO CAPTURE AND CONSERVE the glorious green of leafy soup ingredients such as watercress, spinach, broccoli, or sorrel, it's necessary to break down the acids and enzymes they contain that would otherwise turn them a muddy brown during the cooking process. The solution is to add them to the bubbling soup only once the other vegetables are tender, then cook the soup briefly uncovered, so that these villains of the piece are boiled away.

You can put the same scientific principle to work to preserve the colour of other green vegetables such as peas and beans which, for the sake of convenience, you may want to cook well ahead of a meal. Make sure you have plenty of water actually boiling before you add the vegetables, then cook them uncovered in the same way until tender. Drench them immediately with lots of cold water, then drain well and arrange in a microwave-safe serving dish. Reheat, covered, on 100 percent power for 2–3 minutes and voilà! they're as green as if freshly cooked.

19

GRANDMA'S MILCHIKE SOUP WITH SPRINGTIME VEGETABLES

Evelyn

I ALWAYS ASSOCIATE THIS SIMPLE BUT ELEGANT SOUP with my mother and early summer, because before the days of frozen vegetables, one had to wait for the first garden peas to appear at the greengrocer's. My mother made it exactly as her grandmother had made it in Lithuania.

Makes 6 servings
Keeps up to 3 days under refrigeration.
Freezes up to 2 months.

40 g (1½ oz) butter or margarine
1 onion, peeled and finely chopped
4 medium-sized new potatoes, peeled if necessary
    and diced
225 g (8 oz) fresh or frozen mixed vegetables,
    including if possible baby carrots and spring peas
1 litre (1¾ pints) vegetable stock
1 teaspoon sea salt
¼ teaspoon white pepper
1 teaspoon sugar
300 ml (10 fl oz) milk
2 tablespoons cornflour
For the garnish
1 rounded tablespoon finely snipped fresh chives

Melt the butter in a saucepan over medium heat then add the onion, cover the pan and cook, stirring occasionally, until soft and golden, about 10 minutes. Add the potatoes and mixed vegetables. Cover with the vegetable stock and add the sea salt, pepper and sugar. Lower the heat and simmer, covered, for 30 minutes or until all the vegetables are tender. Stir in the milk mixed with the cornflour and simmer for 3 minutes.

20

Cool, then chill for several hours or overnight.

To serve, bring the soup back to simmering point, then garnish each serving with 1 teaspoonful of the chives.

᠃ SOME FAMILIES MAKE tiny *knaidlach* (see page 11) with butter ᠃ or margarine instead of chicken fat and serve them in this simple but delicious soup.

A SPRING VEGETABLE SOUP FROM PARIS

Judi

THIS MARVELLOUS CREAMY VEGETABLE SOUP stands out from the crowd thanks to the addition of a fresh red pepper, which adds a hint of piquancy to the creamy mixture. Unlike many soups that need to mature for hours for the flavours to develop, this tastes superb within minutes of being made. I do find, however, that allowing the freshly made soup to cool, then reheating it almost immediately, produces a more complex flavour.

Makes 6–8 servings
Keeps 2 days under refrigeration.
Freezes up to 3 months.

225 g (8 oz) young carrots
white part of a fat leek about 110 g (4 oz)
1 large red pepper
½ onion or 3 shallots
225 g (8 oz) potatoes
10 g (½ oz) butter or margarine
About 700 ml (1¼ pints) hot water or vegetable stock
1 bay leaf
1 teaspoon sea salt
¼ teaspoon white pepper
20 grinds black pepper
1 teaspoon dried *fines herbes*
225 ml (8 fl oz) milk
1 tablespoon chopped parsley or
    snipped fresh chives

Peel the carrots. Split the leek and rinse under cold running water. Cut the pepper into quarters, then remove the seeds and white pith. Peel and finely chop the onion or shallots. Peel and thinly slice the potatoes.

22

Cut the carrots, leek and pepper into approximately 2.5 cm (1 in) pieces, then chop finely in a food processor. In a medium saucepan, cook the onion or shallots in the butter over gentle heat, stirring occasionally, until soft but not brown, about 5 minutes. Add the chopped vegetables, stir well, then fry gently for a further minute. Barely cover the vegetables with hot water or stock. Add the bay leaf, salt, peppers and dried herbs, cover and simmer until the vegetables are tender, about 20 minutes.

Remove the bay leaf, then put the vegetables and their cooking liquid in the blender or food processor, and blend or process until puréed.

Put the milk into the same saucepan, add the vegetable purée and bring slowly to a simmer. If the soup seems too thick, add a little more milk. Taste and adjust the seasonings. Stir in the parsley or chives. Allow to cool and let sit for at least 15 minutes for the flavour to develop.

Reheat and serve piping hot with crusty brown bread or croutons.

23

HEARTY HUNGARIAN GOULASH SOUP

Evelyn

THIS GLORIOUS SOUP ENCAPSULATES the very essence of the cuisine of the former Austro-Hungarian Empire. Paprika, caraway seeds, garlic and lemon zest, not to mention pickled cucumber and frankfurters, all jostle for the attention of the palate. If, however, the soup is left for several hours before serving, these different flavours meld together into one harmonious whole. And if you add extra meat and potatoes, you have a true goulash!

Makes 6–8 servings
Keeps up to 3 days under refrigeration.
Freezes up to 2 months.

1 large onion, peeled and finely sliced
2½ tablespoons sunflower oil
1½ tablespoons mild paprika
1 teaspoon wine vinegar
450 g (1 lb) braising steak, cut into 1 cm (½ in) dice
1 rounded tablespoon tomato purée
1 clove garlic, finely chopped
2 teaspoons caraway seeds
1 teaspoon lemon zest
½ teaspoon dried marjoram
hot water or meat stock to cover
450 g (1 lb) potatoes, peeled and cut into 1 cm (½ in) dice
1.2 litres (2 pints) meat or vegetable stock
1 teaspoon sea salt
2 teaspoons light brown sugar
1 tablespoon cornflour mixed with 2 tablespoons cold water

For the garnish
1 small pickled cucumber, drained and diced, or
    2 frankfurters, sliced

24

Fry the onion in the oil over moderate heat, stirring occasionally, for about 10 minutes, until soft and golden, covering for the first 5 minutes. Add the paprika and stir well. Add the vinegar, meat and tomato purée and cook, stirring occasionally, over moderate heat until richly browned, about 5 minutes.

Meanwhile, chop together the garlic, caraway seeds, lemon zest and marjoram, then add them to the meat and barely cover with hot water or stock. Stir well, bring to simmering point, cover and cook for 1 hour or until the meat is barely tender. Add the potatoes together with the stock, sea salt and brown sugar. Cover and simmer 10–15 minutes more, or until the potatoes are tender. Taste and season again if necessary. Stir in the cornflour mixture, then simmer for 3 minutes. Turn off the heat and let sit for several hours for the flavour to develop.

To serve, reheat, together with the diced pickled cucumber or sliced frankfurters, until bubbling throughout.

THE STORY OF THE STONE SOUP

A MAN ONCE CAME to a village claiming he could make soup from a stone. The village folk were impressed and the stranger set up his cooking pot over a fire and added a stone and plenty of water. When it was boiling, he produced a ladle and tasted the soup. 'Delicious!' he announced. 'But, you know, with a little salt it would be just perfect.' Salt was provided and in due course, the stranger tasted his brew again. 'Mmm. Now if I had a couple of carrots, it would be extraordinary'. Carrots arrived and the stone soup continued cooking. When it was time to taste again, the cook declared, 'Superb. If you really want to add the final touch, though, bring me a potato or two . . .' Finally, after several more 'adjustments', he declared the soup ready. The villagers lined up to taste the miraculous stone soup, which was, indeed, quite delicious!

SPANISH SLIM-LINE RED PEPPER SOUP

Judi

FROM THE BASQUE REGION of Spain comes this vibrant, earthy-red soup. It has an intriguing flavour and creamy texture, despite containing no dairy products. It's also completely fat-free. Grilling the peppers adds a little extra time to the preparation but a whole extra depth and dimension to the flavour. It looks spectacular served in rustic bowls on dark plates that contrast with the rich red of the soup.

Makes 6 servings
Keeps 3 days under refrigeration. **Freezes** up to 3 months.

4 large red or orange peppers
2 tablespoons minced dried onion, or 1 large onion,
    peeled and finely chopped
1 large baking potato about 225 g (8 oz), peeled and thinly sliced
1.3 litres (2¼ pints) boiling water
3 vegetable or chicken stock cubes
½ teaspoon sea salt
10 grinds fresh black pepper
1 bay leaf
2 teaspoons dried basil or *fines herbes*

For the garnish
3 slices slightly stale brown bread

Grill and skin the peppers (see page 27). Put in a medium saucepan with all the remaining ingredients except for the garnish and bring to the boil. Cover and simmer until the potato is tender, about 25 minutes. Leave covered until it stops steaming, then remove the bay leaf and purée in a blender or food processor until absolutely smooth. Return to the washed pan and leave overnight.

To serve, reheat the soup over moderate heat, covered, until simmering, then reduce the heat. Meanwhile, toast the bread until a rich brown, sprinkle with a little sea salt, then dice into 1 cm (½ in) pieces. Put the croutons into a small bowl and offer with the soup, allowing people to help themselves.

26

GRILLING PEPPERS: Halve and deseed each pepper, cutting away the white pithy part. Arrange on a grill pan and brush very thinly with oil. Grill under a fierce heat until the skin is blackened and papery in appearance, 10–15 minutes. Remove from the heat and cover the tray with paper towels. After 10 minutes you will find the skin can easily be stripped off with the fingers, revealing juicy, perfectly cooked flesh, ready to be used as directed in the recipe.

HEIMISHE WINTER SOUP
WITH LENTILS, BARLEY
AND BEANS

Evelyn

THIS IS THE MIRACULOUS SOUP 'just like Mama used to make' which Jews in Eastern Europe often used as their main dish of the day. It is capable of infinite variations, by using different lentils, beans and cereals. This type of soup, high in fibre but almost free of fat, measures up to the latest nutritional guidelines! It is loaded with vegetable protein which they used to augment with a little braising steak.

Makes 8 servings

Keeps up to 3 days under refrigeration.

Freezes up to 2 months.

175 g (6 oz) green split peas

125 g (4 oz) red lentils

2 tablespoons pearl barley

scant 50 g (2 oz) dried white beans

225 g (8 oz) braising steak (optional but nice)

2.5 l (4 pints) meat or vegetable stock, or 2.4 l (4 pints) boiling water
    plus 5 stock cubes

2 teaspoons sea salt

10 grinds black pepper

1 teaspoon dried *fines herbes*

2 large carrots, peeled and cut into 2.5 cm (1 in) dice

2 stalks celery, cut into 2.5 cm (1 in) dice

white part of a fat leek, well washed and thinly sliced

large sprig of curly or flat-leaf parsley

1 large carrot, peeled and coarsely grated

28

The day before making the soup, put the split peas, lentils, barley, and beans into a bowl, cover with twice their depth of cold water and leave to soak overnight.

The next day, put the meat, if using, and the stock with the sea salt into a large saucepan and bring to the boil. Skim with a wet metal spoon if using the meat. Tip the split peas, lentils, barley, and beans into a fine sieve to remove any excess soaking water, then put under the cold tap and rinse thoroughly until the water that drains from them is quite clear. Add to the saucepan with the seasonings and all the vegetables except the grated carrot.

Bring back to the boil, then reduce the heat until the mixture is barely bubbling. Cover and simmer for 2 hours, then uncover and add the grated carrot. Continue to cook for 1 more hour, stirring occasionally to make sure the soup does not stick to the bottom as it thickens. The soup is ready when the lentils and peas have turned into a purée. Taste and add more seasonings if required. Remove the parsley sprig. Let the soup sit for several hours for the flavours to develop. Before serving, reheat gently until bubbling, stirring so it does not 'catch' on the bottom of the saucepan.

WHENEVER I MAKE A POT OF SOUP WITH LENTILS, two very different memories come to mind. One is of a field of women in a remote part of southern Turkey, using primitive wooden hand tools to break up the stony soil, ready for sowing the next season's crop of lentils. The other is of a display in the Israel Museum in Jerusalem showing some of the foods discovered in an archaeological dig, which were cultivated and eaten way back in 3000 BCE. And there—among the pistachio shells and the sesame and date seeds—was a little heap of lentils, irrefutable evidence that the lentil is one of the most ancient of food crops that is still eaten today. And in the twentieth century, the Turkish women still use the same methods of cultivation!

For making soup, you have a choice of two different types. There are the familiar red lentils which, along with split peas, butter beans and barley, are an essential ingredient of a true rib-sticking *heimishe* soup, and the brown lentils (more a khaki colour) which are much used in Middle Eastern cookery. There are also the deep green *lentilles du Puy*, costing almost double, which keep their shape during cooking and are used for lentil salads and accompaniments.

29

TUSCAN BEAN SOUP WITH A PARSLEY PESTO

Judi

A MOUTHFUL OF THIS SMOOTH and satisfying soup instantly evokes the hills and farmhouses outside Florence. Puréed beans thicken the soup, making it seem rich and creamy without any flour to add calories, while the pesto sauce transforms a hearty country pottage into something rich and rare. If you're pushed for time, use canned beans.

Makes 6–8 servings
Keeps 3 days under refrigeration.
Freezes up to 2 months.

250 g (9 oz) dried haricot beans
1½ tablespoons olive oil
1 medium onion, peeled finely chopped
1 large carrot, peeled and diced
2 sticks celery, peeled and diced
1.4 litre (2½ pints) hot water
3 vegetable stock cubes
1 tablespoon tomato purée
1 teaspoon salt
15 grinds black pepper
1 tablespoon chopped parsley
For the pesto
1 tablespoon parsley
3 cloves garlic, peeled
½ teaspoon sea salt
50 ml (2 fl oz) extra-virgin olive oil
175 g (6 oz) grated Parmesan cheese

30

The night before, put the beans in a large bowl, generously cover with cold water and leave to soak.

The next day, heat the oil in a large saucepan and fry the onion over moderate heat, stirring, until golden, about 4 minutes. Add the diced carrot and celery, and cook, stirring occasionally, for a further 5 minutes. Add the hot water and stock cubes, the tomato purée, salt, and pepper, and bring to the boil. Meanwhile, drain the beans, rinse under running water, and add them to the saucepan. Cover and simmer very slowly either on top of the stove or in the oven until the beans are absolutely tender, about 1½ hours.

Remove half the beans and a little of the soup and purée in a blender or food processor. Return to the pot with the chopped parsley. Leave for several hours.

To make the pesto, put all the ingredients into the food processor and process until thick and even in texture.

To serve, reheat the soup, taste for seasoning, then garnish each bowl with a generous spoonful of pesto.

IN AN IDEAL WORLD, the onion in any cooked dish would always be fried in some kind of oil or fat so that in the cooking process the starch it contains when raw is changed into sugar, giving it a sweet, mellow flavour. However, if all fats and oils are proscribed for health reasons, commercial minced dried onion is a good substitute.

I use 1 tablespoonful of the dried onion in place of every 150 g (5 oz) 5 ounces of the fresh. It doesn't work so well in dishes where a larger quantity of onion is used as a main ingredient rather than a flavouring, since dried onion, even when reconstituted in the cooking process, does not produce the same bulk or texture as the fresh variety.

31

A taste of things to come:
Enticing Appetisers

'We remember . . . the cucumbers, and
the melons, and the leeks, and the onions, and
the garlic, which we did eat in Egypt freely'

—Numbers 11:5

IT'S NOT TOO FANCIFUL TO ASSERT THAT JEWS HAVE BEEN enjoying a tasty start to a meal ever since they got the idea during the Roman occupation of Palestine many centuries ago.

For it was the Roman Epicureans who first conceived the idea of spicy or salty first courses to stimulate the appetite. These usually contained oil which, by lining the stomach, allowed the consumption of large quantities of alcohol without too many ill effects.

In Czarist Russia, the same idea was enthusiastically taken up by the aristocracy, who found a table laden with tasty starters, *zakuski*, the ideal accompaniment to a glass (or four) of vodka. Delicacies such as blinis with caviar and soured cream were daily fare for them, but even the humblest peasant in the Pale of Settlement relished a plate of schmaltz herring dressed with vinegar to accompany his glass of schnapps.

The taste for these *forspeise* has survived to this day, but has found its expression through many different foods. At one time salted and smoked herring were the favourite starters, but now it is more likely to be smoked salmon or trout.

Other traditional favourites like chopped liver can be fitted into today's lifestyle by reducing their fat content without affecting their flavour or texture.

Starters play a special role in today's entertaining. They make a statement at the beginning of a meal, setting the scene as elegant — perhaps a Smoked Salmon Roulade with a Crushed Pecan Coating; or exotic — a lightly curried Spiced Melon Cocktail (*Indische Melone*); or traditional — like the deliciously simple Chopped Egg and Onion pâté.

They can be a playground for experimentation, trying out something new and radical; or a new slant on an old theme, such as pairing a traditional Chicken Liver Pâté with Pears and a tangy redcurrant sauce.

Starters also serve to mitigate the pang of hunger guests may be feeling, at the same time stimulating their appetite for what is to follow. As such, the old adage that 'hunger is the best seasoning' often applies, so that quite simple appetisers such as fresh, ripe melon and figs in a mint and citrus dressing can have a huge impact for relatively little effort. And in today's world, that has to be good news, for starters!

33

LOWER-FAT CHOPPED LIVER

Gehakte Leber

Evelyn

THE USE OF CHICKEN LIVERS is not traditional but ensures a more delicate flavour than ox liver. The big plus of this recipe is the reduction in the normal fat content. This is achieved by using plenty of onion, which is fried in a covered pan so that the onion is cooked partly by steam and partly by frying in the fat. The caramelising of the onion helps to intensify the wonderful flavour of the dish.

Makes 4–6 servings, 10–12 if used as a spread.
Keeps up to 5 days under refrigeration.
Freezes up to 1 month.

2 tablespoons rendered chicken fat or soft margarine
2 medium-sized onions, coarsely chopped
1 clove garlic, crushed
1 teaspoon sea salt
20 grinds black pepper
good pinch of ground nutmeg
450 g (1 lb) koshered chicken livers
3 large eggs, boiled for 10 minutes, drenched with cold water,
    then shelled and halved
crackers or fingers of challah for serving

To make the pâté, melt the fat in a lidded pan, add the onions and sprinkle with the seasonings. Cover and cook over moderate heat for 15 minutes or until softened and golden-brown, stirring twice. Uncover. If the onions are not a rich brown, continue to cook them uncovered for a further 4 minutes, then add the livers and toss with the onions for 2 minutes more.

Put the contents of the pan into the food processor and process until reduced to a purée, about 30 seconds. Add the shelled and halved eggs and process until they are either finely chopped (use a pulse action for better control) or puréed, as preferred. Taste and add more seasoning if necessary.

34

Turn into a pottery bowl, mark decoratively with the tines of a fork, cover with clingfilm, then refrigerate for at least 6 hours.

Serve with crackers or fingers of challah. A bowl of dill pickles makes a piquant contrast.

~ ONE OF THE MOST delectable dishes in the repertoire of Jewish cuisine, chopped liver used to be a regular on the Shabbat menu. It is said that the dish was invented by the Jewish poultry dealers of Alsace, France, using goose livers. Certainly when it is processed to a smooth consistency, it has a very similar texture to pâté de foie gras, but with hard-boiled eggs and rendered chicken fat replacing the butter of the original.

Be that as it may, every Jewish cook has her or his own version and views on the right texture. Traditional *gehakte leber* used to be made using a *hackmesser*—a one-handed chopping blade. You can often pick these up in a shop selling old kitchen equipment. My mother-in-law gave me one as part of my trousseau to ensure that I always chopped the liver—or the herring or the egg and onion—and never put it through the mincer. However, the advent of the food processor has changed all that: with care, you can now get the same result as when chopping by hand. I have reduced the fat content as far as possible without spoiling the glorious texture.

35

CHICKEN LIVER PÂTÉ WITH PEARS AND A CITRUS AND REDCURRANT SAUCE

Judi

THIS DELICIOUS HORS D'OEUVRE OFFERS the best of both worlds: the rich, nostalgic taste of traditional chopped liver and the fresh, surprising flavours of a fruity, citrus-scented sauce. Sweet ripe pears in a tangy dressing complement the flavours perfectly.

Makes 6–8 servings
Keeps 4 days under refrigeration. **Freezes** up to 1 month.

300 g (10 oz) redcurrant jelly
juice of 1 orange and 1 lemon (150 ml (5 fl oz) altogether)
2 teaspoons cornflour
50 ml (2 fl oz) sweet red wine, such as kiddush wine
4 ripe eating pears such as Williams or comice pears
50 ml (2 fl oz) vinaigrette dressing (page 195)
1 recipe Lower-fat Chopped Liver (page 34)
110g pack mixed salad leaves
paprika
6–8 small sprigs of fresh herbs such as parsley, chervil or dill
6 slices brown bread, toasted

To make the sauce, put the redcurrant jelly into a small pan, add the citrus juices and bring slowly to the boil, whisking gently until the jelly has melted. Mix the cornflour and wine to a smooth liquid and add to the pan, mixing well and bubble over moderate heat until the mixture looks clear, about 3 minutes. Pour into a jug with a narrow pouring spout and chill.

Peel, core and halve the pears, then put in a non-metal container large enough to hold the fruit in 1 or 2 layers. Immediately pour over the vinaigrette, cover and leave to marinate in the refrigerator overnight or at room temperature for several hours.

36

To serve, place 2 scoops of the chicken liver pâté on each serving plate, pour a little sauce around, then arrange 2 pear halves and a small heap of salad leaves at the side, pouring any leftover vinaigrette on to the salad. Dust the pâté with a little paprika, then garnish with a sprig of herbs. Toast the bread and cut into fingers. Wrap while warm in a linen cloth or napkin, place in a basket and pass the warm toast around.

PÂTÉ SCHMATÉ

WITH A TEXTURE that is as smooth as silk, chicken liver pâté in the Jewish style is a fairly new arrival on the Jewish food scene and it's all thanks to the food processor. What gives this dish such a rich flavour is the golden-brown fried onion used in place of the raw onion that's usually added to traditional chopped liver (*gehakte leber*). When the onion is gently fried, its starch content is changed into sugar, producing a sweet, rich flavour (think of steak and onions). The chicken livers are tossed with the browned onion for a few minutes so they also absorb some of the rich, sweet flavours. Because the hard-boiled eggs are so finely puréed, the whites do not become wet in the freezer, so you can safely freeze the pâté for up to 1 month without spoiling the texture.

37

CHOPPED EGG AND ONION

Evelyn

A SCOOP OF THIS PÂTÉ teamed with one of chopped liver (see page 34) and served with fingers of fresh challah makes an elegant starter. Note: for a dairy meal, soft butter can be used instead of the other fats.

Makes 6 servings as a starter, 15 as a spread.
Keeps up to 1 day under refrigeration. **Do not freeze.**

1 bunch spring onions, trimmed, plus 4 inches of the green
8 hard-boiled large eggs, drenched in cold water, then shelled
   and halved
175 g (6 oz) soft margarine or rendered chicken fat
½ teaspoon sea salt
10 grinds black pepper
crackers or challah for serving

Put the spring onions into the bowl of the food processor and pulse for 3 seconds until roughly chopped. Add all the remaining ingredients and pulse for a further 5 seconds, just short of a smooth pâté texture. Turn into a small gratin dish, smooth the top level and mark with a pattern using the blade of a knife. Cover with aluminium foil and chill for at least 1 hour before serving.

  ❧ YOU MIGHT CLASS THIS AS A PÂTÉ—traditionally made, like chopped liver and chopped herring, with a hand-held chopping knife or *hackmesser*. The long and tedious job was often performed by one of the men of the family, using a *hackbrettel*—a wooden chopping board with sides. The food processor does the job in seconds and exactly replicates the texture of the hand-made version.

38

COURGETTE PÂTÉ

Vegetarian 'Chopped Liver'   *Judi*

THIS RICHLY FLAVOURED DISH makes a light but satisfying starter. It's also a great way to use up courgettes that have gone slightly soft. Be generous with the parsley to ensure a pastel-green pâté, prettily speckled with flecks of herbs. Have some fun with your guests: more often than not, no one can guess what the main ingredient is!

Makes 6–8 servings as a starter, 10 as an appetiser on crackers.
Keeps 2 days under refrigeration. **Do not freeze.**

2 tablespoons butter or margarine
1 medium onion, peeled and thinly sliced
700 g (1½ lb) courgettes, trimmed and thinly sliced
½ teaspoon sea salt
10 grinds black pepper
pinch of cayenne pepper (or chilli powder)
1 heaped tablespoon chopped fresh parsley
3 hard-boiled large eggs, shelled and cut in quarters
paprika
brown bread, toasted

Melt the butter or margarine in a medium pan over low heat and cook the onion, stirring frequently until it has turned a rich gold, about 6 minutes. Add the courgettes and seasonings and toss well. Cook over medium heat, shaking the pan occasionally, until the courgettes feel tender when pierced with a sharp knife and are golden brown, about 5 minutes.

Put the parsley in the food processor with the hard-boiled eggs and the cooked vegetable mixture, together with any pan juices. Process until the mixture becomes a smooth pâté, about 30 seconds. Check the seasoning, adding a little more salt or pepper to taste. Turn into a terrine or pottery serving dish, cover and chill for several hours.

To serve, leave at room temperature for half an hour, then lightly sprinkle the top with a little paprika. Serve with lots of warm brown toast.

39

ALSACE HERBED SMOKED SALMON AND CREAM CHEESE TARTE

Evelyn

THIS IS AN UPDATED VERSION of the classic *quiche au fromage blanc* of Alsace — a superb savoury cheesecake, topped just before serving with the finest-quality smoked salmon.

Makes 8 servings. Serve the same day.
Leftovers **keep** up to 2 days under refrigeration. **Do not freeze.**

For the pastry
  125 g (4 oz) plain brown flour
  125 g (4 oz) plain white flour
  ½ teaspoon sea salt
  2 teaspoons icing sugar
  1 teaspoon dried *herbes de Provence*
  1 rounded tablespoon chopped parsley
  1 teaspoon mustard powder
  300 g (10 oz) butter or margarine, chilled and cut in 2.5 cm (1 in) cubed
  1 large egg, beaten with 1 teaspoon wine or cider vinegar
    and 1 tablespoon cold water
For the filling
  350 g (12 oz) cream cheese
  1 tablespoon cornflour
  4 large egg yolks plus 1 whole large egg
  225 ml (8 fl oz) double cream
  1 teaspoon lemon zest
  ½ teaspoon sea salt
  15 grinds black pepper
For the topping
  225 g (8 oz) best smoked salmon, cut in 5 cm (2 in) squares
  225 ml (8 fl oz) reduced-fat soured cream
  8 small fronds fresh dill

40

To make the pastry, put the dry ingredients, herbs and the well-chilled fat into the bowl of the food processor. Mix the egg, vinegar and water, then turn on the machine and pour down the feed tube, pulsing only until the mixture looks like a very moist crumble. Tip it into a bowl and gather together into a dough.

Turn the pastry on to a board or work surface sprinkled with a very light layer of flour. Knead it gently with the fingertips to remove any cracks. Flatten into a 2.5 cm (1 in) thick disc, wrap in aluminium foil or clingfilm and chill in the refrigerator for at least ½ hour. (At this stage it can be frozen for up to 6 weeks or refrigerated for 2 days).

Choose a loose-bottomed flan ring, 23–25 cm (9–10 in) in diameter and 2.5–3 cm (1–1¼ in) deep. Roll the chilled dough into a circle 28–30 cm (11–12 in) in diameter, then ease into the flan ring, pressing it well into the sides. Trim off any excess. Prick the shell all over with a fork, then line with a piece of aluminium foil pressed into its shape. Freeze for 30 minutes (or up to 3 months).

Preheat the oven to 200°C (400°F/Gas 6). Bake the frozen shell for 10 minutes or until the pastry feels dry to the touch. Remove the aluminium foil and bake a further 5 minutes until golden, then remove. Turn the oven down to 190°C (375°F/Gas 5).

To make the filling, put the cream cheese into a bowl and gradually add the remaining ingredients in the order given, using a balloon whisk or hand-held electric whisk to ensure it is smooth. Pour the filling into the baked shell. Bake at 190°C (375°F/Gas 5) for 30 minutes or until puffed and golden, then remove from the oven and cover the top completely with the smoked salmon squares.

Just before serving, drizzle with some of the soured cream and garnish with dill fronds. Serve in wedges accompanied by the remainder of the soured cream.

THERE IS A SCHOOL of thought, particularly in continental Europe, that believes the hotter the dish, the less satisfying the flavour—as though heat acts like an anaesthetic on the taste buds! And perhaps the exception, like soup, proves the rule. Certainly I've found that many dishes only reach their peak 5 or 10 minutes after the cooking process is complete. In this class I would put grilled, fried or baked fish, with or without pastry, as well as 'saucy' pasta dishes such as lasagna and cannelloni, fruit pies and compôtes and savoury tartes baked with an egg and cream filling. This settling period seems to benefit the texture of the dish and definitely improves appreciation of the flavour.

41

SMOKED SALMON ROULADE
WITH A CRUSHED PECAN COATING

Judi

Slices of delicate dill-scented salmon pâté are encrusted with a layer of toasted nuts and parsley and served with a salad fragrant with nut oil. A dramatic starter that looks elaborate but is surprisingly simple to create.

Makes 6–8 servings
Pâté **keeps** 3 days under refrigeration, **freezes** up to 1 month.
Completed roulade **keeps** 2 days under refrigeration. **Do not freeze.**

225 g (8 oz) smoked salmon
100 g (4 oz) cream cheese
50 g (2 oz) soft butter
juice of ½ lemon (about 2 tablespoons)
finely grated zest of 1 lemon
1 tablespoon fresh snipped dill
15 grinds black pepper
For coating the roulade
25 g (1 oz) shelled pecans
2 tablespoons finely chopped parsley
For the garnish
1 small pack mixed salad leaves
2 tablespoons nut oil vinaigrette (see page 196)
8 tiny sprigs fresh dill
½ each red, yellow and green peppers, pith and seeds removed,
    diced as finely as possible

Put the salmon in a food processor with the cheese, butter, lemon juice and zest and dill and process until smooth. Season with the pepper, then turn into a bowl and chill for several hours, until firm.

Spoon the chilled salmon mixture on to a large piece of clingfilm and mould into

42

a cylinder about 5 cm (2 in) in diameter and 30 cm (12 in) long. Chill well until 1 hour before the meal.

To make the coating, toss the nuts in a small, heavy-based pan over a medium heat, shaking all the time, until they smell 'toasty', about 2 minutes. Allow to cool, then chop finely.

Mix the parsley with the toasted nuts and sprinkle evenly on to a piece of aluminium foil at least 30 cm (12 in) long on one side. Carefully remove the roulade from the plastic wrap, then roll it evenly in the nut and parsley mixture. Chill well.

To serve, toss the salad leaves in the nut oil vinaigrette. Cut the roulade into diagonal slices about 2 cm (¾ in) thick (this is heady stuff, so keep the portions dainty!) Place a slice or two of roulade on each serving plate and garnish with a sprig of dill. Arrange a small pile of salad greens at the side, then lightly sprinkle some diced peppers over both the salad and roulade. Serve with brown rolls or challah.

SPICED MELON COCKTAIL

Indische Melone

Evelyn

THIS MELON STARTER—of Viennese origin—has an unexpected, gently flavoured spicy dressing which is wonderfully refreshing. It looks particularly enticing if you use melons with different-coloured flesh, such as honeydew and cantaloupe.

Makes 8–10 servings
Prepared melon **keeps** up to 2 days,
the dressing up to 2 weeks, under refrigeration.

2–3 melons, about 2.25 kg (5 lb) total weight
For the dressing
    300 g (10 oz) redcurrant jelly, melted
    150 ml (5 fl oz) fresh orange juice (about 2 oranges)
    50 ml (2 fl oz) kirsch or white rum
    2 teaspoons Dijon mustard
    2 tablespoons mango or peach chutney
    10 grinds black pepper
For the garnish
    sprigs of fresh mint or chervil
    2 limes

Early in the day (or the day before), scoop out the melons into balls, set in a sieve over a basin and leave to drip for 1 hour, then cover and chill. (This is essential to prevent juice leaching out of the melons, diluting the dressing.)

Whisk together all the ingredients for the dressing and refrigerate until 1 hour before serving, then add the melon balls to the dressing and leave in the least cold part of the refrigerator.

To serve, divide the melon and dressing between 8 large wine glasses and decorate with sprigs of herbs and twists or sections of lime.

44

FRESH FIGS AND MELON WITH A MINT AND CITRUS DRESSING

Judi

A VERY SIMPLE AND REFRESHING SUMMER starter. Any leftover dressing is delicious on a green salad.

Makes 6–8 servings
Keeps 4 hours under refrigeration; serve the same day.
Dressing **keeps** 1 week under refrigeration.

For the dressing
> 1 teaspoon finely grated orange zest
> 50 ml (2 fl oz) fresh orange juice
> 1 teaspoon lemon juice
> 1 tablespoon white wine vinegar
> 2 teaspoons honey
> ½ teaspoon Dijon mustard
> 15 grinds black pepper
> 3 tablespoons extra-virgin olive oil
> 3 tablespoons sunflower oil
> 1 tablespoon finely chopped fresh mint

For the salad
> 2 small very ripe cantaloupe melons
> 12 fresh figs; if not available, 450 g (1 lb) seedless
> black grapes can be substituted

For the garnish
> 1 small bag of mixed salad leaves
> small sprigs of fresh mint

Put all the dressing ingredients, except the fresh mint, in a screw-top jar and shake vigorously until thickened, about 1 minute. Leave overnight to mature.

Several hours before the meal, halve the melons and scoop out the seeds. Cut

45

into crescents about 1 cm (½ in) thick, then remove the peel from each crescent. Lay on a dish, cover with clingfilm and refrigerate.

An hour before the meal, wash the figs and pat dry, then cut into halves or quarters depending on their size. Arrange a fan of melon crescents on each plate with the figs (or grapes) at the base of the fan. Garnish with a little bouquet of the salad leaves and a sprig of mint.

To serve, add the chopped mint to the dressing, then drizzle over the fruit and leaves. Serve with warm brown rolls.

SEPHARDI CHEESE PUFFS

Evelyn

THESE TRADITIONAL DELICACIES have been westernised in recent years and can now be made with easier-to-handle puff pastry instead of filo. They're irresistible. If you can, use a plastic wonton shaper, available from Chinese stores.

Makes 16 cocktail servings
Uncooked puffs **keep** up to 1 day under refrigeration.
Freeze up to 3 weeks. **Do not freeze** cooked puffs.

300 g (10 oz) mature Cheddar cheese
2 large eggs
good pinch of sea salt
1½ sheets, about 350 g (12 oz), puff pastry, defrosted but still very cold
5 tablespoons white sesame seeds

Cut the cheese into pieces that will fit the feed tube of the food processor, then freeze for 1 hour so they won't 'gum up the works'. Grate the frozen cheese using the fine grater disc, then turn into a bowl.

In a small bowl, whisk the eggs, then take out 3 tablespoonfuls and reserve for glazing the puffs. Stir the remaining eggs into the cheese with a pinch of salt and mix to a sticky paste.

Roll out the defrosted pastry to about 3 mm (⅛ in) thick. Using a 6 cm (2½ in) biscuit cutter, stamp out 50 rounds of pastry. Put a rounded teaspoonful of filling into the center of each round, fold over into a half-moon shape and seal the edges. Glaze with the reserved egg and sprinkle with the sesame seeds. Arrange on baking trays lined with baking parchment and refrigerate till required.

Twenty minutes before you want to serve the puffs, preheat the oven to 230°C (450°F/Gas 8). Put the puffs in the oven, then immediately turn the heat down to 220°C (425°F/Gas 7) and bake for 15 minutes, until golden brown and well risen.

Serve as freshly baked as possible as a cocktail snack. Do not reheat as they become tough.

47

FRENCH CHEESE PUFFS

Petites Gougères

Judi

THESE DELICIOUS LITTLE CHOUX PASTRIES, seasoned with tangy cheese and mustard, can be served hot or cold and are delicious with a glass of chilled white wine. They make a convenient party dish as they can be made several weeks ahead and frozen.

Makes 40 puffs
Freezes up to 6 months.

300 ml (10 fl oz) water
125 g (4 oz) butter
1 teaspoon sea salt
pinch of nutmeg
pinch of white pepper
pinch of cayenne pepper
1 teaspoon Dijon mustard
150 g (5 oz) plain white flour
4 large eggs
125 g (4 oz) coarsely grated aged Gruyère or Emmenthaler cheese
    (if not available, extra mature Cheddar can be substituted)
For the topping
1 large egg mixed with ½ teaspoon water
50 g (2 oz) coarsely grated Gruyère or Parmesan cheese

Preheat the oven to 220°C (425°F/Gas 7). Lightly grease 2 large baking trays.

Heat the water, butter, seasonings and mustard in a medium saucepan over low heat, stirring until the butter has melted and the water is bubbling, about 2 minutes. Remove from the heat and add the flour all at once. Mix thoroughly with a wooden spoon, then return to moderate heat and cook, stirring, for 1–2 minutes, until the mixture forms a ball that leaves the sides of the saucepan clean and resembles firm mashed potato.

48

Remove from the heat and make a well in the centre. Add the eggs one at a time, beating after each addition to incorporate thoroughly. (This can also be done in the food processor.) When ready, the mixture will be glossy and fall lazily from the lifted spoon. Finally beat in the coarsely grated cheese.

Using a pastry bag with a 1 cm (½ in) plain round tube, squeeze the mixture in little mounds about 2.5 cm (1 in) in diameter and 1 cm (½ in) high on to the pre-pared baking trays. Leave about 5 cm (2 in) between each for expansion. Alternatively, drop heaped teaspoonsful of the mixture directly on to the baking trays.

Glaze the top of each puff with the egg-water mixture. (Avoid letting it drip down the side as this stops the puffs rising.) Sprinkle with the grated Gruyère or Parmesan.

Bake for 20–25 minutes or until crisp to the touch and a rich golden brown. Turn off the oven, take out the trays of puffs and immediately pierce the side of each one with a sharp knife to release the steam. Return to the oven and leave with the door ajar for 10 minutes to dry the puffs out slightly and prevent them from becoming soggy.

Serve hot from the oven or at room temperature. If frozen, put in a 220°C (425°F/Gas 7) oven for 3–4 minutes to thaw and recrisp at the same time.

49

TURKISH MUSHROOMS

Evelyn

Baby mushrooms are infused with wine, herbs and spices and gently sweetened with sultanas and orange segments. This delicately seasoned starter is equally easy to prepare in the microwave or on top of the stove.

Makes 6–8 servings

Keeps up to 4 days under refrigeration. **Do not freeze.**

900 g (2 lb) small white mushrooms
1 tablespoon tomato purée
1 tablespoon minced dried onion
1 teaspoon ground coriander
1 fat garlic clove, crushed
150 ml (5 fl oz) dry white wine such as Chardonnay or Sauvignon Blanc
3 tablespoons extra-virgin olive oil
pinch of cayenne pepper
1 teaspoon sea salt
15 grinds black pepper
8 sprigs parsley
1 bay leaf
25 g (1 oz) sultanas
1 large unpeeled lemon, thinly sliced

For the garnish
2 oranges, peeled and in segments
parsley sprigs

Trim the mushroom stalks level with the base of the caps, then wipe with a damp cloth. (Keep the stalks for another use, such as for soup or a stew.)

In a large microwave-safe bowl, put the remaining ingredients except for the sultanas and lemon slices and mix well. Cover with a plate and microwave on full power for 3½ minutes. Add the mushrooms, sultanas and lemon slices, stir well, then cover and microwave for 6½ minutes longer, stirring halfway through.

50

If cooking on top of the cooker, put all the ingredients (except the mushrooms, sultanas and lemon slices) in a saucepan and mix well. Bring to the boil, then lower the heat, cover and simmer for 5 minutes. Uncover and add the mushrooms, sultanas and lemon. Spoon the liquid over, then cover and simmer for 8–10 minutes more or until the mushrooms are just tender.

When the mushrooms are cooked, turn into a bowl and allow to cool, stirring once or twice. When cold, refrigerate overnight.

To serve, remove the parsley and bay leaf, then divide into the little soufflé dishes or place in one large serving dish. Garnish with the orange segments and sprigs of parsley.

51

CALIFORNIA SALAD WITH RASPBERRIES AND GLAZED PECANS

Judi

THIS COLOURFUL, FRUITY SALAD with its lightly caramelised nuts makes a spectacular start to a dinner party. If you can, buy a pack of six or seven different salad leaves that includes more unusual varieties such as spinach, lamb's lettuce and rocket, which have soft, broad leaves to which the dressing can easily cling.

Makes 6–8 servings
Once dressed, **use** within 1 hour.

For the dressing
 2 tablespoons walnut or hazelnut oil
 50 ml (2 fl oz) sunflower oil
 2 tablespoons extra-virgin olive oil
 1 tablespoon raspberry or cider vinegar
 juice of ½ lemon (about 2 tablespoons)
 1 teaspoon honey or light brown sugar
 1 teaspoon whole-grain mustard (or English mustard powder)
 pinch of sea salt
 10 grinds black pepper

For the salad
 5 g (¼ oz) butter or margarine
 1 teaspoon light brown sugar
 50 g (2 oz) shelled pecans (use walnut halves if not available)
 225–300 g (8–10 oz) mixed salad leaves
 175 g (6 oz) fresh raspberries
 10 stalks fresh chives, each cut into 3 pieces

52

Place all the dressing ingredients together in a screw-top jar and shake until thickened, about 1 minute. Chill, preferably overnight.

In a small non-stick frying pan over moderate heat, melt the butter or margarine and sugar, then add the pecans. Toss for a minute until evenly glazed. Allow to cool in the pan.

To serve, tear up the salad leaves and toss with enough dressing to coat. Divide the dressed salad on the individual plates and arrange some raspberries, chives and pecans decoratively on top. Serve chilled with warm, country-style bread such as *ciabatta*, or brown or light rye bread rolls.

Something Light:
Dairy Dishes, Eggs, and Tartes

'A land flowing with milk and honey'

—Exodus 3:8

WITH THE EXCEPTION OF THE FESTIVAL OF SHAVUOT, WHEN milk and milk products are the traditional celebration foods, dairy dishes used to play a relatively minor role in Jewish cuisine. Not anymore.

With a wondrous array of cheeses and herbs, not to mention all manner of vegetables, readily available in every season of the year and lighter dairy and egg entrées in favour in both Ashkenazi and Sephardi families, a mouth-watering new repertoire of dishes has been plucked from communities all over the world to add to the classics.

So while Evelyn offers an onion tarte from the Alsatian cuisine of western France, filled with the delicious cheese custard typical of that part of Europe, Judi also cooks up a tarte, but with a tomato, olive and fresh basil filling, bursting with the sunny flavours of Provence—which has a long but lesser-known Jewish history. Communities lived there under the protection of the Pope even when they were banished from other French territories.

Sephardi cooking has a culinary heritage with strong Moorish and Spanish roots, as well as those of host countries of the Middle East and North Africa. From these we have chosen two tasty *eggahs* or baked omelettes. Evelyn's traditional choice, a Tunisian version, has a mouth-watering filling of sautéed aubergine, fresh herbs and, yes, raisins, while Judi gives this ancient idea a modern fillip with the addition of tuna and Cheddar cheese, served in bite-sized squares.

The festival of Shavuot has always been dairy's 'big day' in Jewish cuisine. No Shavuot table is complete without that exquisite delicacy, the cheese blintze, which combines a paper-thin crêpe with an creamy cheese filling, the whole baked or fried to a golden crispness. Judi's choice is a light-as-air cheese soufflé, equally symbolic of the holiday but perhaps more in tune with modern palates.

55

TUNISIAN BAKED OMELETTE WITH TOMATOES AND AUBERGINE

Badinjan Kuku

Evelyn

THIS IS ONE of the many variations of baked omelette which are a feature of different Sephardi cuisines. It makes a satisfying vegetarian main course but is also ideal for a cocktail snack. Use very fresh free-range eggs if you can.

Makes 4–5 servings
Eat the same day. Leftovers **keep** 2 days in the refrigerator.
Do not freeze.

2 medium aubergines, cut into 2.5 cm (1 in) cubes
sea salt
3 tablespoons extra-virgin olive oil
1 large beefsteak tomato, sliced
1 small onion, peeled and finely chopped
1 medium clove garlic, peeled and finely chopped
2 tablespoons finely chopped dill or parsley
2 tablespoons raisins
pinch of ground saffron (optional)
10 grinds black pepper
1 teaspoon sea salt
6 large eggs, beaten

Put the diced aubergine on a large plate or in a colander and sprinkle liberally with salt. After 30 minutes, rinse well with cold water, drain thoroughly and dry. (This dramatically reduces the amount of oil they will absorb when fried.)

Heat the oil in a large frying pan over a low heat, add the well-dried aubergine cubes, tomato, onion and garlic. Cook gently, stirring, for 5 minutes. Stir in the dill, raisins, saffron, black pepper and sea salt.

Preheat the oven to 190°C (325°F/Gas 3). Oil a gratin dish or aluminium foil

56

dish approximately 25 cm (10 in) in diameter or 23 cm (9 in) square. Stir the vegetable mixture into the beaten eggs, turn into the baking dish and bake, uncovered, for 35–40 minutes, or until firm to a gentle touch. Leave to cool before cutting.

To serve as a main dish, cut into large squares. As an accompaniment, cut into 2.5 cm (1 in) cubes and spear each cube with a cocktail stick. Serve hot or at room temperature.

I FIRST TASTED THIS at the home of a Spanish *marquesa* in Seville whose family claimed direct descent from Marrano Jews. The mixture is certainly very similar to the *eggah* or baked omelette made by Sephardi Jews whose ancestors were expelled from Spain at the end of the fifteenth century.

The dish probably has an even older, North African origin, however, having become naturalised in Spain during the Moorish occupation. It is really a savoury egg and vegetable cake which can be eaten warm or cold, either as a supper dish or — as I had it in Spain — speared on cocktail sticks at a drinks party. It's also wonderful for picnics.

BAKED CHEESE AND TUNA SQUARES

Judi

THIS IS A DELICIOUS COMBINATION of flavours, derived from the traditional Sephardi *eggah*, or baked omelette. The texture, however, is more akin to a quiche than an omelette, firm yet creamy. You can vary this dish by using 75 g (3 oz) of fried sliced mushrooms or a can of asparagus tips in place of the tuna.

Makes 4–5 servings
Keeps 2 days under refrigeration. **Do not freeze.**

3 large eggs
175 g (6 oz) mature or extra-mature Cheddar cheese, grated
1 fat spring onion, finely chopped
1 × 175 g (6 oz) can tuna, drained and roughly flaked
2 tablespoons milk or single cream
½ teaspoon sea salt
10 grinds black pepper
pinch of paprika
½ tablespoon soft butter or margarine
1 tablespoon snipped fresh chives, or ½ teaspoon dried

Preheat the oven to 180°C (350°F/Gas 4).

Whisk the eggs to blend, then stir in 150 g (5 oz) of the cheese and all the other ingredients.

Turn into a well-greased ovenproof dish, or a baking tin lined with baking parchment, approximately 20 × 23 cm (8 × 9 in) and at least 5 cm (2 in) deep. Sprinkle with the remaining cheese.

Bake for 30 minutes or until just firm to the touch and a rich brown on top. Do not overcook or it will become dry and rubbery. Allow to cool slightly before cutting.

To serve as a starter, cut into 7.5 cm (3 in) squares, then carefully remove from the tin with a spatula. Serve slightly warm or at room temperature with tomatoes, bread or a green salad. For a snack, cut into 4 cm (1½ in) squares, pierce with cocktail sticks and serve on a platter.

58

books
for
giving

TOKENS

ONION TARTE FROM ALSACE

Tarte à l'Oignon   *Evelyn*

THIS MAKES AN UNUSUAL STARTER or, in larger portions, a perfect vegetarian main course. The onion is cooked till it melts and turns a pale golden brown — the flavour is too intrusive if overbrowned.

Makes 6–8 servings

Leftovers **keep** up to 2 days under refrigeration. **Do not freeze.**

1 recipe brown shortcrust pastry (page 40),
     in a 20–23 cm (8–9 in) loose-bottomed flan tin

For the filling

700 g (1½ lb) peeled and finely chopped onions

1 tablespoon sunflower oil

65 g (2½ oz) butter

2 tablespoons plain flour

For the pastry case

2 large eggs

150ml (5 fl oz) single or double cream

1 teaspoon sea salt

10 grinds black pepper

¼ teaspoon nutmeg

75 g (3 oz) finely grated mature Cheddar cheese

Put the pastry-lined flan tin in the freezer while the filling is being prepared. Put the onions in a lidded frying pan with the oil and 40 g (1½ oz) of the butter, cover and cook very slowly over low heat, stirring occasionally, until absolutely tender and golden brown — this may take 45 minutes. Stir in the flour and cook for 3 minutes longer.

Preheat the oven to 190°C (375°F/Gas 5).

In a large bowl, whisk the eggs to blend, then stir in the cream and seasonings.

59

continued

Add the cooked onion and half the cheese. Spoon into the raw pastry case, sprinkle with the remaining cheese and dot with the remaining butter.

Bake for 25–30 minutes or until the tarte turns a rich brown. It will stay puffed for 10 minutes in the turned-off oven.

Serve hot with a simple green salad. The tarte can be reheated gently until warm to the touch, either loosely covered with aluminium foil in a moderate oven or uncovered in the microwave.

ASK ANY JEWISH COOK to name the most important flavouring ingredient in his or her cooking and I'd guess that in ninety-nine cases out of a hundred the answer would be—an onion. And if you turn to the Bible, to Numbers, Chapter 11, you'll find the Jewish housewives even of that day lamenting its absence in the wilderness of Sinai!

What makes the onion so special that it's remained a fashionable food for so long? It's mainly its starch content, which is converted into sugar during the frying process, giving a wonderful depth of flavour to any savoury dish. But that's not the end of the story: The longer you cook an onion, the deeper becomes the flavour, as the sugar begins to caramelise. Finally, the onion 'melts' into a rough purée, leaving only the flavour to betray its presence in the dish.

For two of the best examples, you need to go to the French rather than the traditional Jewish cuisine. Onion soup needs to be supped on a cold winter's night to appreciate why it is the favourite 'tipple' of the market porters of Paris. Onion tarte, as it's prepared in Alsace, is altogether more elegant if equally satisfying fare which makes an unusual starter or, in larger portions, a perfect vegetarian main course.

60

PROVENÇAL SUN-DRIED TOMATO, OLIVE AND BASIL TARTE

Judi

ALL THE SCENTS AND TASTE sensations of Provence in midsummer are captured in this exquisite tarte. For best results, serve it about 10 minutes after taking it from the oven. You can get it oven-ready several hours in advance, however. For a vegetarian version, omit the anchovies. This dish is equally delicious made with two crusts, like a pie, or just one, like a pizza. For the open version, we halve the amount of pastry and reduce the baking time by 10 minutes.

Makes 5–6 servings
Filling **keeps** 3 days under refrigeration.
Do not freeze.

1 large onion, peeled and finely chopped
1 garlic clove, peeled and chopped
1½ tablespoons olive oil
450 g (1 lb) vine-ripened tomatoes, chopped, or 1 × 400 g (14 oz) can
    chopped tomatoes, drained
2 teaspoons plain or sun-dried tomato purée
1 bay leaf
½ teaspoon sea salt
15 grinds black pepper
1 teaspoon sugar
1 teaspoon dried basil
1 × 50 g (2 oz) can anchovy fillets
175–200 g (6–7 oz) fat black olives (kalamata are ideal), stoned
12 fresh basil leaves, coarsely chopped
2 sheets, about 450 g (1 lb), puff pastry, defrosted but still
    very cold
1 large egg yolk mixed with 3 teaspoons cold water, for glazing

61

continued

In a heavy, 20 cm (8 in) covered frying pan over moderate heat, gently cook the onion and garlic in the olive oil, until soft, about 5 minutes. Remove the lid and cook uncovered for 1–2 minutes so that they turn a golden colour. Add the tomatoes, tomato purée, bay leaf, salt, pepper, sugar and dried basil. Stir well, then simmer for 5 minutes over a low heat. Drain the anchovies, chop coarsely, then add to the pan together with the olives and simmer for a further 5 minutes. Stir in the basil leaves. Allow to cool completely.

Preheat the oven to 200°C (400°F/Gas 6).

For a two-crust version, roll out 1 sheet of the puff pastry to fit a shallow pie dish, about 24 cm (9½ in) in diameter. Line the base and sides with the pastry, allowing for some shrinkage during cooking. Spoon in the filling, then dampen the edges. Roll out the second sheet of pastry for the top crust, then lay it gently on top. Press the two edges together to seal well, then trim off any excess with a sharp knife. Brush the top evenly with the egg glaze.

For a single-crust version, roll out 1 sheet of the puff pastry to a circle about 25 cm (10 in) in diameter or a rectangle about 12 × 25 cm (5 × 10 in) and transfer to a nonstick baking sheet. Spoon on the filling, leaving 1 cm (½ in) clear at the edges, then bunch up the pastry around the edge to form a rough rim about 1 cm (½ in) high.

Bake for 25 minutes, until a rich, golden brown. Allow to cool for 5–10 minutes before serving. Serve with a green salad.

THIS DELICIOUS TARTE ORIGINATES IN the Provençal town of Nyons, famed for its tiny black olives. I was first put off making it myself by the thought of stoning nearly half a pound of olives! Nowadays, however, you can buy good-quality stoned black olives. They're often Greek or Moroccan rather than French, but work equally well in this dish. My favourite are oil-cured olives, marinated with garlic and herbs such as thyme and rosemary. (Be careful not to use those with a bitter taste.) The flavours of the tarte are enriched by using good-quality canned tomatoes and sun-dried tomato paste.

62

ISRAELI CREAM CHEESE PANCAKES

Chremslach

Evelyn

THESE TENDER PANCAKES, crisp on the outside and fluffy in the centre, make a light alternative to potato latkes that are traditional fare at Hanukkah. They were invented by the Israelis in the early years of the State when meat was at a premium—they called them 'cheese steaks'. Our family love them so much, we eat them as a light lunch at any time of the year.

Makes 4 servings
Serve hot off the pan. Uncooked batter **keeps** 1 hour under refrigeration.
Do not refrigerate or **freeze** once cooked.

225 g (8 oz) cream cheese at room temperature
2 large eggs
50 g (2 oz) plain flour
½ teaspoon baking powder
1 teaspoon sugar
½ teaspoon sea salt
2 tablespoons sunflower oil plus ½ tablespoon butter, or all oil

For serving
125 g (4 oz) sugar mixed with 1 teaspoon ground cinnamon

Mix the cinnamon and sugar together and set aside. Put the cheese in a mixing bowl. In a separate bowl, beat the eggs with a rotary whisk until fluffy, then stir into the cheese together with the flour, baking powder, sugar and salt. Don't worry if there are small lumps of cheese—they will end up as little creamy nuggets that add to the texture of the finished pancakes.

Put the oil and butter into a large nonstick frying pan over moderate heat. The minute the butter starts to foam, drop tablespoons of the cheese mixture into the pan, flattening slightly with the back of the spoon, leaving at least 1 cm (½ in) between pancakes (if necessary, cook in 2 batches). Fry gently until risen and golden brown on one side, about 4 minutes, then turn over with a spatula and cook until the second side is brown, a further 2 minutes.

Serve hot from the pan, sprinkled with the cinnamon-sugar mixture.

GREEK SPINACH AND FETA CHEESE SPIRAL

Spanakopita *Judi*

THE PERFECT DISH when you need a truly dramatic centrepiece for a vegetarian meal, or as part of a buffet—a golden, flaky spiral the size of a large pizza! It does take more time and patience than our other starters, but your efforts will be handsomely rewarded. If you can find Greek strained yogurt, use it in the dill and yogurt sauce that accompanies the spiral.

Makes 6–8 servings
Serve cooked spiral the same day. Raw spiral **freezes** for up to 1 month.

For the yogurt sauce
225 g (8 oz) natural yogurt, or soured cream
2 teaspoons fresh snipped dill, or ½ teaspoon dried
½ teaspoon sea salt
8 grinds black pepper

For the spiral
450 g (1 lb) frozen leaf spinach, or 900 g (2 lb) fresh, rinsed
140 g (4½ oz) butter
2 small bunches spring onions, including 5 cm (2 in) of the green tops, finely sliced
2 large eggs, beaten
225 g (8 oz) feta cheese, crumbled
3 tablespoons chopped fresh dill, or 1 tablespoon dried
½ teaspoon sea salt
20 grinds black pepper
½ teaspoon grated nutmeg
12 sheets filo pastry, approximately 350 g (12 oz)
3 tablespoons sesame seeds

64

To make the yoghurt sauce, mix all the sauce ingredients together and chill for several hours.

To make the spiral, roughly chop the fresh spinach, then toss in a nonstick pan or wok over medium heat until wilted and tender, about 5 minutes. Drain well and chop finely. If using frozen leaf spinach, defrost, then squeeze well in a sieve to remove the moisture and chop finely.

Put the chopped spinach into a large mixing bowl.

Heat 15 g (½ oz) of the butter in a pan over moderate heat and cook the spring onions, stirring, until soft, about 5 minutes. Add this to the spinach together with the beaten eggs, crumbled cheese, herbs and seasonings, mixing well. Spoon into a 35 cm (14 in) piping bag fitted with a 2.5 cm (1 in) plain nozzle.

To assemble the spiral, grease a 28–30 cm (11–12 in) pizza pan or the base of a loose-bottomed flan tin, sitting on a baking tray. Melt the remaining butter (most easily done in the microwave).

Stack the sheets of filo one on top of the other and immediately cover with a slightly damp tea towel to prevent their drying out.

Place a filo sheet on a board with the long edge toward you. Brush lightly all over with melted butter, then cover with a second sheet and brush with butter in the same way.

Leaving clear 4 cm (1½ in) of pastry nearest to you, pipe a long strip of the filling from one edge of the sheet of pastry to the other. Fold the lower edge of the pastry to enclose this filling, then roll up like a thin Swiss roll. Cover the finished roll with a damp tea towel and repeat this with the remaining sheets of filo. There will now be six long rolls.

Take one roll and brush it lightly all over with melted butter, then carefully curl it into a tight spiral and place it in the centre of the prepared pan. Take another roll, brush that in the same way, then curl it around the outside of the first spiral, making sure the end butts up tightly against the inner spiral. Continue buttering and curling the rolls in the same way, until you have made a giant spiral that completely covers the base of the pan or flan tin. Scatter with sesame seeds. At this stage the *spanakopita* can be frozen or chilled overnight.

To cook, preheat the oven to 190°C (375°F/Gas 5). Bake the spiral for 40–45 minutes, until it becomes rich golden brown in colour.

To serve, transfer on to a circular wooden board or platter, leave to cool for 15 minutes, then serve in wedges with the dill sauce.

65

LIGHT CHEESE BLINTZES

Evelyn

ONE OF THE GLORIES of Jewish cuisine! Follow to the letter the instructions for frying the pancakes and you can't go wrong.

Makes 12 blintzes or 6–8 servings
Keep filled but unbaked blintzes up to 1 day under refrigeration.
Freeze empty blintzes up to 2 months, filled blintzes up to 3 weeks.

For the batter
  125 g (4 oz) all-purpose flour
  2 large eggs
  ½ teaspoon sea salt
  125 ml (4 fl oz) milk
  125 ml (4 fl oz) water
  25 g (1 oz) butter, melted, or 2 tablespoons sunflower oil
For the filling
  450 g (1 lb) cream cheese or sieved cottage cheese
  2 tablespoons soured cream or Greek yoghurt
  1 teaspoon sugar
  pinch of salt
For frying
  50 g (2 oz) butter, melted
  2 teaspoons sunflower oil
For the topping
  150 ml (5 fl oz) soured cream, or *smetana*

In a blender or food processor, blend or process all the batter ingredients except the butter or oil until a smooth batter is formed. Transfer to a bowl. Leave the batter for half an hour, though it can be refrigerated overnight if more convenient.

In another bowl, combine all the filling ingredients and set aside until required.

When ready to fry the pancakes, stir the batter well. It should be the consistency of single cream. If too thick, stir in 1 tablespoon water. Pour the batter into a jug.

66

Heat a 15–18 cm (6–7 in) diameter omelette pan with rounded sides over moderate heat for 3 minutes, then pour in a teaspoonful of sunflower oil. Swirl the oil round the base and sides of the pan, wiping out any excess with a wad of paper towels. With the same wad of towels, coat the insides of the pan very thinly with butter, then pour in a thick layer of batter, swirling it around so that it covers the sides as well as the base of the pan. The heat will immediately set a thin layer, so that any excess can be easily poured back into the jug. You will get a pancake so thin that by the time the sides begin to curl from the pan, the bottom will be brown and the top side dry. Turn this pancake out, brown side down, on to a sheet of greaseproof baking parchment.

Butter the pan again and repeat the process until all the pancakes have been made—there should be 12. As each pancake stops steaming, stack one on top of the previous one, browned side down. At this stage, the pancakes can be frozen, refrigerated overnight or filled.

To fill the blintzes, place a pancake, browned side up, on a board and spread 1 tablespoonful of the filling over it. Tuck in the sides and roll up into a long, thin roll. Repeat with each pancake. The blintzes can now be refrigerated overnight or frozen until time to be fried or baked.

To fry, heat the melted butter and sunflower oil in a wide pan. The moment the butter stops foaming, put in the blintzes, joined side upward. Cook gently for 3 minutes, until golden brown, then turn and cook the second side.

To bake, preheat the oven to 190°C (375°F/Gas 5). Use only 50 g (2 oz) butter. Arrange the blintzes 2.5 cm (1 in) apart on a baking tray lined with baking parchment. Brush each blintze thoroughly with the melted butter and bake for 20 minutes, until crisp and golden brown.

Baked or fried blintzes may be kept hot for up to 15 minutes in the oven at 160°C (325°F/Gas 3). Serve with ice-cold soured cream or smetana.

FANNY AND HELEN WERE SISTERS of diminutive height but prodigious intelligence. They not only made wonderful blintzes, but had the rare ability to explain the whys and wherefores of their technique. Their secret was to pour a goodly amount of batter into a hot, greased pan and immediately pour the excess back into the jug, leaving the thinnest layer to set on the base of the pan.

The Yiddish word for crêpes or pancakes is *bletlach* or 'skeleton leaf', and when you hold one made in this way up to the light, it really is leaf-thin and you can see your hand through it.

CHEESE SOUFFLÉ WITH FRESH HERBS

Judi

SOUFFLÉ MAKING HAS TRADITIONALLY STRUCK fear into the hearts of many home cooks. Think of a soufflé, however, as simply a thick sauce lightened with beaten egg white. As long as you don't overbeat the egg whites and above all don't open the oven for a peek before the allotted time, there's no reason why you can't produce a perfectly risen soufflé every time. The outside will be crisp, the inside silky-soft and slightly trembling, or, as the French say, *baveuse*. But make sure your guests wait for the soufflé, not the other way round!

Makes 4–5 servings
Serve immediately.

For coating the dish
> 1 teaspoon butter
> 1 tablespoon grated Parmesan cheese

For the soufflé
> 40 g (1½ oz) plain flour
> 50 g (2 oz) butter or margarine
> 300 ml (10 fl oz) cold milk
> ½ teaspoon sea salt
> 10 grinds black pepper
> pinch of cayenne pepper or hot paprika
> pinch of ground nutmeg
> 2 teaspoons Dijon mustard
> 2 tablespoons finely chopped fresh chives
> 4 large eggs, separated, plus 1 large egg white
> good pinch of cream of tartar or salt
> 175 g (6 oz) coarsely grated mature cheese, such as Cheddar

Preheat the oven to 200°C (400°F/Gas 6) and put in a baking tray to warm up.

Grease a straight-sided ovenproof dish 7.5 cm (3 in) deep and 20 cm (8 in) in diameter with the 1 teaspoon butter and sprinkle with the grated Parmesan.

68

Put the flour, butter and cold milk into a heavy-based medium saucepan and bring to the boil over low heat, whisking constantly with a batter or balloon whisk. Add the seasonings and mustard, then simmer for 3 minutes, stirring constantly with a wooden spoon. Remove from the heat and stir in the chives.

Have ready a large bowl in which you intend to whisk the egg whites (a copper bowl is ideal). Separate the eggs, then drop the yolks one at a time into the hot sauce, stirring well after each addition, while you drop its companion white into the bowl. Add the extra egg white to the bowl, together with the cream of tartar or salt and whisk until the whites stand up in floppy but still glossy peaks when the beaters are withdrawn. Be careful not to whisk beyond this stage—if the meringue becomes watery, the soufflé will not rise properly.

Stir a quarter of the meringue into the sauce, followed by all but 1 tablespoonful of the grated cheese. Spoon the remaining meringue on top and, using a rubber spatula, fold it into the sauce as gently as possible so that the mixture becomes an even colour but remains fluffy in texture, no more than 1 minute of folding. If the mixture starts to deflate, err on the side of caution and stop folding, even if the colour is not yet even.

Coax the mixture gently into the prepared dish. With the tip of a round-bladed knife, make a shallow groove around the edge of the mixture 2.5 cm (1 in) away from the rim of the dish. (This helps it to rise into a 'top hat' shape.) Sprinkle with the remaining grated cheese. At this point the soufflé can be covered with a large bowl and left to stand for up to 1 hour before baking.

When ready to bake, put on the baking tray in the preheated oven, then turn the heat down to 190°C (375°F/Gas 5). The soufflé will be ready to eat in 35 minutes, by which time the top will be a crusty brown.

To serve, spoon out on to individual plates and eat at once!

Perfect Pasta: Oodles of Noodles

'Of wheaten flour shalt thou make them'

—Exodus 29:2

ALMOST EVERY WORLD CUISINE HAS A VERSION OF *LOKSHEN*, or to give it its more generally used name today, pasta. It was originally a 'survival' food that could be made with nothing more than flour and water, but which packed a hefty protein and carbohydrate punch.

Auntie Mary, whose family came from Moscow to England at the turn of the century, would toss her homemade *lokshen* with margarine and serve it piping hot but simply seasoned. Judi gives this traditional dish a new twist by seasoning the noodles with mouthwatering sesame seed paste (tahini), an idea that is common to both Hong Kong and Israel.

This is one of many instances where traditional dishes have been modified over the years, as different communities are affected by (usually forced) migration to new climates and living conditions. To see why a satisfying and warming dish like *lokshen* kugel was a winner, you have only to imagine life in a *shtetl* or small village in the Pale of Settlement in Eastern Europe, where bitter winters had to be endured with minimal heating and inadequate clothing, and every journey was taken on foot or in an open cart.

But today's lifestyle of heated homes and cars demands lighter dishes such as Judi's pasta shells filled with a delicious combination of mushrooms and mozzarella cheese, while Auntie Mary would surely be both astonished and charmed by the irresistible combination of smoked salmon, lemon and bow tie pasta!

GRANDMA'S LOKSHEN KUGEL

Evelyn

I HAVE OMITTED the traditional chicken crackling (*gribenes*) from the recipe since such a dose of concentrated saturated fat is unwelcome today. Serve this with the main course as a replacement for potatoes or rice.

Makes 4–5 servings

Keeps up to 2 days under refrigeration.

Freezes up to 3 weeks.

cold water
2 teaspoons sea salt
175 g (6 oz) medium egg noodles
4 tablespoons rendered chicken fat or soft margarine
2 large eggs
15 grinds black pepper

Preheat the oven to 150°C (300°F/Gas 2).

Half fill an 20 cm (8 in) diameter saucepan with cold water, add 1 teaspoon sea salt and bring to the boil. Add the noodles and stir until the water comes back to the boil. Half cover the pot and allow to boil steadily for 8 minutes. (Do not cover tightly or the water will froth over the sides of the pot.)

Taste a piece of noodle. It should be bite-tender. Turn the noodles into a metal sieve but do not rinse under the tap because the starch on the outside of the noodles helps to 'set' the pudding. Allow the noodles to drain completely, then put in a bowl.

Put the chicken fat or margarine into an ovenproof casserole dish and leave in the oven for a few minutes. Meanwhile, beat the eggs with the remaining 1 teaspoon salt and the pepper and pour over the drained noodles. Take the hot dish out of the oven, swirl the fat to coat the sides, then pour it on to the noodle mixture. Stir well, then spoon into the casserole dish.

Bake for 1½ hours or until crisp on top and set inside. *Lokshen* kugel can be cooked in a 110°C (225°F/Gas ¼) oven overnight, but twice the quantity of ingredients must be used if the dish is not to turn out dry.

72

IN THE JEWISH KITCHEN, the noodles (*lokshen*) that are the essential ingredient of any self-respecting chicken soup, are always made from flour and water, with or without eggs.

The Chinese, who are equally partial to noodles, have different ideas. Instead of wheat flour, Western-style, they may use ground mung beans to produce the shiny, brittle 'cellophane' noodles which are often added to stir-fry dishes. I've been experimenting with great success with yet another kind, made from ground rice and water alone—no eggs. This makes them useful for people who cannot tolerate either the eggs or the wheat flour in normal noodles. After soaking them for 5 minutes in boiling water, you simply add them to the soup and by the time it comes back to the simmer they are deliciously tender.

BAKED PASTA SHELL WITH A MUSHROOM AND MOZZARELLA FILLING

Judi

Amouthwatering MÉLANGE of mushrooms, ground almonds, spinach and cheese enclosed in giant shells of pasta under a golden, cheesy crust, this dish could persuade even the most ardent meat lover that vegetarian food can be just as satisfying as a plate of meat and potatoes!

Makes 4–6 servings
Ready-to-bake casserole **keeps** 24 hours under refrigeration.
Leftovers **reheat** well in the microwave.
Do not freeze once baked.

2 teaspoons salt
24 large pasta shells, approximately 6 cm (2½ in)
    in length
For the filling
    450 g (1 lb) frozen leaf spinach
    225 g (8 oz) white closed cup mushrooms,
    40 g (1½ oz) butter
    2 cloves garlic, peeled and finely chopped
    1½ teaspoons sea salt
    40 g (2 oz) ground almonds
    225 ml (8 fl oz) single cream
    1 tablespoon chopped parsley
    1 tablespoon snipped chives
    ½ teaspoon ground nutmeg
    20 grinds black pepper
    ½ teaspoon paprika
    175 g (6 oz) grated mozzarella or other mild but well-flavoured cheese,
        such as Gruyère or Gouda

74

Bring a large pot of water, at least 2.4 litres (4 pints) in capacity, with 2 teaspoons salt to a full, rolling boil, then add the pasta shells and boil until tender, 12–14 minutes. Drain in a colander, flood with cold water to cool and drain again.

Meanwhile, allow the spinach to defrost at room temperature or in the microwave for 2 minutes on full power.

Chop the mushrooms coarsely by hand or food processor. In a medium frying pan, melt 15 g (½ oz) butter, add the mushrooms and half the chopped garlic, sprinkle with a pinch of the salt and cook over moderate heat, stirring occasionally, until they are nicely browned and any liquid has evaporated, about 6 minutes.

Empty the mushrooms and their fat into a large bowl. Chop the drained spinach in the food processor for 5 seconds, then cook in the same pan with the remaining butter until it is absorbed and no liquid remains in the pan. Add the spinach mixture to the mushrooms, followed by the ground almonds, 2 tablespoons of the cream, the herbs, ¼ teaspoon nutmeg, half the remaining salt, 15 grinds pepper, paprika and all but a generous 25 g (1 oz) of the grated cheese. Mix well, then taste and add more seasoning if necessary.

Preheat the oven to 200°C (400°F/Gas 6) and butter a gratin dish large enough to hold the tightly packed stuffed shells side by side, about 30 × 18 cm (12 × 7 in).

Divide the filling between the shells, arranging them in the dish with the 'stuffed' side downward. To the remaining cream, add the rest of the garlic and nutmeg, the remaining salt and 5 grinds of pepper. Pour this mixture over the shells, then scatter with the remaining cheese.

Bake in the oven for 15–20 minutes until a rich golden brown. Or microwave, covered, on full power for 5 minutes, then uncover and grill for 5 minutes, until rich brown.

To serve, arrange 4 shells on each serving plate and spoon some of the sauce around them. Serve with a crisp green salad.

AUNTIE MARY'S SAVOURY NOODLES

Lokshen

Evelyn

THIS IS A SIMPLE LAST-MINUTE DISH to serve with braised meat or a casserole instead of rice or potatoes. As a variation, 1 tablespoon shredded basil can be stirred in just before serving in place of the parsley.

Makes 4–5 servings
Keeps up to 2 days under refrigeration.
Freezes up to 6 weeks.

1 litre (1¾ pints) boiling water
1 chicken or beef stock cube
175 g (6 oz) broad egg noodles
5 g (¼ oz) margarine
1 tablespoon chopped parsley
15 grinds black pepper

Preheat the oven to 110°C (225°F/Gas ¼).

Bring the water to the boil in a large pot, then add the stock cube and the noodles. Partially cover, lower the heat and simmer for 10 minutes. While the noodles are cooking, put the margarine in the warm oven in an ovenproof dish. Drain the noodles (reserving the stock for other use) and add to the margarine with the parsley and pepper. To serve, toss well, then serve piping hot.

Variation

For a milk meal, boil the noodles in good vegetable stock. Heat 50 g (2 oz) butter in the serving dish, then blend with the noodles, parsley and black pepper.

76

I HAVE AN EARLY MEMORY of my Auntie Mary cutting the *lokshen* (the name is derived from a Turkish word for noodles—*lakcha*) for Shabbat meals. Her hand with the knife moved so surely and swiftly that it appeared as no more than a blur to my child's eye. Then she would hang the fine ribbons over a wooden clothes-drying rack draped with snowy tea towels to dry, ready to be put into the chicken soup or made into savoury or sweet *lokshen* kugel.

This was a chore that had to be done each week in every Ashkenazi Jewish household, until the advent of factory-made, packaged noodles. Those who can remember tell me that the texture and taste of the home-made variety was incomparably superior, but I had to wait for many years before I could judge for myself. Now, the fact that all the major supermarkets and delicatessens are offering this wonderful fresh pasta is not to belittle the dry variety, which is particularly useful to serve with a thick sauce. The pasta is allowed to dry until it feels brittle. The drying process extends its life and also the cooking time, which may be anything from 3 to 15 minutes, depending on quality and size. But even with dried pasta, there are differing degrees of excellence. Look for the words 'durum wheat' or 'durum semolina' on the packet; they are your guarantee that the pasta will cook to perfection and still have a little 'bite' left in it.

Dry or fresh, the pasta must be able to 'swim' in the saucepan, which means using one that can hold 6 litres (10 pints) if you are cooking 450 g (1 lb) of pasta. Don't be tempted to break long strands of pasta—such as spaghetti—to get them into the pot. Instead, lower them gently into the boiling water and, as they soften, they will coil around on themselves, fitting the pan to perfection. A few drops of oil added to the cooking water will avoid any danger of sticking.

NOODLES IN TAHINI SAUCE, HONG KONG STYLE

Judi

THIS IS A WONDERFUL DISH to add sparkle to cold meats and poultry. The recipe hails from Hong Kong, where it is made with a paste of roasted sesame seeds, but I find tahini paste works equally well. You can add a little cooked chicken to turn this into a more substantial dish. For a spicier version, use hot sesame oil.

Makes 4 servings
Leftovers **keep** 2 days under refrigeration and can be reheated.
Freezes up to 1 month.

225 g (8 oz) flat egg noodles
3 teaspoons dark sesame oil (see page 79)
For the sauce
    1 rounded tablespoon tahini
    1 tablespoon soy sauce
    1 teaspoon sugar
    225 ml (8 fl oz) chicken or vegetable stock
    good pinch of sea salt

Cook the noodles as directed on the packet until tender. Drain thoroughly, reserving 125 ml (4 fl oz) of the cooking liquid, then turn into a warm dish and toss with the sesame oil.

Meanwhile, mix the sauce ingredients in a small saucepan and heat gently until bubbling.

To serve, toss the sauce mixture with the noodles and serve at once. If you prefer a moister texture, add a little of the reserved cooking liquid.

78

SESAME OIL, WIDELY USED in Asian cooking, comes in two forms. The pale, straw-coloured version looks very much like sunflower oil. It's mild in flavour and good for frying or in salad dressings, imparting a subtle, slightly nutty flavour.

Dark sesame oil, on the other hand—made from the roasted seeds—is a very different animal, thick and fragrant—a condiment rather than a cooking medium. You'll find dark sesame oil in small bottles and a little goes a long way. (Hot sesame oil, a version infused with chillis, is delicious but incendiary!) Don't try substituting light for dark or vice versa, as these two incarnations of the oil are quite different in character and impact. They do, however, share two useful characteristics—a high smoke point, around 200°C (400°F) and a high level of polyunsaturated fat, making them a healthy and delicious addition to one's culinary repertoire.

AUSTRIAN NOODLES
WITH PARMESAN AND WALNUTS

Nussnudeln   *Evelyn*

THIS DISH HAS A VIENNESE BACKGROUND. A perfect accompaniment to grilled or baked fish, it is light and full of flavour. The nuts and bread crumbs add a pleasing crunchiness.

Makes 6 servings
Serve immediately.

350 g (12 oz) fresh tagliatelle
100 g (3½ oz) butter
½ teaspoon sea salt
15 grinds black pepper
50 g (2 oz) walnuts, finely chopped
50 g (2 oz) finely grated Parmesan cheese
50 g (2 oz) dried breadcrumbs

Cook the noodles as directed until tender then drain.

To make a *beurre noisette*, melt 50 g (2 oz) of the butter in a small pan and cook over medium heat until it turns pale brown, 2–3 minutes.

Melt the remaining butter in a large pan and add the hot noodles, tossing until they are evenly coated and glistening. Stir in all the remaining ingredients except the *beurre noisette*.

To serve, turn into a hot serving dish and pour the *beurre noisette* over the noodles. Serve immediately.

80

BOW TIE PASTA WITH
CREAM CHEESE AND WALNUTS

Judi

IN TRUE ITALIAN TRADITION a few simple ingredients are combined to create a whole that is far greater than the sum of its parts. The pasta is enveloped in a velvety sauce laced with toasted walnuts. It's truly delicious for a light supper when calorie and cholesterol counting are off the menu, although in Italy this would be merely an appetiser!

Makes 6–8 servings
Serve at once. **Do not freeze.**

450 g (1 lb) bow tie pasta (farfalle)
125 g (4 oz) shelled walnuts
50 g (2 oz) butter
250 g (9 oz) full-fat cream cheese, or mascarpone (if available)
125 g (4 oz) freshly grated Parmesan cheese
1 teaspoon sea salt
15 grinds black pepper

Boil the pasta in plenty of water with ½ teaspoon salt until bite-tender, 10–12 minutes. Drain.

Toss the walnuts in a heavy-bottomed frying pan over moderate heat until they smell 'toasty,' about 2 minutes, then roughly chop and set aside.

In an ovenproof dish (enamelled cast iron is ideal), melt the butter and the cheese over low heat, stirring from time to time, about 3 minutes. Do not allow to boil. Into this mixture put the well-drained cooked pasta. Mix gently, adding 25 g (1 oz) of the Parmesan and seasoning with ½ teaspoon salt and 10 grinds pepper. Finally, stir in the chopped walnuts, making sure the pasta is evenly coated with the sauce.

Serve at once, offering the remaining Parmesan to sprinkle on the top and passing the pepper mill.

81

CHEESY TUNA GRATIN

Evelyn

IF CANNED TUNA HAD BEEN AROUND in my grandmother's day, I'm sure she would have incorporated it into her *lokshen* kugel. What's more, with the addition of hard-boiled eggs and grated cheese, this becomes a stylish main dish that graces even the most elegant buffet.

Makes 4–6 servings
Keeps up to 2 days under refrigeration.
Freezes without the eggs up to 3 months.

3 large eggs
225 g (8 oz) uncooked fusilli pasta or short-cut macaroni
1 tablespoon sea salt
4 spring onions (optional)
50 g (2 oz) butter
2 rounded tablespoons plain flour
600 ml (1 pint) milk
15 grinds black pepper
¼ teaspoon white pepper
½ teaspoon paprika
1 tablespoon Dijon mustard
1 × 75 g (3 oz) grated Gruyère or mature Cheddar cheese
50 g (2 oz) grated Parmesan cheese
3 tablespoons single cream
1 × 175 g (6 oz) tuna, preferably oil-packed,
  drained and flaked
2 teaspoons finely chopped parsley

For the topping
  2 tablespoons sesame seeds

Put the eggs in a small saucepan of warm water. Bring to the boil, then immediately turn off the heat, cover and let sit for 15 minutes. Drain off the hot water and run cold water into the saucepan for 2 minutes. Shell the eggs, which will still be slightly soft in the centre, then slice.

Cook the pasta according to directions, adding 2 teaspoons of the sea salt to the water, then drain.

Cut the white part of the spring onions (if using) into 1 cm (½ in) slices and the green part into very fine slices like snipped chives. Melt half the butter in a pan over medium heat, then cook the white part of the spring onions, stirring until slightly coloured, about 3 minutes. Add the flour, the remaining butter, the milk, the seasonings, the remaining teaspoon of sea salt and the mustard. Whisk over gentle heat till it starts to thicken, about 5 minutes, then boil for 2 minutes. Remove from the heat, add three-quarters of the cheeses and the green part of the spring onions and stir. Then gently stir in the cream, followed by the tuna and eggs.

Add the sauce mixture to the pasta with the finely chopped parsley and mix gently. Transfer to a buttered gratin dish no more than 5 cm (2 in) deep. Sprinkle with the remaining cheese and the sesame seeds.

To serve immediately, brown under a hot grill. To serve later, reheat for 4 minutes in the microwave, then transfer to the grill and brown until the top is crisp and dark golden.

TAGLIATELLE WITH
LEMON AND SMOKED SALMON

Judi

W HENEVER I GET A CALL in the late afternoon from my husband to tell me he's bringing a colleague home for a working supper, this quick, stylish dish is my salvation. It takes only moments to make, but never fails to impress. You can use the cheaper smoked salmon pieces (off-cuts), but make sure they don't smell 'fishy.'

Makes 6 servings
Leftovers **keep** 2 days in the refrigerator.
Do not freeze.

350 g (12 oz) fresh tagliatelle or other ribbon-shaped pasta,
 or 225 g (8 oz) dried
225 ml (8 fl oz) single cream
¼ teaspoon nutmeg
20 grinds black pepper
½ teaspoon paprika
finely grated zest of 1 lemon
125 g (4 oz) freshly grated Parmesan cheese
2 tablespoons snipped fresh dill or fresh chives
225 g (8 oz) smoked salmon, cut in slivers,
 or smoked salmon pieces
pinch of sea salt, if necessary
For the garnish
 small bowl of grated Parmesan
 freshly ground black pepper

Cook the pasta in boiling salted water according to directions.
 While the pasta is cooking, put the cream, the seasonings and and the lemon zest

into a small saucepan. Heat very gently until steaming, about 5 minutes. Keep warm over very low heat. Do not boil.

Drain the pasta over a bowl, reserving the cooking liquid.

Transfer the pasta to a warm serving dish and pour on the hot cream mixture, followed by 25 g (1 oz) of the Parmesan, the herbs and the salmon. Stir gently, then add the reserved cooking liquid 1 tablespoon at a time until the sauce is creamy, without being sticky. (The pasta will continue to absorb liquid as it sits, so you may need to add more cooking liquid if it is not served within a couple of minutes.) Check the seasoning and add salt if necessary.

Serve immediately, offering extra Parmesan to sprinkle on top and passing the pepper mill.

85

A Fine Kettle of Fish:
A Variety of Fish Dishes

'Whatsoever passes through the paths of the sea'

—Psalms 8:8

EVELYN'S MOTHER USED TO RECOUNT HOW, IN THE DAYS BEFORE the First World War, *her* mother would send her to the fish market— together with several of her younger siblings to help carry the load— to buy 6 kg (14 lb) of fish! The fish would be chopped by hand, formed into patties and fried in a monster iron frying pan, very similar to ones found in the tombs of the Pharaohs in ancient Egypt.

How Grandma would have welcomed today's food processors and electric deep-fryers to speed the job of cooking enough fish to feed her family of eight over a whole weekend! 'Chopped and fried' has been a traditional Anglo-Jewish favourite for over a hundred years, but a lighter version which avoids any frying has the fish poached with a superb tomato and pepper sauce.

The unusual Halibut in a Velvet Lemon Sauce is Evelyn's choice for a Seder meal, as the glorious sweet-and-sour sauce can be part of either a chicken or a fish menu, while Judi's choice, fillets of salmon topped with an unusual sun-dried tomato crust, makes a perfect dish for Rosh Hashanah.

The strudel has long been a favourite way of making a little expensive filling stretch to feed a large family. Evelyn has kept to tradition but used a luxurious salmon filling, while Judi's dramatic *Salmon en Croûte* is in a similar genre but with a more contemporary spirit.

SOLE GRATIN IN A LIGHT CREAM SAUCE

Evelyn

A DISH WITH THE MOST GLORIOUS of flavours. Cream plus a little fried onion is transformed into a superb creamy sauce enveloping the fish and the potatoes as they bake. Ideal for a Shavuot meal for family and friends.

Makes 6–8 servings
Serve immediately. **Do not freeze.**

900 g (2 lb) new potatoes, scrubbed
6–8 × 175 g (6 oz) fillets of lemon sole or plaice
   (or 12–16 smaller ones), washed and skinned
300 ml (10 fl oz) double cream
1½ teaspoons sea salt
¼ teaspoon white pepper
1 medium onion, peeled and finely chopped
25 g (1 oz) butter
For the topping
75 g (3 oz) grated Cheddar or Gruyère cheese

Cook the potatoes in their skins in boiling water until barely tender, about 15 minutes. Skin if desired, then cool and slice 2 cm (¾ in) thick.

Lightly salt the fish and season the cream with the salt and pepper.

Gently fry the onion in the butter until soft and golden, about 5 minutes.

Take a dish about 4 cm (1½ in) deep and wide enough to hold the folded fillets in one layer. Butter it well. Arrange the potato slices evenly over the bottom. Lay the folded fillets side by side on top and scatter with the fried onion. Finally, spoon over the seasoned cream and scatter evenly with the grated cheese. Place a sheet of buttered greaseproof paper or baking parchment lightly on top. The dish can now be refrigerated for up to 12 hours. Leave at room temperature for 1 hour before baking.

Preheat the oven to 160°C (325°F/Gas 3). Bake for 30 minutes, until the sauce is bubbling very slightly and the fish has lost its glassy appearance. Take off the paper and, if the dish is too pale, grill gently for 3–4 minutes until it turns a rich golden brown.

Serve immediately, accompanied by green vegetables such as Minted Peas and Cucumber with Shallots (page 176).

87

NORMANDY-STYLE FISH WITH CIDER AND APPLES

Judi

Fish fillets are poached in dry cider infused with herbs and spices, enveloped in a velvety cream sauce made from the concentrated cooking juices, then grilled to a golden brown. Poached apples add an unusual finishing touch.

Makes 6–8 servings
Refrigerate leftovers 2 days. **Freezes** up to 1 month.

2 tart green apples, such as Granny Smith
squeeze of lemon juice
900g–1.4 kg (2–3 lb) white fish fillets, such as haddock, lemon sole,
    or halibut, skinned
450 ml (16 fl oz) dry cider (or substitute 350 ml (12 fl oz) cups dry
    white wine and 125 ml (4 fl oz) apple juice)
1 teaspoon sea salt
1 teaspoon whole black peppercorns
pinch of white pepper
1 bay leaf
sprig of parsley
For the sauce
    25 g (1 oz) butter
    25 g (1 oz) plain flour
    150 ml (5 fl oz) double cream
For the topping
    40 g (1½ oz) grated Cheddar or other mature cheese

Peel and core the apples, then cut into eighths. Put the apple sections in one layer in a lidded frying pan, then add a squeeze of lemon juice and enough water to cover the base of the pan. Cover and poach gently until tender, 6–7 minutes, turning once, or cook, covered, in the microwave, sprinkled with the lemon juice but without water, for 3–4 minutes. Drain and reserve.

Cut the fish into 6 or 8 pieces, salt lightly and leave to drain in a colander for 10 minutes. Put the cider (or wine and apple juice), the seasonings and the herbs into

88

a wide pan, bring to the boil over gentle heat, then add the fish. Cover and cook at barely a bubble until the fish looks creamy and flakes easily with a fork, 10–12 minutes.

Lift the cooked fish out with a slotted fish slice or spatula, drain thoroughly on paper towels then arrange in a buttered gratin or similar shallow ovenproof dish. Cover with aluminium foil to keep warm.

Strain the fish poaching liquid into a small saucepan and boil vigorously for 3–4 minutes until only about 300 ml (10 fl oz) remain.

Meanwhile, to make the sauce, put the butter and flour on to a plate and work them into a smooth paste using a flexible knife or spatula. Add this *beurre manié* 1 teaspoon at a time to the reduced poaching liquid in the saucepan, whisking constantly over low heat. Bubble gently for 3 minutes, then stir in the cream and bubble again until the sauce is thick enough to coat the back of a wooden spoon, about 2 minutes.

Pour the sauce over the fish, scatter with the grated cheese and arrange the drained apple decoratively around the edge. At this stage, the dish can be left, covered, for up to 2 hours.

Grill gently until a rich golden brown, about 5 minutes and serve at once.

If made earlier, reheat for 15–20 minutes in the oven at 180°C (350°F/Gas 4) until bubbly round the edges, or for 5 minutes, covered, at full power in the microwave. Remove the aluminium or clingfilm and grill for 5 minutes until golden brown. Serve with new potatoes and a delicately flavoured vegetable dish.

NORMANDY BOASTS ONE OF THE FINEST cuisines in France, yet it is one of the few regions that doesn't produce any wine. Instead, acres of orchards cover the countryside, producing superb apples and a deliciously fruity, dry cider. It is also renowned for its wonderful dairy products.

Dishes cooked *à la normande* feature butter, cream, dry cider and apples. In days gone by, meals in the region were characteristically punctuated by *le trou normand* — a small glass of Calvados, apple brandy, served between courses to aid digestion and stimulate the appetite. Nowadays, the *trou* or hole is more likely to be a refreshing sorbet, liberally sprinkled with Calvados, a memorable combination!

89

CHOPPED AND
FRIED FISH

Evelyn

THIS IS THE FAVOURITE Anglo-Jewish technique for cooking gefilte fish mix.

If you are chopping the fish in the food processor, be very careful not to over-process it to the purée stage, as this makes the mixture too 'pasty'.

Makes 12–14 patties, or 6–8 servings
Keeps up to 3 days under refrigeration.
Freezes up to 6 weeks raw or cooked.

For the fish mix
1 medium onion, peeled and roughly chopped
2 large eggs
2 teaspoons sea salt
pinch of white pepper
2 teaspoons sugar (or reduced-calorie equivalent)
1 tablespoon vegetable oil
50 g (2 oz) fine matzah meal
450 g (1 lb) haddock fillet, skinned
450 g (1 lb) cod fillet, skinned
For the coating
matzah meal or fine dry breadcrumbs
For frying
sunflower oil

Put the onion into the food processor, together with the eggs, seasonings, sugar and oil, then process until reduced to a purée. (If you wish to make a larger quantity but are using a standard-size processor you will need to do this in two batches.) Pour this purée into a large bowl and stir in the matzah meal. Leave to swell for 10 minutes.

If possible, buy minced fish at the fishmongers. Otherwise, cut the fish into

90

2.5 cm (1 in) dice and put in the processor, half-filling the bowl each time. Process for 5 seconds, until it is finely chopped, then add to the matzah meal mixture and blend in, using a large fork. Mix thoroughly—if preparing a large quantity, this is most easily done with the widespread fingers of one hand. The mixture should be firm enough to shape into a soft patty or ball. If it feels too 'cloggy', rinse out the processor bowl with a tablespoon or two of water and stir that in. If it feels very soft, stir in a tablespoon or two of matzah meal. Leave for half an hour, or overnight (under refrigeration) if preferred.

Dip the hands into cold water and form the mixture into patties about 6 × 4 × 2 cm (2½ × 1½ × ¾ in). The fish can now be cooked, or frozen raw or cooked.

To freeze cooked or raw, arrange the patties side by side on a tray lined with greaseproof paper or aluminium foil. Put the tray, uncovered, in the freezer for 2 hours or until the patties are firm to the touch. They can now be packed in a plastic bag or individually wrapped in Clingfilm to make it easy to remove a few at a time.

Frying the patties is most easily done in an electric deep-fryer, but you can use a deep frying pan. In either case, coat the patties evenly, either with fine dry bread-crumbs (easily prepared in the food processor from dry stale challah) or matzah meal.

To use a deep-fryer, remove the basket, then heat the oil to 190°C (375°F/Gas 5). Cook 5 or 6 patties at a time, allowing 5–6 minutes or until a rich golden brown.

To use a deep frying pan, heat 2.5 cm (1 in) deep oil until it is hot enough to brown a 2 cm (1 in) cube of bread in 30 seconds. Gently lower in enough patties to fill the pan without overcrowding—usually 5 or 6 in a 23 cm (9 in) pan. Cook steadily over moderate heat, turning every 2–3 minutes, until the patties are an even brown, 7–8 minutes in all. In either case, drain the patties by standing them up around the sides of a dish lined with crumpled paper towels.

Serve warm (never hot), or at room temperature or, if previously frozen, defrost and recrisp at 180°C (350°F/Gas 5) for 20–25 minutes or until heated through and crisp to the touch. Absolutely delicious with beetroot-and-horseradish sauce (*chrane*), mayonnaise or dill pickles.

CHOPPED AND FRIED GEFILTE FISH is delicious both warm and at room temperature, and can be served for family meals, informal picnics and elegant lunches. It keeps its flavour in the refrigerator for several days and in the freezer for several months. And it only needs a little recrisping in the oven to bring it back to its just-fried condition.

Forming the mixture into patties can only be done with wetted hands. At this point, disposable latex gloves come into their own. As they are thin and clingy, there is no loss of feeling and if they're dipped in cold water between each patty, the job is done in record time!

92

GEFILTE FISH PROVENÇAL

Judi

Tender, tasty patties of white fish are poached in a juicy tomato and pepper sauce, spiked with black olives. The dish combines the nostalgia of traditional gefilte fish with the irresistible flavours of Provence.

Makes 6–8 servings
Keeps 4 days under refrigeration. **Freezes** up to 2 months.

1 tablespoon olive oil
1 onion, finely chopped
1 green or red pepper, seeded and thinly sliced
2 tablespoons ketchup
1 × 400 g (14 oz) can Italian-style chopped or puréed tomatoes
2 teaspoons sun-dried tomato paste (optional)
12 black olives, herb-marinated if possible, stoned and halved
(optional)
1 teaspoon sea salt
1 teaspoon light brown sugar
10 grinds black pepper
1 bay leaf
pinch of dried *herbes de Provence*
6–8 raw patties of gefilte fish (page 90)

To make the sauce, heat the oil in a large, deep frying pan over low heat and cook the onion, stirring occasionally, until transparent, about 6 minutes. Add the pepper and fry gently for 3–4 minutes, then add all the remaining ingredients except the fish patties. Stir well and bubble until reduced to a thick coating consistency, about 10 minutes.

Preheat the oven to 150°C (300°F/Gas 2).

Arrange the patties in a shallow ovenproof dish, pour over the sauce and loosely cover with aluminium foil. Bake for 1 hour, basting once or twice.

Serve at room temperature (never hot) with plenty of brown bread to mop up the juices and side salads such as Fennel, Almond and Black Grape Salad (page 193) and Doris's German Cucumber Salad (page 200).

93

FRESH SALMON STRUDEL
PERFUMED WITH DILL

Evelyn

THIS IS MY INTERPRETATION OF A strudel in which paper-thin slices of fresh salmon fillet are encased in pastry and—an Israeli touch—served with a cool, pale-green avocado mayonnaise.

Makes 6–8 servings
Best **served** freshly baked.
Leftovers **keep** up to 2 days under refrigeration.

900 g (2 lb) thick salmon fillet with skin on
1 packet filo pastry
50 g (2 oz) unsalted butter, melted
sea salt
freshly ground black pepper
75 ml (3 fl oz) dry vermouth or dry white wine
2 tablespoons finely chopped dill

For the mayonnaise
1 large, very ripe avocado, peeled, stoned and cut in 2.5 cm (1 in) cubes
1 tablespoon fresh lemon juice
4 rounded tablespoons mayonnaise
2 rounded tablespoons reduced-fat yogurt
10 grinds black pepper
½ teaspoon sugar

Slice the salmon on the diagonal as is done with smoked salmon, using a flexible serrated knife. The slices should be 5 mm (¼ in) thick.

For the strudel you will need 3 layers of filo, each made up into an 45 cm (18 in) square. Depending on the size of each sheet of filo, you may need to make up the squares by piecing 1½–2 sheets together.

Brush the first square thinly but evenly with melted butter, arrange another 45 cm (18 in) square on top and brush that, then do the same with the third square.

94

Leaving 2.5 cm (1 in) clear at either side, 2.5 cm (1 in) at the top edge and 5 cm (2 in) at the bottom, cover evenly with the salmon slices. Season lightly with sea salt and a few grinds of black pepper. Sprinkle with the wine, then scatter the dill on top.

Turn in the 2.5 cm (1 in) of clear pastry over the salmon at either side, then roll up into a strudel and arrange with the seal-side down on a well-buttered baking tray. Brush the strudel top sparingly with more butter (too much fat prevents even browning). Make diagonal cuts through the top layer to mark out the 8 portions. The raw strudel can now be refrigerated for several hours, then left at room temperature for 1 hour before baking.

When ready to cook, preheat the oven to 200°C (400°F/Gas 6). Bake the strudel for 20–25 minutes, or until crisp and golden brown.

To make the mayonnaise, purée the avocado and the lemon juice in the food processor, then pulse in all the remaining ingredients until absolutely smooth. Chill for several hours.

To serve, allow the strudel to cool for 10–15 minutes, then slice and serve with the avocado mayonnaise.

A BOUQUET OF FRESH HERBS

ONCE UPON A TIME, fresh herbs—mainly parsley—were strictly seasonal and only used by the teaspoon. Now that they've become a year-round staple and we've learned to love what they can do to boost the flavour of even a simple soup, we're using them by the tablespoon or by weight—25 g (1 oz) is equivalent to 4 level tablespoons.

To keep them fresh for up to a week, I remove and discard any coarse stalks from herbs such as parsley, basil, coriander, tarragon and chervil, then place them in a large plastic bag together with a tablespoon of cold water, blow into the bag until it balloons out, then close tightly, shake well and refrigerate. It's magic!

Once chopped in quantity, herbs are best frozen; their maximum life in the refrigerator is rarely more than 3 days. After that they become indistinguishable in smell and taste from grass cuttings.

95

FILLET OF FRESH SALMON
IN PUFF PASTRY

Salmon en Croûte   *Judi*

THIS IS MY DINNER PARTY TOUR DE FORCE, golden puff pastry encasing succulent layers of salmon, spinach and a creamy herb mousse.

Makes 6–8 servings
Keeps 1 day under refrigeration.
Do not freeze.

2 × 450 g (1 lb) fillets of salmon cut from the centre to the tail, skinned
5 g (¼ oz) butter
2 spring onions, white part and 2.5 cm (1 in) of green part, finely sliced
1 clove garlic, finely chopped
225 g (8 oz) fresh spinach, washed and chopped,
    or 125 g (4 oz) frozen leaf spinach, chopped
10 grinds black pepper
2 teaspoons sea salt
For the cream cheese mixture
110 g (4 oz) cream cheese
1 large egg, beaten
1 teaspoon sea salt
pinch of white pepper
1 tablespoon chopped fresh chives or dill
pinch of paprika
1 tablespoon chopped fresh tarragon
    (use more chives if not available)
For the pastry case
2 sheets, about 450 g (1 lb), puff pastry,
    thawed but still very cold
For the garnish
few sprigs fresh dill or tarragon

96

Rinse the fish under running water, sprinkle lightly with sea salt then leave to drain in a colander.

In a medium frying pan, melt the butter over gentle heat, add the spring onions and cook, stirring until soft, about 3 minutes. Add the garlic followed by the spinach, the black pepper and 1 teaspoon of the sea salt, mixing well to coat the leaves with the buttery juices. Cook, stirring, over moderate heat until there is no visible liquid in the pan, about 5 minutes. Remove from the heat and allow to cool.

In a bowl, mix the cream cheese with 1 tablespoon of the beaten egg, ½ teaspoon salt, the white pepper, chives and paprika.

Line a baking tray large enough to hold the fish with baking parchment

Roll each sheet of pastry into a rectangle about 25 cm (1 in) wider than the fish on each side. Lay one piece of pastry diagonally on to the baking tray. Spread with half the cream cheese mixture in the shape of the fillets, leaving a 2.5 cm (1 in) margin on all sides, then sprinkle with half the chopped tarragon.

Blot the fish with paper towels, then lay one fillet on the cream cheese and tarragon. Sprinkle with a little sea salt, then spread the spinach mixture on top of the fish. Lay the second piece of fish on top with the thicker end over the thinner end of the bottom piece, to even out the thickness of the two pieces. Spread with the remaining cream cheese mixture, then lay the second piece of pastry on top.

Trim the excess pastry on all sides — you can create a curved 'fish' shape if you wish — then press the two pieces together gently with a fork to seal and brush evenly with beaten egg.

At this point the dish can be refrigerated for up to 3 hours, but should be allowed to stand at room temperature for 15 minutes before baking.

Preheat the oven to 220°C (425°F/Gas 7). Bake for 15 minutes, then reduce the heat to 190°C (375°F/Gas 5) and continue to bake for a further 25–30 minutes until the pastry is a rich golden brown. Allow to cool for a few minutes before serving.

To serve, transfer the fish on to a long serving platter and garnish with a few sprigs of fresh herb. Serve in angled slices with new potatoes and a side dish such as Minted Peas and Cucumber with Shallots (page 176) or Shades of Green Tossed Salad (page 189).

IMMIGRANT'S FISH PIE

Evelyn

A MORE SOPHISTICATED VERSION of an early Anglo-Jewish dish which provided a tasty but economical meal for immigrant families, who were taught the rudiments of British cooking in an effort to Anglicise them. This version, with its filling of three varieties of fish folded into a delicious sauce and topped with fluffy mashed potatoes, is ideal to serve as the main dish at an informal supper. It can be prepared up to 24 hours in advance, then baked as required.

Makes 6 generous servings
Leftovers **keep** up to 3 days under refrigeration.
Freezes up to 1 month.

1 small onion, peeled and thinly sliced
8 black peppercorns
2 bay leaves
2 sprigs parsley
350 g (12 oz) cod, skinned
175 g (6 oz) smoked haddock fillet, skinned
425 ml (15 fl oz) milk
350 g (12 oz) salmon fillet, skinned
squeeze of lemon juice

For the topping
1 kg (2¼ lb) boiling potatoes, peeled and cut into quarters
6 tablespoons milk
25 g (1 oz) butter
2 teaspoons sea salt
pinch of white pepper

For the sauce
25 g (1 oz) butter
25 g (1 oz) plain flour
½ teaspoon sea salt
20 grinds black pepper
shake of white pepper

98

125 g (4 oz) grated mature Cheddar cheese
2 tablespoons chopped fresh dill or parsley
squeeze of lemon juice

Divide the onion slices, peppercorns, bay leaves and parsley evenly between a large pan and a large saucepan. Add the cod and the haddock to the pan and pour in the milk. Put the salmon into the saucepan, barely cover with water and add the squeeze of lemon juice. Bring both pans slowly to the boil, remove from the heat, cover and let stand for 10 minutes (longer will do no harm).

Put the potatoes for the topping in a saucepan with enough boiling water to cover. Add the sea salt, bring to the boil again, then cover and boil steadily for 15–20 minutes or until tender when pierced with a sharp knife.

Preheat the oven to 190°C (375°F/Gas 5). Lightly butter a large oven-to-table dish, about 30 cm (12 in) long and about 5 cm (2 in) deep.

Meanwhile, remove the cod and haddock from the pan with a slotted spoon, then strain the milk into a measuring jug. There should be about 425 ml (15 fl oz). If less, make up the difference with a little extra milk. Set aside for making the sauce. Remove the salmon from the saucepan with a slotted spoon and discard its cooking water and the flavourings from both pans. Remove any skin and small bones from all the fish, then flake the flesh very coarsely with a fork and arrange in an even layer in the baking dish.

For the sauce, melt the butter in a large saucepan, stir in the flour and cook over low heat for 1 minute, then gradually stir in the hot strained milk. Bring to the boil, whisking constantly, then reduce the heat and simmer for 2 minutes. Remove from the heat and season with the sea salt and the peppers, then stir in the grated cheese, dill or parsley and lemon juice. Pour over the fish.

For the topping, drain the cooked potatoes and return them to a low heat. Trickle the milk down the inside of the pan and when it begins to steam, start whisking the potatoes (preferably using a hand-held electric mixer), adding the butter and the salt and pepper, and continue whisking until smooth and creamy.

Spread the potatoes evenly on top of the fish and mark decoratively with a fork. Bake for 30–35 minutes, or until the top is a rich golden brown and you can just see the filling bubbling up a little at the side.

Allow to cool for 5 minutes, then serve with a green salad or green vegetable .

FISHERMAN'S CASSEROLE

Marmite du Pêcheur

Judi

Succulent white fish fillets and tender vegetables are poached in a light cream sauce. This is a comforting dish, perfect for an informal supper on a cold, dark night.

Makes 6–8 servings
Leftovers **keep** 2 days under refrigeration. **Do not freeze.**

675–900 g (1½–2 lb) white fish such as hake, sea bass or plaice,
  skinned and filleted
½ large carrot, peeled
½ medium onion, peeled
50 g (2 oz) butter
1 teaspoon sea salt
pinch of white pepper
1 small bay leaf
10 black, white, or pink peppercorns
2 teaspoons cornflour
1 × 175 ml can evaporated milk or 150 ml (5 fl oz) single cream
150 g (5 oz) frozen peas
900 g (2 lb) scraped new potatoes boiled until tender, or 1 large can,
  about 900 g (2 lb), new potatoes, drained
2 teaspoons chopped curly or flat-leaf parsley

Wash and salt the fish, then cut the thick fillets such as hake into 6–8 pieces and roll up the thinner ones such as plaice.

Grate the carrot and the onion finely. Melt the butter in a flameproof casserole or a frying pan with a well-fitting lid. The minute the butter has melted, but before it starts to change colour, add the grated vegetables. Stir for 1–2 minutes to allow them to absorb some of the butter and begin to soften, then add the fish, turning it over so that it becomes coated with the buttery vegetables.

100

Now add just enough water to cover the bottom of the dish or to a depth of 5 mm (¼ in). Sprinkle the fish with the salt and pepper, and add the bay leaf and the peppercorns at the side of the pan. Cover, then simmer on a very low heat for 15 minutes, or until the fish looks creamy all through. Remove the bay leaf and peppercorns.

Put the cornflour in a bowl and stir in the evaporated milk or cream. Add to the fish, stirring well, then turn up the heat a little and allow to bubble gently for 3 minutes.

Finally stir in the frozen peas, drained potatoes and chopped parsley. Leave covered on a very low heat for 3–4 minutes, until the vegetables are heated through. Serve immediately.

A *MARMITE* is a covered earthenware or metal casserole. The name comes from the old French word for 'hypocrite,' since the covered pot hides its true contents! In French fishing villages this dish would be made with a medley of whatever the local *pêcheurs*, fishermen, brought in that day.

JUICY GRILLED KEBABS
WITH A SESAME CRUNCH
COATING

Evelyn

WHEN SUMMER COMES AROUND AND YOU FEEL like heating up the barbecue again, this is a deliciously different way to cook firm fish such as salmon, halibut or hake fillet. A sesame and bread crumb coating keeps the fish moist while adding an extra layer of flavour. The kebabs cook in just minutes.

Makes 6–8 servings
Leftovers **keep** 1 day in refrigerator.
Do not freeze.

16 wooden or metal skewers, about 25 cm (10 in) long
675–900 g (1½–2 lb) thick fish fillets, skinned
1½ teaspoons sea salt
good pinch of white or black pepper
50 g (2 oz) melted butter, or 125 ml (4 fl oz) olive oil
125 g (4 oz) fresh white breadcrumbs
2 teaspoons finely grated lemon zest
50 g (2 oz) sesame seeds
32 small mushrooms

For the dill sauce
6 rounded tablespoons mayonnaise
4 tablespoons chopped fresh dill
½ teaspoon Dijon mustard
150 ml (5 fl oz) soured cream

If using wooden skewers, soak for at least 30 minutes in water to cover before using.

Cut the fish into 5 cm (2 in) cubes and sprinkle with the salt and pepper. Put the melted butter or olive oil in a small bowl. In another bowl, mix the breadcrumbs,

102

lemon zest and sesame seeds. Cut the stalks of the mushrooms level with the edge of the caps.

Put the fish cubes into the butter or oil and turn to coat on all sides, then dip in the breadcrumb mixture and lay on a board. Toss the mushrooms in the butter or oil. Thread the fish and mushrooms alternately on the skewers, leaving room in between so that the fish can cook evenly.

Grill on the barbecue for 3–5 minutes, turning once or twice. The kebabs may also be cooked under the grill for 8–10 minutes, turning once.

In a bowl, beat all the dill sauce ingredients together.

Serve the kebabs with the dill sauce, either hot or at room temperature up to 2 hours later.

NUTS ABOUT NUTS

A MIRACULOUS METAMORPHOSIS takes place when nuts and seeds such as sesame or sunflower are toasted or roasted. Their rather bland flavour when raw intensifies as the rich oil content browns and some of their water content evaporates. And not only is the flavour vastly improved, so is the colour. Because of the high percentage of oil, it's not really necessary to use additional fat for the process. As the seeds or nuts heat through, some of their own oil comes to the surface and does the browning job instead.

Small quantities can be 'dry-fried' in a heavy (preferably non-stick) pan or under the grill. Larger quantities are most evenly toasted in a thin layer in the oven at 220°C (425°F/Gas 7) for 15–20 minutes, stirring once or twice. Once they've been given this gilding treatment, they can be stored in an airtight container for future use.

Golden sesame seeds by themselves make a superb crunchy coating for portions of salmon fillet. My friend, the food writer Richard Crawley, first brushes the salmon pieces, each weighing 125–150 g (4–5 ounces, with a thin coating of flour, dips them in egg and finally in golden sesame seeds, then pan-fries them in shallow oil for 2–3 minutes on each side until they turn a rich brown.

103

MIRACULOUS FISH

Judi

THIS IS ONE OF THOSE DISHES THAT HAS BECOME an all-time greatest hit in the repertoire of every cook who's tried it, and has an unbelievable impact for the minuscule effort involved. A cheese and mayonnaise topping keeps the fish wonderfully moist and juicy, while adding a terrific flavour that tastes neither of mayonnaise nor of cheese. Almost any white fish will do, although avoid cod, which tends to get watery when grilled.

Makes 4 servings
Leftovers **keep** 1 day under refrigeration. **Do not freeze.**

4 large fillets of white fish such as plaice or hake, skinned
sea salt
white pepper
1 tablespoon fresh lemon juice
3–4 tablespoons mayonnaise
For the topping
    125 g (4 oz) grated extra mature Cheddar cheese

Wash the fillets, season lightly with salt and pepper on both sides, then arrange side by side in a lightly buttered baking tray. (If using a nonstick tray, there is no need to grease it.)

Sprinkle each fillet with a little lemon juice, then spread each with a thin but even coating of mayonnaise. Sprinkle evenly with the cheese, making sure the fish is entirely covered.

Place the pan 5 cm (2 in) below a hot grill until the topping is a rich golden brown and the fish flakes easily with a fork, about 6 minutes.

Serve with boiled or baked potatoes and a juicy vegetable such as Fragrant Green Beans à la Côte d'Azur (page 179).

104

HALIBUT IN A
VELVET LEMON SAUCE

Evelyn

THIS CLASSIC ANGLO-JEWISH PASSOVER dish should be refrigerated for 24 hours to allow the delicate sauce to flavour the fish. The contrast between the sweet-and-sour sauce and the gently flavoured fish is mouthwatering. Fresh salmon steaks may be substituted.

Makes 6–8 servings
Keeps up to 4 days under refrigeration.
Do not freeze.

For poaching the fish
   water to cover the fish, approximately 425 ml (15 fl oz)
   1 large onion, peeled and thinly sliced
   125 g (4 oz) sugar
   2 teaspoons sea salt
   pinch of white pepper
   6–8 pieces of halibut on the bone, about 700–900 g (1½–2 lb)
      total weight
For the sauce
   2 large eggs
   5 tablespoons fresh lemon juice
   2 teaspoons potato flour, mixed to a liquid
      with a minimum of cold water
For the garnish
   parsley
   sections of fresh lemon, skin left on

In a lidded pan wide enough to hold all the fish in a single layer, bring the water, onion, sugar and seasonings to the boil. (Adding the sugar at this stage greatly improves the fish without noticeably sweetening it.) Lower the heat while you prepare the fish.

continued

105

Wash and salt the fish and put in the pan. Bring the poaching liquid back to the boil, then lower the heat so that it is barely bubbling. Partly cover and simmer very gently for 20 minutes. Lift out the fish with a slotted spoon or fish slice, draining any liquid back into the pan.

Place the fish in an oval serving dish about 4 cm (1½ in) deep. Remove any skin but leave in the bone, then leave to cool while you make the sauce.

To make the sauce, boil the remaining fish poaching liquid for 3 minutes to concentrate the flavour, then strain it and measure out 225 ml (8 fl oz). Beat the eggs thoroughly with a rotary whisk, then whisk in the fish liquid, the lemon juice and the potato flour liquid. Alternatively, mix all the sauce ingredients for 10 seconds in a blender or food processor. This makes it easier to thicken the sauce without fear of it curdling.

Put this liquid into a thick-bottomed saucepan and cook gently over low heat until the sauce thickens to the consistency of a coating custard—you will need to stir it constantly. Do not let it boil or the eggs may curdle. To make the sauce in the microwave, cook the blended ingredients, uncovered, in a jug or bowl on 50 per cent power for 2 minutes, whisk well, then cook for a further 2–3 minutes until thickened to the consistency of a coating custard.

Taste the sauce and add extra lemon juice, if necessary, to make it equally sweet and sour. Pour the sauce over the fish, coating it completely. Leave in the refrigerator overnight, covered with aluminium foil.

Serve at room temperature, garnished with the parsley and lemon sections.

106

DÉLICES OF SALMON
UNDER A SUN-DRIED TOMATO CRUST
WITH A BASIL CREAM SAUCE

Judi

SUN-DRIED TOMATOES—originally a way of preserving a glut of summer vegetables by farmers in Calabria in southern Italy—became an expensive fashion food in the early 1990s. Happily, they have once again found their rightful place as a superb flavouring agent at an every-day price. In this dish they add an intense, earthy undertone to the cheese-and-crumb crust.

Makes 6–8 servings
Best **served** the same day. Leftovers **keep** 2 days under refrigeration.
Uncooked pastry **freezes** up to 1 month.

6–8 thick salmon fillets, 150 g (5 oz) each, skin removed
sea salt
For the crust
75 g (3 oz) mild Cheddar cheese
3 tablespoons sun-dried tomato paste or sun-dried tomatoes in oil
225 g (8 oz) fresh white breadcrumbs
125 g (4 oz) very cold butter, cut in 2 cm (1 in) chunks
good pinch of sea salt
2 tablespoons mayonnaise
For the basil sauce
40 g (1½ oz) butter, softened
25 g (1 oz) plain flour
150 ml (5 fl oz) dry white wine
150 ml (5 fl oz) vegetable stock
150 ml (5 fl oz) double cream
150 ml (5 fl oz) soured cream
salt and white pepper (optional)
8 fresh basil leaves, finely chopped

107

continued

At least 20 minutes before preparing the crust, cut the cheese into pieces that will fit the feed tube of your food processor, put in the freezer to chill for 15 minutes then grate finely in the food processor.

Pulse all the crust ingredients (including the chilled cheese) in the food processor for a few seconds, until the mixture forms a ball around the blade. Lift out, cover with clingfilm, flatten slightly and chill for 30 minutes.

Have ready a lightly buttered baking tray. Arrange the salmon fillets on it, sprinkle lightly with salt, then spread each piece of fish with a thin layer of mayonnaise. Sift a very thin layer of flour on a pastry board. Roll out the chilled tomato crust 8 mm (⅜ in) thick, then cut into neat portions to cover each piece of salmon. Pat firmly in place. The salmon can now be refrigerated for several hours, then left at room temperature for 1 hour before cooking.

To make the sauce, mash together the soft butter and flour with a fork or knife on a plate until a smooth, thick paste is formed, about 1 minute.

Heat the wine and stock over gentle heat until simmering, then add the butter-flour paste, 1 teaspoon at a time, whisking well between each addition. Slowly stir in the double cream and soured cream and bubble gently until the sauce is thick enough to coat the back of a spoon, about 2 minutes. Taste and add a little salt and white pepper if necessary, then stir in the finely chopped basil. The sauce can be left under refrigeration, without the basil, for up to 8 hours.

At least half an hour before serving, preheat the oven to 220°C (425°F/Gas 7). Bake the fish for 10 minutes, then leave to rest for 15 minutes before serving.

To serve, add the basil leaves to the sauce and reheat gently if it was made earlier in the day. Serve the fish warm or at room temperature, accompanied by the warm sauce and a selection of salads such as Perfect Potato Salad (page 194) and Shades of Green Tossed Salad (page 189), or vegetables such as new potatoes and Minted Peas and Cucumber with Shallots (page 176).

108

A Bird in the Hand:
Wonderful Ways with Chicken

'Fowl that may fly above the earth in the open firmament of heaven'

—Genesis 1:20

OUR LOVE AFFAIR WITH THE CHICKEN IS COMMON TO BOTH Sephardi and the Ashkenazi cuisines, probably because the birds could be kept even in the smallest of back yards and fattened very satisfactorily on kitchen scraps. The daughter of a local family who emigrated from Lithuania to the East End of London in the 1920s told us that chicken was so much a part of her family's diet that even when they lived in a tiny flat in a tenement block with no back yard, a live bird would be kept under the kitchen table ready for a festival or Shabbat meal!

Every Jewish community has its own way with a chicken. The Poles and Hungarians favour intensely flavoured casseroles, such as *Gedaempte Chicken* or the rich red paprika-scented chicken from Hungary, that were often cooked in the village baker's oven. For modern appetites, a dish of grilled chicken in a lime and chilli marinade with a pineapple and coriander salsa, or succulent chicken portions in a crunchy sesame coating, may strike a lighter note yet still follow the spirit, if not the letter, of the original.

109

SUCCULENT ROAST CHICKEN WITH A LEMON AND HERB STUFFING

Evelyn

THIS IS THE BEST METHOD I know to achieve a succulent, tasty bird. To keep the breast meat juicy, the chicken is cooked breast-side down and turned over to complete the browning only for the last 20 minutes. Positioning the bird on a poultry rack allows heat to circulate around it and also prevents the bird from reabsorbing the fat as it melts from the skin. When calculating the serving time, allow an extra 15 minutes for letting the bird rest out of the oven before it is carved.

Makes 6 servings

Leftovers **keep** up to 3 days under refrigeration.

Freezes up to 6 weeks.

For the stuffing

125 g (4 oz) fresh breadcrumbs (4 large slices of bread)

½ teaspoon sea salt

½ teaspoon paprika

15 grinds black pepper

1 teaspoon dried *herbes de Provence*

2 tablespoons finely chopped curly parsley

2 teaspoons grated lemon rind

75 g (3 oz) margarine

2 teaspoons olive oil

1 small onion, peeled and chopped

For the bird

1 2–2.25 kg (4½–5 lb) roasting chicken

sea salt

1 fat clove garlic, halved

olive oil for brushing

freshly ground black pepper

350 ml (12 fl oz) strong chicken stock, hot

110

For the gravy

    2 teaspoons cornflour
    2 to 3 tablespoons water or white wine

Preheat the oven to 200°C (400°F/Gas 6). In a roasting pan that will just hold the bird comfortably, put a poultry rack.

First make the stuffing. Put the breadcrumbs, seasonings, herbs and rind into a bowl. Heat the margarine with the oil in a small pan over moderate heat. Add the onion and cook gently until soft and golden, about 5 minutes. Pour the contents of the pan over the seasoned crumbs. Toss lightly until all the crumbs are coated.

Salt the cavity of the bird, then stuff lightly with the prepared stuffing and, if necessary, tie up the cavity with kitchen twine. Make a shallow cut on each side of the bird where the leg joint meets the breast and insert half a clove of garlic in each slit.

Brush the bird all over with olive oil and season with a sprinkling of sea salt and freshly ground black pepper. Pour the hot stock into the roasting pan, then lay the bird upside down on the poultry rack. (If it doesn't sit comfortably, arrange it on its side.) Roast for 20 minutes per 450 g (1 lb), plus an extra 20 minutes. (For a 2.25 kg/5 lb bird, the total cooking time will be 2 hours.) Baste the bird every half hour with the stock, then 20 minutes before the end of the cooking time, turn it over (a large wooden or metal spoon inserted in the body cavity makes the job easier) and cook breast side up for the remaining time.

Remove the chicken from the oven and lift it on to a carving dish or board, cover lightly with aluminium foil (to keep the heat in) and make the gravy. Pour off any free fat from the roasting pan and, if the stock has dried up, add enough boiling water to bring it back to the original 350 ml (12 fl oz). Stir well to loosen any of the crisp bits on the bottom, then pour into a small saucepan. In a small bowl, mix the cornflour and water or wine together to make a smooth liquid. Add to the saucepan, bring to the boil and simmer for 3 minutes. Taste and correct the seasoning if necessary.

To serve, detach the legs and wings, carve the breast and serve garnished with 1 tablespoon of stuffing and 1–2 tablespoons of gravy. Omitting the (alas, delectable) skin from each serving will halve the calorie content.

111

SPATCHCOCK CHICKEN
WITH PROVENÇAL HERBS

Poulet en Crapaudine   *Judi*

THE QUICKEST WAY to cook an entire chicken on the barbecue is to split and flatten it so that it looks like a butterfly — or, as the French, less romantically, call it, a *crapaud* or toad! By any name, however, this is a spectacular way to serve barbecued chicken. Marinating the bird in lemon and herbs produces well-flavoured, succulent flesh.

Makes 3–4 servings
Keeps 2 days under refrigeration.
Freeze leftovers for 2 months.

1 × 2 kg (4½ lb) chicken
For the marinade
  2 teaspoons sea salt
  20 grinds black pepper
  1 teaspoon dried *herbes de Provence*
  juice of 2 lemons
  1 tablespoon soy sauce
  2 tablespoons olive oil

To prepare the chicken, with poultry shears or a sharp heavy knife, make 2 parallel cuts on either side of the backbone and remove it. Flatten the chicken into a butterfly shape with your hands.

Mix together the marinade ingredients in a non-metallic dish large enough to hold the chicken when flattened. Place the flattened chicken in the dish with the marinade. Leave for 30 minutes to 1 hour, turning it over once.

Heat the barbecue or grill. To barbecue, place the chicken on the barbecue rack skin side up (only the bony underside should be in contact with the heat) and cook for 25–35 minutes, covered if a lid is available.

To grill, place on a grill pan with the skin side down about 8 cm (3 in) from the

112

heat and grill for 20–30 minutes.

To check that it is cooked right through, pierce a leg with a skewer—the juice should run clear. Turn the bird over and barbecue or grill for a further 2–3 minutes, uncovered, to crisp the skin (watch carefully, as the skin burns easily once it is in direct contact with the heat). Transfer the chicken to a platter and cover with aluminium foil to keep warm.

To serve, use the shears or a sharp, heavy knife to cut into serving portions. It's delicious either hot from the grill or at room temperature. Serve with a dressed green or mixed salad, a juicy side dish such as Marinated Roast Peppers (page 187) and rice or potatoes.

~ THE FRENCH KING Henry IV won eternal fame and approval ～ with his famous remark that every citizen in his kingdom should have a chicken to put in their pot every Sunday. From the Jewish point of view, however, he got the day wrong—he should have made it Friday!

The reasons for chicken on the Friday night menu in Ashkenazi households are well documented. It was one of the cheaper and more delicious protein foods available in nineteenth-century Eastern Europe. In addition, the canny housewife could devise three different courses from just one bird—an hors d'oeuvre (chopped liver), a soup and a casserole—not to mention the free schmaltz (fat) which every Jewish cook treasured before the cholesterol era.

What did surprise me when researching food customs in households where one partner came from the Sephardi community and one from the Ashkenazi, was the large number where chicken was on the menu on Friday night in both traditions—albeit stuffed and flavoured in different ways.

113

SLOW-COOKED CHICKEN
ON A BED OF POTATOES

Gedaempte Chicken

Evelyn

THE POTATOES ARE COOKED IN THE JUICES of the chicken—a very old technique in Jewish kitchens—which gives them a wonderful flavour. This is a very good-tempered dish which can be kept warm in a low oven without overcooking the bird. I have given quantities for 8–10 servings, as it is an ideal dish for a family get-together or an informal supper party.

Makes 8–10 servings
Keeps up to 2 days under refrigeration.
Leftovers **freeze** up to 6 weeks.

2 × 1.4–1.6 kg (3–3½ lb) chickens, cut into 8 to 10 pieces, skinned
125 ml (4 fl oz) olive oil
3½ teaspoons sea salt
30 grinds black pepper
1.4 kg (3 lb) baby new potatoes
2 rounded teaspoons margarine
2 medium onions, peeled and finely chopped
2 bay leaves
2 teaspoons cornflour
425 ml (15 fl oz) chicken stock

For the garnish
2 tablespoons chopped fresh tarragon

Preheat the oven to 180°C (350°F/Gas 4).

Dry the chicken pieces thoroughly.

Heat the oil in a large frying pan over moderate heat, then cook the chicken, stirring, until golden brown on all sides, about 10 minutes. Remove from the pan and drain on paper towels. Sprinkle with 1½ teaspoons of the sea salt and the black pepper.

114

In a large pot, cover the potatoes with cold water, add the remaining 2 teaspoons sea salt and bring slowly to the boil. Cook for 5 minutes, until almost tender when pierced with a slim, pointed knife. Drain well and leave covered with a tea towel to absorb any remaining moisture.

To the oil remaining in the pan, add the margarine and cook the onions and the partly cooked potatoes together over moderate heat, until golden, about 5 minutes, keeping them moving in the pan so that they brown evenly. (You may need to do this in two batches). Arrange them in a large casserole dish and sprinkle very lightly with sea salt. Lay the chicken pieces on top, tuck in the bay leaves, cover and transfer to the oven. Cook covered for 35 minutes or until the juices run clear when a leg piece is pierced.

Lift the chicken and vegetables out of the casserole dish and set aside. In a small bowl, stir the chicken stock into the cornflour and mix until smooth. Add to the cooking pan, bring to the boil on top of the stove and bubble for 2–3 minutes. Tip this sauce into a bowl, return the potatoes and chicken to the casserole dish then pour over the sauce.

Scatter with the chopped tarragon and serve from the casserole dish.

HUNTER'S CHICKEN
WITH FRESH HERBS AND MUSHROOMS

Chicken Chasseur
Judi

THE FRESH, FRAGRANT HERBS THAT GROW on French hillsides give this earthy rosemary- and thyme-scented casserole its glorious flavour. In days gone by, a sauce of mushrooms, shallots and wine was served with game, the fruits of the hunter, or *chasseur*. The sauce is richest and most intense if made the day before and reheated. If you plan to do this, be careful not to overcook the chicken when reheating.

Makes 8 servings

Keeps 3 days under refrigeration. **Freezes** up to 3 months.

For the coating
- 3 tablespoons plain flour
- 1 teaspoon sea salt
- 10 grinds black pepper
- 1 teaspoon paprika

For the chicken
- 50 ml (2 fl oz) olive oil
- 1 large chicken, 2.3–2.7 kg (5–6 lb), cut into 6 portions, or 8 chicken pieces (legs, thighs and breasts), skinned
- 2 cloves garlic, peeled and finely chopped
- 4 shallots, finely chopped
- 2 tablespoons brandy (optional)
- 225 g (8 oz) very small white mushrooms (or larger mushrooms cut into quarters)
- 450 g (1 lb) ripe tomatoes, diced, or ½ × 400 g (14 oz) can chopped tomatoes with juice
- 2 teaspoons fresh thyme, stripped from stalk
- 2 teaspoons finely chopped fresh rosemary
- 225 ml (8 fl oz) white wine

116

425 ml (15 fl oz) strong chicken stock

2 teaspoons dark brown sugar

1 teaspoon paprika

1 teaspoon sea salt

For the garnish

1 tablespoon fresh chopped parsley

1 tablespoon chopped fresh tarragon

Put the flour, salt, pepper and paprika in a plastic bag, then shake each chicken piece in the seasoned mixture to coat evenly.

Heat the oil in a large frying pan or lidded sauté pan over moderate heat for 2 minutes. Add the chicken legs and thighs (they should sizzle). After 3 minutes add the breasts. Fry, uncovered, turning until a rich golden brown on all sides, about 4 minutes. If necessary, reduce the heat to prevent the oil from smoking. Do not crowd or the chicken will not brown—if the pan is not large enough, fry in 2 batches. Remove the chicken, drain on paper towels then transfer to a plate.

Pour off all but 1 tablespoon oil from the pan and cook the garlic and shallots over gentle heat, stirring, until golden, about 4 minutes. Pour in the brandy, if using and bubble for 1 minute until it has almost evaporated, stirring well to loosen any of the brown bits in the pan. Add the mushrooms, tomatoes and the rest of the ingredients. Bring to the boil and simmer for 5 minutes, until thickened to a coating consistency. Taste and adjust the seasoning, then return the chicken with any juices to the pan and stir gently to cover with the sauce.

Cover and cook on low heat for 30 minutes, until a leg is tender when pierced with a sharp knife. For the best flavour, allow to cool and refrigerate overnight.

To serve, if refrigerated, reheat gently until the sauce is steaming and the chicken is heated through, about 8 minutes on the stove, 5 minutes in the microwave on full power. Just before serving, sprinkle with the chopped parsley and tarragon.

HUNGARIAN CHICKEN CASSEROLE

Csirke Paprikás

Evelyn

A LUSCIOUS CASSEROLE REDOLENT of the flavours that epitomised the cuisine of the former Austro-Hungarian Empire. In the classic dish, soured cream is stirred in at the end to thicken the sauce, but I use cornflour as a substitute. The brightest and best Hungarian paprika is called *kulonleges*, which has a delicate rather than a fiery flavour.

Makes 6–8 servings
Keeps up to 3 days under refrigeration.
Freezes up to 6 weeks.

2 × 1.6 kg (3½ lb) chickens, backbone removed and each cut in
    4 portions (or 8 chicken portions on the bone), lightly salted
3 tablespoons sunflower oil
2 medium onions, finely chopped
3 level tablespoons Hungarian paprika
300 ml (10 fl oz) chicken stock
4 medium green or red peppers, seeds and pith removed,
    cut into fine strips
2 teaspoons dark brown sugar
1 × 400 g (14 oz) can chopped tomatoes
2 teaspoons cornflour mixed with 2 tablespoons cold water
1 teaspoon sea salt
10 grinds black pepper

Dry the chicken pieces with paper towels. Heat the oil in a large frying pan over moderate heat and cook the chicken in it until golden brown on all sides, 5–6 minutes. Remove and drain on paper towels.

In the same pan in the remaining oil, gently cook the onions, covered, until softened and golden, 10–15 minutes. Stir in the paprika and chicken stock, and cook a further 2 minutes.

118

Add the chicken, the pepper strips, brown sugar and tomatoes. Cover and cook very gently for 25–30 minutes, until the chicken is cooked through — there will be no sign of pinkness when a piece is nicked with a sharp knife. Lift the chicken pieces on to a warm platter.

Add the cornflour mixture to the pan. Simmer for 3 minutes or until thickened to a coating consistency. Then add the sea salt and black pepper, taste and adjust the seasoning if necessary.

Spoon the sauce over the chicken and serve with Auntie Mary's Savoury Noodles (page 76) or plain boiled white or brown rice.

PAPRIKA — the spice made from the dried and pulverised flesh of sweet peppers — comes in no less than six different strengths in its native Hungary. The mildest, *kulonleges* (which I'm told translates as 'delicate and of exquisite flavour'), is the one most similar to that sold as 'sweet paprika'.

Should you visit Hungary, don't miss the opportunity to bring home a few packs of *kulonleges*. You might also try *edes-nemes* (noble, sweet), *tozsa* (rose) and *csemege* (mild). Unless your family have cast-iron stomachs though, I'd keep away from *eros* — the hot one!

119

FRENCH-STYLE CHICKEN WITH A RICH RED WINE SAUCE

Poulet Grande Dame

Judi

THE SIMPLE BUT DELICIOUS FLAVOURS of what the French call *poulet bonne femme,* or housewife's chicken, have been elevated into a grand dinner party dish that combines robust peasant flavours with urban sophistication. A whole chicken is part braised, part roasted in stock and red wine on a bed of carrots and tiny potatoes. Before going into the oven, the bird is browned in a pan. The result is a rich brown skin and succulent, aromatic flesh imbued with the earthy flavours of all its cooking companions.

Makes 6–8 servings

Leftovers **keep** 3 days under refrigeration. **Freezes** up to 2 months.

1.1–1.4 kg (2½–3 lb) small new potatoes, cleaned but not peeled

For the chicken

1 × 2.3–2.7 kg (5–6 lb) chicken

1 tablespoon plain white flour

1 tablespoon paprika

2 teaspoons sea salt

20 grinds black pepper

1 lemon, cut in half

3 tablespoons olive oil

For the vegetables

1 large onion, thinly sliced

2 cloves garlic, halved

3 medium carrots, peeled and sliced in rounds

1 teaspoon sea salt

10 grinds black pepper

4 sprigs parsley

2 bay leaves

225 ml (8 fl oz) rich fruity red wine such as Cabernet Savignon

120

For the gravy

    2 teaspoons cornflour mixed to a thin liquid
       with a little wine or water
    water as needed
    pinch of sugar
    salt and freshly ground black pepper if needed

Preheat the oven to 200°C (400°F/Gas 6).

Cover the potatoes with cold water and 1 teaspoon of the sea salt, bring to the boil and simmer over moderate heat until almost tender, about 10 minutes. Drain.

Place the chicken on a board. Mix together the flour, paprika, 1 teaspoon sea salt and the pepper, and sprinkle evenly over the chicken. Place the lemon halves inside the cavity, then tie the legs together with kitchen twine to keep the bird in shape.

Heat the oil in a large frying pan over moderate heat for 1 minute, then add the bird and fry over gentle heat, turning at 5-minute intervals, until it is a rich gold on all sides, about 20 minutes altogether. Remove from the pan and leave on a large plate.

To prepare the vegetables, in the remaining oil in the pan, cook the onion over moderate heat until soft and golden, about 4 minutes. Add the garlic, followed by the carrots and the partly cooked potatoes, stirring well. Season with the salt and pepper, then continue to cook until the potatoes take on a little colour, about 5 minutes. Add the parsley and bay leaves.

Transfer the vegetable mixture, along with any residue on the bottom of the pan, to a large casserole. Place the chicken breast-side-up on top of the vegetables, together with any juice that has come out of it while resting.

Cover the casserole and put in the oven. After 15 minutes, by which time it should be sizzling nicely, turn the heat down to 160°C (325°F/Gas 3). After a further 30 minutes, add the wine and baste the chicken. Baste again 40 minutes later, remove the lid and turn the oven back up to 200°F (400°F/Gas 6). Cook for a further 15–20 minutes. At this point the chicken should be a rich brown and a leg will waggle easily. The total cooking time will be about 2 hours.

Remove the bird from the casserole and allow to rest in a warm place, lightly covered with aluminium foil, for at least 10 minutes (and up to 20) before carving.

Remove the vegetables with a slotted spoon and transfer to a covered serving dish, then return to the oven and reduce the temperature to 140°C (275°F/Gas 1) to keep them warm.

121

continued

To make the gravy, add enough water to the cooking pan to make up to 425 ml (15 fl oz). Bring to the boil on the stove, stirring to loosen any brown bits, then pour into a small saucepan. Whisk in the cornflour liquid and bubble over moderate heat, whisking until smoothly thickened, about 3 minutes. Add the sugar and season with salt and black pepper if necessary. Keep at a very gentle simmer until the chicken is ready to serve.

Present the chicken, then carve. Pour a little of the sauce over each portion. Serve with a simply cooked green vegetable such as peas or French beans.

OVEN-FRIED SESAME CHICKEN
WITH A TARRAGON SAUCE

Judi

THESE CRUNCHY PORTIONS of chicken are coated with a mixture of bread-crumbs, sesame seeds and herbs. They're as crisp as if they had been deep-fried but are cooked with only 50 ml (2 fl oz) of oil. They make excellent freezer fillers as they can be frozen ready-coated but raw, or cooked. The chicken is equally delicious hot or cold.

Makes 6 servings
Serve same day once cooked.
Freezes up to 3 months cooked or raw.

5 tablespoons freshly squeezed lemon juice
½ teaspoon sea salt
1 × 1.4–1.6 kg (3–3½ lb) chicken cut into 6 pieces,
    or 6 boneless breast portions, skinned if preferred
For the coating
125 g (4 oz) dry breadcrumbs or matzah meal
1 large egg
3 tablespoons sunflower oil
1 tablespoon dark sesame oil
20 grinds black pepper
½ teaspoon sea salt
1 tablespoon dried mixed herbs or *herbes de Provence*
zest of 1 lemon, finely grated
75 g (3 oz) sesame seeds
½ teaspoon paprika
For the sauce
2 shallots, peeled and finely chopped, or the finely chopped whites of
    4 large spring onions
2 tablespoons margarine or sunflower oil
3 tablespoons medium dry sherry (optional)

123

continued

150 ml (5 fl oz) dry white wine or vermouth

150 ml (5 fl oz) chicken stock

2 teaspoons cornflour mixed to a thin liquid with a little wine or
  chicken stock

1 teaspoon Dijon mustard

good pinch of nutmeg

good pinch of white pepper

1 large egg yolk

2 tablespoons chopped fresh tarragon

For the garnish

6 small sprigs fresh tarragon

One hour before cooking, put the lemon juice and ½ teaspoon salt into a flat dish, turn the chicken pieces in it, then leave to marinate. Turn once or twice during the hour.

Preheat the oven to 200°C (400°F/Gas 6). If the breadcrumbs or matzah meal are very pale, spread them out on a baking tray, put in the oven as it heats up and toast until they are golden brown (this gives a better colour to the cooked chicken). Have ready a lightly greased baking tray large enough to hold the chicken portions, well spaced, side by side.

Whisk the egg and oils together with the pepper and ½ teaspoon salt until well blended, then put in a shallow dish large enough to hold a portion of chicken. Mix the crumbs or matzah meal, dried herbs, lemon zest, sesame seeds and paprika in a dish of a similar size. Lay each chicken joint in turn in the egg mixture, using a pastry brush to coat evenly, then roll in the seasoned crumbs, again to coat evenly. Pat off any excess with the hands.

Arrange on the baking tray and cook for 35–40 minutes (25–30 minutes if using boneless breasts), until a rich brown (there is no need to turn the chicken as it will brown evenly on all sides). The chicken can then be kept hot and crisp for up to 30 minutes at 120°C (250°F/Gas ½).

The sauce can be made at any convenient time up to 24 hours before serving. In a medium saucepan or deep frying pan over moderate heat, fry the shallots or spring onions in the margarine or oil until softened and golden, about 3 minutes. Add 2 tablespoons of the sherry if using and bubble until it has almost evaporated. Add the white wine and the stock, then simmer, uncovered, over gentle heat for 5 minutes. Add the cornflour liquid, mustard, nutmeg and white pepper, and simmer

124

for 3 minutes, stirring constantly, then remove from the heat and whisk in the remaining 1 tablespoon sherry if using, the egg yolk and the chopped tarragon. Refrigerate if not serving immediately and reheat when needed.

To serve, spoon a swirl of the hot sauce on each dinner plate and top it with a chicken piece garnished with a sprig of tarragon.

125

CHICKEN AND MUSHROOM PUFF

Feuilletée

Evelyn

JUICY PIECES of chicken and vegetables in a velvety sauce are encased in a crisp puff pastry rectangle. It's a great way of using up leftover chicken and gravy from a roast or casserole (or left-over turkey), although the dish is so good I often poach chicken specially for it. Don't be tempted to leave out any of the seasonings, which are what gives this dish its impact. For a family supper, you can also make this in a conventional round pie dish.

Makes 4–6 servings
Filling **keeps** 1 day under refrigeration.
Do not freeze.

For the filling
- 225 g (8 oz) tiny white mushrooms, stalks removed (or larger mushrooms cut in quarters)
- 40 g (1½ oz) margarine
- 125 g (4 oz) fresh or frozen green beans, cut in 2.5 cm (1 in) pieces
- 2 small carrots, peeled and thinly sliced
- 1½ teaspoons sea salt
- 2 teaspoons dark sesame oil
- 2 shallots or 4 spring onions, white part only, peeled and finely chopped
- 2 tablespoons flour
- 150 ml (5 fl oz) strong chicken stock, heated
- 150 ml (5 fl oz) dry white wine
- 50 ml (2 fl oz) dry sherry or vermouth (optional)
- good pinch of nutmeg
- good pinch of white pepper
- 1 teaspoon soy sauce
- 1 teaspoon anchovy-free Worcestershire sauce (optional)
- ½ teaspoon paprika
- 1 tablespoon sun-dried tomato paste (optional)
- 10 grinds black pepper

126

1 teaspoon sugar

1 tablespoon chopped parsley

350 g (12 oz) cooked chicken or turkey, removed from the bone and
cut in bite-sized pieces, plus any left-over gravy or sauce

For the pastry case

2 sheets puff pastry, about 450 g (1 lb), thawed but still very cold

1 large egg yolk mixed with 1 teaspoon water and a pinch of sea salt

2 tablespoons sesame seeds

To make the filling, in a large frying pan over moderate heat, cook the mushrooms in 25 g (1 oz) of the margarine, shaking from time to time, for about 3 minutes. Add the green beans and carrots, season with ½ teaspoon sea salt and cook a further 3 minutes. Transfer the vegetables with a slotted spoon to a bowl.

Add the remaining margarine and the sesame oil to the pan, add the shallots or spring onions and cook them over moderate heat, covered, until soft and golden, about 3 minutes. Stir in the flour, mix well and cook gently for 1 minute. Whisk in the hot stock, white wine, and the sherry or vermouth if using, the remaining sea salt and all the rest of the seasonings. Whisk constantly until thickened, then simmer for 3 minutes, stirring from time to time. Remove from the heat, then add the vegetables, the parsley and the chicken with any left-over gravy and mix gently. Allow to cool.

To make the filled puff, lightly oil a baking tray measuring at least 38 × 23 cm (15 × 9 in). Roll each sheet of pastry into a rectangle measuring approximately 35 × 20 cm (14 × 8 in). Lay one rectangle on the baking tray and spread with the cooled filling, leaving a 2 cm (¾ in) margin of pastry clear on all sides. Dampen the margin with a little water, then lay the second rectangle carefully on top. Seal the two layers of pastry by pressing down with the side of the hand, then scallop the edges with the back of a knife blade. Finally, with a very sharp knife, make 3 or 4 V-shaped slashes in the top of the pastry to allow steam to escape. The uncooked *feuilletée* can now be refrigerated for up to 4 hours.

To bake, preheat the oven to 230° (450°F/Gas 8). Paint the top of the *feuilletée* with the egg glaze as evenly as possible, then scatter with the sesame seeds.

Bake for 15 minutes, then turn the temperature down to 200°C (400°F/Gas 6) and cook for a further 15–20 minutes, until well risen, crisp to the touch and richly browned.

Serve within 15 minutes, cut in diagonal slices about 4 cm (1½ in) thick, with salad, rice or potatoes.

127

SPICE-ROASTED CHICKEN WITH AN APRICOT AND BULGUR STUFFING

Evelyn

A GLORIOUS BLEND of spices in both the bird and the stuffing lend more than a touch of Oriental magic to this superb dish. The stuffing can be put inside the bird, but the chicken will cook more quickly—and be easier to serve—if the stuffing is cooked separately alongside, as in this recipe. One option is to double the amount of stuffing and use it as an accompaniment rather than as a garnish; another is to serve the stuffed bird with plain boiled new potatoes.

Makes 6–7 servings
Leftovers **keep** up to 4 days, tightly wrapped and under refrigeration.
Freezes up to 2 months.

1 × 2.3–2.4 kg (5–5½ lb) roasting chicken

For coating the bird

finely grated zest and juice of 1 lemon (save half of each for the
   stuffing)

1 tablespoon olive oil

1 teaspoon ground turmeric

1 teaspoon ground cumin

For the stuffing

1 tablespoon olive oil

1 small onion, peeled and finely chopped

1 medium clove garlic, peeled and finely chopped

2 teaspoons fresh ginger, peeled and finely chopped

175 g (6 oz) uncooked bulgur (cracked wheat)

175 g (6 oz) ready-to-eat dried apricots, coarsely chopped

350 ml (12 fl oz) chicken stock

2 tablespoons pine kernels, toasted (page 103) (optional)

½ teaspoon sea salt

8 grinds black pepper

128

For the gravy

    3 tablespoons water or wine

    225 ml (8 fl oz) chicken stock

    2 teaspoons cornflour mixed to a liquid with

        3 tablespoons hot water

Preheat the oven to 190°C (375°F/Gas 5).

Arrange the chicken in a roasting tin, preferably on a poultry rack to prevent the bird absorbing too much fat. Mix the coating ingredients thoroughly, then brush all over the bird. Cover very loosely with aluminium foil and roast for 1½ hours, basting occasionally.

Meanwhile, make the stuffing. Heat the oil in a large frying pan over medium heat. Add the onion and cook, stirring, until golden, about 5–6 minutes. Add the garlic and ginger and cook a further 2–3 minutes, until they take on a little colour and the onion has turned a golden brown. Add the bulgur, chopped apricots and stock. Stir well, then cover and cook for 10 minutes, until the stock has been absorbed. Stir in the lemon zest and juice saved from the coating, the pine kernels, salt and pepper. Turn into a greased casserole dish and cover with aluminium foil.

After the chicken has been roasting for 1½ hours, remove the aluminum foil from the bird. Return it to the oven together with the stuffing casserole and cook both for a further 30 minutes or until the bird is a rich brown and the juices run clear (not pink) from the leg when it is pierced with a skewer. Take out and let stand for 15–20 minutes before carving.

To make the gravy, drain the fat from the roasting pan and add 3 tablespoons water or wine. Heat gently on top of the cooker, scraping the base of the pan with a wooden spoon to release any browned residue. Pour into a small saucepan and add the chicken stock and the cornflour liquid. Mix well and simmer gently over low heat until thickened — about 2 minutes. Taste and add extra salt and pepper if necessary.

Cut off the chicken legs and thighs and carve the breast. Serve with the gravy and the stuffing.

GRILLED CHICKEN IN A LIME AND CHILLI MARINADE WITH A PINEAPPLE AND CORIANDER SALSA

Judi

CHICKEN PIECES BURST with vibrant flavours in a dish inspired by the cuisine of south-east Asia. Cool chunks of fresh pineapple in a tangy marinade with a hint of cardamom add an exotic note, although the chicken is delicious on its own. For a decorative presentation, the cooked breasts can be sliced and arranged on a bed of salad leaves tossed with slices of ripe mango and dressed with a little vinaigrette.

Makes 4 servings
Keeps 2 days under refrigeration.
Chicken **freezes** up to 1 month. **Do not freeze** salsa.

4 boneless chicken breast halves, skinned and trimmed of fat

For the marinade

juice of 3 limes

2 cloves garlic, crushed with the back of a knife but not chopped

2 teaspoons peeled and grated fresh ginger

1 teaspoon sugar

2 tablespoons soy sauce

2 teaspoons dark sesame oil

1 medium red or green chilli, seeded and finely chopped

1 teaspoon tender fresh lemon grass, sliced paper thin (optional)

10 grinds black pepper

1 teaspoon sea salt

For the salsa

2 cardamom pods

½ medium pineapple, peeled and cut into 1 cm (½ in) cubes

1 small fresh red chilli, seeded and finely sliced (optional)

1 tablespoon fresh lime juice

¼ teaspoon ground cumin

130

½ teaspoon sea salt

1 teaspoon sugar

¼ medium green pepper, finely diced

1 tablespoon fresh chopped coriander

For the garnish

a few sprigs fresh coriander or flat-leaf parsley

wedges of lemon or lime

To make the marinade, combine all the ingredients in a wide, shallow bowl and mix well. Put in the chicken breasts and marinate at room temperature for at least 30 minutes, or in the refrigerator for at least 1 hour, turning two or three times. At this point, the marinated chicken may be left in the refrigerator for up to 2 hours before cooking.

To make the pineapple salsa, split the cardamom pods and remove the tiny dark seeds. Combine the seeds and the other salsa ingredients, except the coriander, in a non-metallic bowl. Stir gently, then refrigerate for at least 30 minutes.

Remove the breasts from the marinade, reserving any remaining liquid. To grill, arrange side by side in a grill pan and grill 10 cm (4 in) from the heat for 8–10 minutes, turning once.

To barbecue, arrange the breasts side by side on a preheated barbecue and cook, covered if a lid is available, for 8–10 minutes, turning over after 5 minutes. Baste with a little of the marinade three or four times during cooking.

With either method, nick one breast to make sure no pink remains, then transfer the chicken to a cutting board and leave to rest for 5 minutes.

Strain any remaining marinade into a small pan, add 1 tablespoon of water, bring to the boil and simmer for 1–2 minutes. Check the seasoning, adding a little salt or sugar if necessary.

To serve, add any juice from the chicken to the hot marinade. Stir the tablespoon of coriander into the pineapple salsa. Cut the breasts at an angle across the grain into 1 cm (½ inch) slices. Arrange on a warm platter and pour the hot marinade over the chicken. Garnish with the coriander sprigs and lime wedges. Serve with the chilled pineapple salsa.

BIBLICAL CHICKEN IN AN ORANGE, HONEY AND RAISIN SAUCE

Evelyn

A DISH THAT ENCAPSULATES the spirit of Rosh Hashanah cooking—sweet with honey and the fruits of the season—this is also an ideal way to keep chicken breasts tender and juicy. They are first lightly fried to give them colour, then left to soak in the delicious sauce for a while. A final short cooking completes the process.

Makes 6–8 servings

Keeps up to 2 days under refrigeration. **Freezes** up to 2 months.

2 tablespoons plain flour

1 teaspoon sea salt

10 grinds black pepper

6–8 partly boned chicken breasts, trimmed of rib cage and skinned

50 g (2 oz) margarine

1 tablespoon sunflower or olive oil

75 g (3 oz) slivered almonds

For the sauce

300 ml (10 fl oz) dry white wine plus 175 ml (6 fl oz) chicken stock,
    or 475 ml (16 fl oz) chicken stock

150 ml (5 fl oz) orange juice

2 teaspoons grated lemon zest

2 tablespoons honey

40 g (1½ oz) raisins or sultanas

1 × 8 cm (3 in) cinnamon stick

2 teaspoons cornflour mixed with 1 tablespoon cold water
    or chicken stock

For the garnish

2 small oranges, peeled, cut in segments

Season the flour with the salt and pepper. Flatten the chicken breasts gently between the hands, one at a time, then coat with the seasoned flour (the easiest way is to shake them one by one in a small plastic bag).

In a large frying pan, heat the margarine and oil over moderate heat until the foam subsides, then immediately add the slivered almonds and cook gently until golden brown. Remove the almonds, drain on a paper towel and set aside.

Add the chicken to the hot fat in the pan and cook over moderate heat on each side for about 3 minutes or until golden. Remove from the pan and pour away any excess fat without discarding the savoury brown bits at the bottom.

To make the sauce, add the wine (if using) to the pan, stirring well and bubble for 3 minutes to intensify the flavour, then add the stock, orange juice, lemon zest, honey, raisins or sultanas and cinnamon stick.

Bring the sauce to the boil and add the chicken breasts in a single layer. Spoon the liquid over, then cover the pan and take it off the heat. Leave for at least 30 minutes. If the pan won't hold all the chicken breasts in a single layer, arrange them side by side in a roasting tin, pour over the hot sauce and leave covered with aluminium foil.

Shortly before serving, bring the sauce slowly back to simmering point, stir in the cornflour mixed with the water or stock and simmer for 3 minutes. Nick a breast to check there's no sign of pinkness. If there is, simmer for 3 more minutes.

Lift the chicken out and arrange on a warm serving plate. Add salt and pepper if necessary, then spoon the sauce over.

Decorate the dish with the orange segments and the slivered almonds. Serve accompanied by plain boiled rice or new potatoes. To reheat if cold, cook, covered, at 180°C (350°F/Gas 4) for 25 minutes or until bubbly.

GOLDEN LEMON CHICKEN

Judi

GOLDEN CHICKEN BREASTS glazed with a sublime lemony sauce belie the fact that this is one of the simplest home-made chicken dishes ever. Just a few simple ingredients come together to create a dish that has a huge impact for surprisingly little effort. The breasts take on a beautiful golden glaze as they and the lemon halves bake in the exquisite lemon syrup. The inside of the lemon is delicious to eat. This recipe can also be made with boneless chicken breasts, in which case, reduce the oven cooking time to 15–20 minutes. Be sure to use very fresh lemons.

Makes 6–8 servings
Keeps 3 days under refrigeration.
Do not reheat once cooked.
Freezes up to 2 months.

225 g (8 oz) plus 1 tablespoon sugar
600 ml (20 fl oz) water
3 large lemons
6–8 boneless chicken breasts
½ teaspoon sea salt
15 grinds black pepper
flat-leaf parsley

Preheat the oven to 230°C (450°F/Gas 8).

Place the sugar in an 20 cm (8 oz) saucepan with the water and slowly dissolve over a low heat. Bring to the boil and bubble for 3 minutes. Pierce the skin of the lemons with a fork or skewer and place in the sugar syrup. Cover, bring to the boil then simmer over low heat for 20 minutes.

Remove the lemons, then halve when cool. Bubble the liquid over moderate heat for about 12 minutes more, or until reduced by half (about 300 ml/10 fl oz) and a golden caramel colour. To check the colour, take the pot off the heat and allow the bubbles to settle.

134

Season the chicken breasts with the salt and pepper. Place them skin side down in a roasting tin that is just large enough to hold them in a single layer with the lemon halves. Pour the sugar syrup over the chicken and lemons. Place the pan in the oven and cook for 30–35 minutes, turning the breasts over halfway through cooking. Nick a breast to make sure that it is cooked right through to the centre. The chicken can now be kept warm at 140°C (275°F/Gas 1).

Alternatively, if the chicken is cooked before your guests arrive, take out of the oven then return to a moderate oven while you are eating the first course. Do not leave the chicken in the oven continuously once cooked or it will be overdone.

Transfer the chicken and sauce to a serving dish and garnish with the lemon halves and the parsley. The lemon can be eaten if the skin is tender; otherwise each guest can scoop out the delicious inside. Quick Couscous (page 219) and any green vegetable go well.

A Meat-lover's Paradise:
Succulent Beef and Lamb

'And God made the cattle . . . and God saw that it was good'

—Genesis 1:25

BECAUSE IN MOST JEWISH COMMUNITIES ONLY THE forequarter cuts of beef are available, traditional ways tend to involve cooking these tougher cuts in some kind of liquid to tenderise them. This produces some wonderful dishes such as the Greek-Jewish Red Wine Beef Casserole, *Stifado* and, of course that perennial classic, *Tsimmes* with dumplings. However, perhaps it's time to introduce Jewish gourmets to the Italian accents of Low-fat Braised Steak with Oregano and Tomatoes or to Daube, the rustic herb and red wine stew from Provence.

Even the humble minced beef, usually associated with nothing

136

more exotic than meat loaf or hamburgers, lends itself to delicious new interpretations such as *Bobotie*, the curried beef gratin from South Africa, or Florentine Meatballs with Renaissance Spices, with their crunchy oatmeal and coriander seed crust.

When it comes to lamb, the prime kosher roasting joint—the shoulder—is considered the sweetest cut by butchers everywhere. But wait till you've tasted a boned shoulder when it's stuffed with a pinwheel of fresh herbs. It's not exactly *heimishe*, as the only herbs available in Eastern Europe for most of the year were dill, garlic and bay leaf, but it is a recipe that has been adopted by the Anglo-Jewish community.

137

SAVOURY BEEF STRUDEL
WITH PINE KERNELS

Evelyn

T HIS DISH IS a universal favourite. The combination of the crisp puff pastry and the tasty meat filling make what is essentially a family-style dish into one fit for the Succot table.

Makes 2 strudels, or 6–8 servings
Will **keep** under refrigeration 2 days raw or 3 days cooked.
Freezes raw up to 2 months.
For best results, do not reheat but **serve** fresh from the oven.

1 tablespoon sunflower oil
1 medium onion, peeled and finely chopped
1 large red pepper, finely chopped
700 g (1½ lb) minced beef
1 heaped tablespoon tomato purée or ketchup
½ teaspoon sea salt
15 grinds black pepper
pinch of grated nutmeg
2 teaspoons soy sauce
2 teaspoons anchovy-free Worcestershire sauce
2 teaspoons finely chopped parsley
2 sheets, about 450 g (1 lb), puff pastry, thawed but still very cold

For the glaze
1 large egg, beaten
1 rounded tablespoon sesame seeds

Preheat the oven to 220°C (425°F/Gas 7).

Put the oil in a medium frying pan and add the onion and pepper. Cook over moderate heat until the onion softens, about 3 minutes, then add the meat and stir with a fork until it loses its redness and starts to brown. Add the tomato purée or

138

ketchup, seasoning, soy sauce, Worcestershire sauce and parsley. Cover and simmer gently for 20 minutes, until thick but still juicy. Allow to cool.

Roll 1 sheet of the puff pastry into a rectangle 40 × 25 cm (16 × 10 in). It must be so thin that you can see the board through it. Spread half the cooled meat mixture over the pastry, leaving a 2.5 cm (1 in) margin all the way round. Turn the ends in to seal, then roll up like a slightly flattened Swiss roll. Transfer to an ungreased baking tray, seam side down, brush evenly with beaten egg, then sprinkle with half the sesame seeds. Make cuts 5–6 cm (2–2½ in) apart, through the top layer of pastry to prevent the strudel from bursting and also to make it easy to portion when cooked. Repeat the process with the remaining pastry and filling.

Bake the strudels for 10 minutes, then turn the oven down to 200°C (400°F/Gas 6) and bake for a further 15–20 minutes, until crisp and golden brown.

Serve warm in slices. Accompany with Creamy Puff Perfect Mashed Potatoes (page 173) and a lightly cooked green vegetable.

ROAST BEEF
WITH A PEPPER AND HERB COATING
ON A BED OF ROASTED VEGETABLES

Judi

ROAST BEEF IS, of course, a British classic. Over the years, however, it has been adopted as a special-occasion family favourite by the Anglo-Jewish community. In this version, a thyme and crushed peppercorn coating brings out the flavour of the meat while adding a piquant crustiness to each slice. Ask the butcher for a wing rib of beef that has been hung for at least 10 days, with the bones shortened so that it will stand evenly in the roasting pan. The cooking times given below produce a roast that is a rich brown on the outside and a pale pink within. If you prefer your beef rare, reduce the cooking time by 10 minutes. The sauce can be made with left-over wine that has gone slightly vinegary. Instead of the black, green and white peppercorns in the recipe, you can substitute 3½ teaspoons of the multi-coloured peppercorn mixtures available in most supermarkets.

Makes 8 servings with leftovers, delicious cold
Leftovers **keep** 3 days under refrigeration. **Do not freeze.**

1 × 3 kg (7 lb) wing rib of beef
2 teaspoons black peppercorns
1 teaspoon green peppercorns
½ teaspoon white peppercorns
1 small sprig of fresh thyme, leaves stripped from stalks
1 teaspoon sea salt
2 tablespoons olive oil
450 g (1 lb) young carrots, peeled if necessary and trimmed
225 g (8 oz) tiny onions or shallots, peeled
For the sauce
150 ml (5 fl oz) full-bodied red wine such as Cabernet Sauvignon
425 ml (15 fl oz) beef or vegetable stock
1 teaspoon wholegrain mustard
1 teaspoon dark or light brown sugar
2 teaspoons cornflour mixed to a liquid with 2 tablespoons cold water

140

Leave the meat at room temperature for 1 hour. Preheat the oven to its highest temperature, 240°C (475°F/Gas 9).

In a mortar (or a small, strong bowl) coarsely crush the peppercorns, thyme and sea salt with the pestle or the end of a rolling pin. Brush the meat lightly with the olive oil, then rub with the pepper mixture and transfer to a roasting tin.

Place in the very hot oven for 30 minutes, then turn the heat down to 180°C (350°F/Gas 4) and continue to cook for a further 1½ hours. Baste the meat at 30-minute intervals, most easily done with a basting syringe. When cooked, the internal temperature for medium beef should read 70°C (150°F) on a meat thermometer.

While the meat is cooking, blanch the carrots in a pot of boiling water for 5 minutes and the peeled onions or shallots for 3 minutes (use the same water). As each vegetable is blanched, transfer to a colander, drench in cold water, then drain well and pat dry.

Twenty minutes before the meat is done, add the vegetables to the roasting pan, turning them so they are coated with the juices. When the meat is done, lift it on to a carving dish, cover lightly with aluminium foil and leave in a warm place (either a warming oven or the back of the cooker) for 20–30 minutes to rest before carving (this will make the meat juicier and easier to carve). Remove the vegetables with a slotted spoon and place in a dish lined with paper towels to remove the excess fat, then transfer to a dish, cover with foil and keep hot in a low oven 110°C (225°F/Gas ¼).

To make the sauce, skim as much fat as possible from the surface of the roasting tin. Place the tin on the cooker over moderate heat, pour in the wine, then stir well with a wooden spoon to deglaze the pan. When all the brown bits have been stirred into the wine, bubble for 2 minutes, then turn into a small saucepan. Add the stock and simmer for 5 minutes, then stir in the mustard, sugar and cornflour liquid. Bubble for 3 minutes, until thickened and glossy. Season to taste with additional salt, pepper and brown sugar, and transfer to a sauce boat or small jug.

For the most elegant presentation, have ready a large, preheated platter. Present the roast to your guests, then return to the kitchen and carve into 1 cm (½ in) thick slices. Arrange on the hot platter, spooning over any juices that have come out of the meat and surround with the roasted vegetables. Serve at once, accompanied by the sauce. Delicious with Swedish 'Fan' Potatoes (page 167) or No-fat Crispy Roast Potatoes (page 169) and a vegetable dish such as Fragrant Green Beans à la Côte d'Azur (page 179) or Butternut Squash and Spiced Apple Purée (page 174).

141

BEEF-FILLED CABBAGE LEAVES IN A SWEET-AND-SOUR SAUCE

Holishkes

Evelyn

THE SWEET-AND-SOUR sauce and the juicy filling taste even better if this dish can be left under refrigeration for 2 days before it is served either hot or at room temperature.

Makes 4 servings, 6 as a starter
Keep up to 3 days under refrigeration.
Freeze cooked up to 6 weeks.

1 firm head white cabbage
For the stuffing
   450 g (1 lb) raw minced beef
   2 tablespoons matzah meal
   1 teaspoon sea salt
   pinch of white pepper
   1 large egg, beaten
   ½ onion, peeled and grated
For the sauce
   2 tablespoons wine vinegar
   3 tablespoons golden syrup
   1 bay leaf
   5 peppercorns
   1 teaspoon salt
   350 ml (12 fl oz) beef stock or thin gravy

Freeze the cabbage for 24 hours, then defrost overnight at room temperature or for 30 minutes on Defrost in the microwave. The leaves will then peel off easily.

   The next day, preheat the oven to 180°C (350°F/Gas 4). In a large bowl, mix all the stuffing ingredients together.

142

Detach 12 large leaves from the defrosted cabbage. Cut out and discard any thick stalk. Stuff each leaf, one at a time, by placing 1 tablespoon of stuffing in the center, turning in the sides and rolling up into a bundle. Lift each bundle and give a gentle squeeze with the palm of the hand to seal it. Lay the bundles side by side, with the seal underneath, in a shallow, lidded or aluminium foil-covered casserole dish.

Mix all the sauce ingredients together and spoon over the bundles. Add extra stock if necessary so that they are barely covered. Cover with the lid or aluminium foil.

Cook the stuffed cabbage leaves in the oven for 30 minutes. The sauce will then be simmering. Turn the oven down to 150°C (300°F/Gas 2) and continue to cook for a further 2 hours.

Fifteen minutes before the end of the cooking time, uncover the dish and turn the heat up to 180°C (350°F/Gas 4) to brown the tops of the cabbage bundles and thicken the sauce.

Allow 2–3 *holishkes* per person for a main dish, 1–2 as an appetiser. Serve warm (the dish reheats well).

SUCCOT MEANS STUFFED cabbage 'bundles' in the majority of Jewish homes, celebrating this Autumn harvest festival with the good things of the earth.

My mother-in-law called the dish *'gevikilte* cabbage', and stewed the bundles in a slightly spicy sweet-and-sour sauce containing vinegar and golden syrup. This was 'Moscow style'. On the other hand, Auntie Rose, who was a marvellous *Roumanische* cook, always made her sauce with tomatoes, lemon juice, and, a more modern touch, brown sugar and the dish was called '*holishkes*'.

In both cases, the inimitable flavour of the meat stuffing and the sauce was only produced by long, slow cooking until even the cabbage began to caramelise a little.

143

SOUTH AFRICAN
CURRIED BEEF GRATIN

Bobotie   *Judi*

Aᴊᴜɪᴄʏ, ꜱᴘɪᴄᴇᴅ minced beef mixture is baked beneath a savoury 'custard'. It's easy enough to put together quickly for a family meal, but also works well as a party dish. Lamb is normally used in South Africa, but as it can be fatty I prefer to use lean minced beef.

Makes 4–6 servings
Keeps 2 days under refrigeration. Do not freeze.

2 tablespoons pine kernels, slivered almonds or cashews
1 medium onion, peeled and finely chopped
1 tablespoon sunflower oil
900 g (2 lb) lean minced beef
1 teaspoon sea salt
20 grinds black pepper
1 tablespoon curry paste or 2 teaspoons curry powder
3 tablespoons apricot preserve or mango chutney
2 tablespoons fresh lemon juice

For the topping
3 large eggs
325 ml (11 fl oz) canned coconut milk
1 teaspoon sea salt
2 teaspoons soy sauce
½ teaspoon paprika
pinch of chilli powder
10 grinds black pepper
2–3 bay leaves

144

Preheat the oven to 180°C (350°F/Gas 4).

Toast the nuts in a heavy-based frying pan over moderate heat, tossing frequently, until they smell 'toasty', about 3 minutes.

In a large pan over moderate heat, cook the onion in the oil, stirring until golden brown, about 5 minutes. Add the minced beef and fry, stirring once or twice, until well-browned, about 3 minutes. Add the salt, pepper, curry, preserve or chutney and lemon juice. Cook gently for 5 minutes, then stir in the toasted nuts.

Transfer to a casserole 18 cm (7 in) in diameter and about 5 cm (2 in) deep, or a small gratin dish and keep warm while you make the topping.

In a bowl, whisk the eggs with the coconut milk. Add the salt, soy sauce, paprika, chilli powder and black pepper. Mix well, then pour the coconut custard (it will be thin) evenly over the meat mixture. Arrange the bay leaves on top.

Bake for 30 minutes, until the top has set and is golden brown. Allow to cool for 5 minutes before serving. Serve with rice and a green vegetable such as peas.

BOBOTIE (pronounced bo-*boh*-ti) probably found its way into South African cuisine from Malaysia and is particularly popular around the Cape area. It's generally unknown in the Jewish kitchen because the traditional recipe contains meat and milk. Substituting creamed coconut (or coconut milk) for its dairy counterpart, however, produces a delicious kosher version of this wonderful dish.

PICKLED BRISKET,
ANGLO-JEWISH STYLE

Evelyn

THIS IS MY once-a-year treat for my family. It's become almost a ritual in our house—and yes, it is a chore, particularly if you are mixing your own pickling solution. But the pleasure to be found in every mouthful makes it all worthwhile. The Saltpetre gives the meat its rich red colour and also helps to preserve it.

Makes 8–10 servings as a cold cut, with extra for sandwiches
Keeps up to 4 days under refrigeration.
Freezes up to 2 months.

2 fat garlic cloves, peeled
1 tablespoon mixed pickling spice
2 bay leaves, crumbled
1 teaspoon crushed black peppercorns
75 g (3 oz) Demerara or light or dark brown sugar (page 147)
175 g (6 oz) sea salt
2 teaspoons saltpetre
2.3–2.7 kg (5–6 lb) corner of brisket, not rolled

For cooking the meat
1 large onion, peeled and halved
2 bay leaves

I find it convenient to pickle and cook the meat in the same dish—a cast-iron, enamelled casserole. Otherwise an earthenware dish can be used for pickling (don't use metal, which might react with the saline solution). Put the garlic, pickling spice, bay leaves and peppercorns into a mortar or strong small bowl and crush coarsely with a pestle or the end of a rolling pin. Add the crushed spices to the casserole along with the sugar, salt and saltpetre. Add the meat and turn to coat with the mixture, rubbing it well into all the surfaces of the meat. Leave to stand for 1 hour, then add cold water to come just to the top of the meat. Liquid will also ooze out of it as the

146

days go by. Refrigerate for 10 to 14 days, or leave in a cool larder or pantry, turning daily.

To cook, take the meat from the liquid and wash well. Pour out the liquid from the dish and put the meat back. Cover with cold water and bring slowly to the boil on top of the cooker. Skim off any scum with a spoon dipped in cold water. Now add the onion and 2 bay leaves. Cover and simmer very gently for 4 hours. You can do this on top of the cooker, but it is easier to keep it at the right temperature in a low oven at 150°C (300°F/Gas 2). Reduce the heat to 140°C (275°F/Gas 1) if necessary to keep it barely bubbling.

When cooked, lift the meat out on to a cutting board. Part of it can now be carved rather thickly and served warm. After dinner, fit the rest into a bowl and cover with a plate and several weights. Leave under pressure until quite cold, then wrap in aluminium foil and refrigerate. Use as required.

Serve warm, preferably with latkes or chips, or cold in rye bread or challah sandwiches, with mustard and pickles.

DEMERARA SUGAR, a dry, coarse-textured, light-brown, raw sugar, comes from the Demerara area of Guyana, West Africa. With its gentle flavour and the ease with which it dissolves in a hot liquid, it is considered by connoisseurs to be the ideal complement to coffee.

Its large crystals, golden brown colour and appetising aroma add a delicious flavour and pleasing crunchiness to streusel toppings and biscuits. It's also good sprinkled over breakfast cereals, fruits and hot oatmeal. Unlike moist brown sugar, it does not go hard when stored.

147

LOW-FAT BRAISED STEAK WITH OREGANO AND TOMATOES

Judi

THE BEEF IS braised in an herbed tomato sauce that tastes so good you won't believe it's virtually fat-free! You won't be sealing in the flavour as you do when browning the meat first, so you must add it to a sauce that's already bubbling to seal the beef by the heat alone. As flavour is the name of the game here, have a good smell of your dried herbs and be ruthless about throwing out any that have lost their fragrance or smell like dried grass!

Makes 4–6 servings
Keeps 3 days under refrigeration. **Freezes** up to 2 months.

4–6 slices braising steak, about 2 cm (¾ in) thick, 175 g (6 oz) each
For the sauce
    2 teaspoons finely chopped dried onion
    3 cloves garlic, crushed
    400 g (14 oz) can chopped tomatoes with their liquid
    125 ml (4 fl oz) dry red wine or beef stock
    ½ teaspoon sea salt
    1 teaspoon sugar
    15 grinds black pepper
    1 teaspoon dried oregano
    ½ teaspoon paprika
    1 bay leaf
    2 tablespoons chopped parsley
    25 g (1 oz) black olives, stoned (optional)

Preheat the oven to 150°C (300°F/Gas 2).

Put all the sauce ingredients into a lidded ovenproof casserole pan and bubble, uncovered, over moderate heat, for 3–4 minutes. Add the beef, top up if necessary with stock so that it is barely covered and bring back to a simmer. Cover and transfer to the oven.

Cook for 2½ hours until the meat is meltingly tender. Serve with peas and rice or mashed potatoes.

148

GREEK-JEWISH RED WINE BEEF CASSEROLE

Stifado   *Evelyn*

IN GREECE this wonderfully spiced dish is always eaten with crusty country bread to soak up every last spoonful of the sauce. It is generally cooked on top of the cooker, but I find it is easier to regulate the heat in the oven, where the dish also needs less attention. The meat must be cooked very gently so that it becomes meltingly tender in a rich dark-brown sauce and the shallots or onions stay whole.

Makes 8–9 servings
Keeps up to 4 days under refrigeration.
Freezes up to 2 months.

675 g (1½ lb) shallots or small pickling onions
1.8 kg (4 lb) braising steak, cut in 4 cm (1½ in) cubes
2 tablespoons olive oil
very hot water
3 tablespoons tomato purée
350 ml (12 fl oz) fruity red wine
3 cloves garlic, crushed
3 bay leaves
2 cinnamon sticks or 3 teaspoons ground cinnamon
1 teaspoon ground cumin
1½ tablespoons light brown sugar
3 teaspoons sea salt
20 grinds black pepper

To skin the shallots, plunge for 2 minutes in boiling water, drain then cover with cold water. The skins can then be easily removed. If using pickling onions, peel as normal.

Preheat the oven to 160°C (325°F/Gas 3). Heat the oil in a flameproof casserole

149

dish and quickly brown the meat on all sides, 5–6 minutes for each batch. You will need to do this in several batches so as not to crowd the pan. Barely cover the meat with very hot water, cover the dish and transfer to the oven. Cook for 1 hour, then turn the oven down to 150°C (300°F/Gas 2). Uncover the casserole and add all the remaining ingredients. Stir gently, then cover and simmer for a further 1½ hours. (If the casserole is bubbling too fiercely at any time, reduce the heat to 140°C (275°F/Gas 1). Add a little extra boiling water if the liquid has reduced too much — it should be a rich, thick gravy.

Serve with mashed potatoes or rice.

Tagliatelle with Lemon and Smoked Salmon (page 84)

Butternut Squash and Spiced Apple Purée (page 174)

Hearty Hungarian Goulash Soup (page 24)

Fresh Asparagus and Saffron
Risotto (page 210)

Biblical Chicken in an Orange,
Honey, and Raisin Sauce
(page 132), with roasted
potatoes (page 169)

Roast Boned Lamb Stuffed with a Pinwheel of Fresh Herbs (page 162), Swedish "Fan" Potatoes (page 167), and Minted Peas and Cucumber with Shallots (page 176)

Provençale Sundried Tomato, Olive, and Basil Tarte (page 61)

Moroccan-Style Carrot, Raisin, and Toasted Nut Salad (page 198)

Individual Mocha Soufflés (page 229)

Caramel Glazed Upside-Down Pear
Tarte (page 232)

PROVENÇAL BEEF WITH WINE AND HERBS

Daube à la Provençal

Judi

A RICH, EARTHY CASSEROLE that transports you to the smells and tastes of home cooking in the hamlets of Provence. The dish is best made several days ahead; each time it is reheated, the flavour becomes deeper and more intense.

Makes 8–10 servings
Keeps 3 days under refrigeration.
Freezes up to 2 months.

1.8 kg (4 lb) braising steak, cut into 5 cm (2 in) cubes

For the marinade

peeled zest of 1 orange (without the pith)
12 black peppercorns, slightly crushed with the end of
    a rolling pin or in a mortar
2 bay leaves
2 cloves garlic
large sprig of parsley
300 ml (10 fl oz) dry red wine such as Cabernet Sauvignon

For braising the beef

2 tablespoons olive oil
1 tablespoon brandy (optional)
1 large onion, peeled and thinly sliced
1 carrot, peeled and thinly sliced
½ teaspoon paprika
2 teaspoons sea salt
20 grinds black pepper
1 red pepper, diced
25 g (1 oz) black olives, stoned (optional)
175 g (6 oz) small white mushrooms, quartered
1 sprig parsley
1 bay leaf

151

continued

1 teaspoon cornflour mixed to a thin liquid with a little water or wine

At least 24 hours (or up to 3 days) before you intend to serve, combine the marinade ingredients in a pot and heat until boiling, then allow to go quite cold. (I do this in the same enamelled cast-iron casserole in which I intend to cook the meat.) Put the beef into the marinade and leave in the refrigerator, basting several times with the juices and turning the meat so that the marinade can soak in.

On the day it is to be cooked, leave at room temperature for 1 hour before cooking. Preheat the oven to 150°C (300°F/Gas 2).

Lift the meat from the marinade and dry it thoroughly with paper towels. (This is essential so that it will brown.) Strain the marinade into a small bowl.

Wash out the casserole and in it heat the 2 tablespoons of olive oil. Put the meat into the hot fat and cook it at a moderate sizzle, turning it to brown on all sides, about 3 minutes. Add the brandy, if using and continue to fry the meat until the liquid has disappeared. Add the onion and carrot, cooking gently until they are limp and brown, about 6 minutes. Sprinkle the meat with the paprika, salt and black pepper. Add the sliced pepper, olives if using, mushrooms and herbs, then pour in the reserved marinade, cover and bring to the boil. Transfer to the oven and cook for 3 hours.

Add the cornflour liquid, stir well and bring back to a simmer on top of the cooker.

Allow to cool and refrigerate overnight or up to 3 days before serving. Reheat and serve from the cooking pot. If it seems a little dry, add a dash of red wine or stock. Daube is traditionally served with *macaronade*—short-cut macaroni that has been moistened with gravy from the casserole, but it is equally delicious with boiled or mashed potatoes.

THIS FRENCH 'STEW' IS a wonderful example of the newly-popular Cuisine Grandmère – close relative of such traditional Jewish dishes as tsimmes, braised steak, cholunt – as well as similar casseroles such as Lancashire hotpot, Irish stew and Moroccan tagine. All these slowly simmered dishes were 'invented' by generations of grandmothers to solve the conundrum of how to make a tasty dish for a large family using the cheaper cuts of meat.

All these dishes share one golden rule – they must be cooked for a long time over low heat with the liquid at barely a bubble so that the meat becomes meltingly tender and all the flavours become married together.

The daube has one flavour advantage over most such peasant-style stews – it uses liberal quantities of the local (and therefore low cost) red wine. The word 'daube' describes both the method of cooking and the casserole dish in which it is left to simmer gently over many hours.

Variations of daube appear throughout France – every family has its own recipe. In the south west – around Bordeaux – a version is prepared using the local geese that takes no less than three days to make!

153

BEEF AND SWEET CARROT CASSEROLE WITH DUMPLING

Tsimmes mit Halke

Evelyn

To ACHIEVE THE GLORIOUS FLAVOUR of this once-a-year treat, it is essential to cook for the full length of time given in the recipe. During this time, the sugar in the carrots begins to caramelise and they and the potatoes turn golden brown. The dumpling is optional but divine.

Makes 6 servings as a main course, 8 as a side dish —
but you can never make enough *tsimmes* to satisfy everyone!
Keeps 4 days under refrigeration.
Do not freeze as it tends to go watery and mushy.

900 g (2 lb) slice of brisket, cut into 4 cm (1½ in) cubes
1.4 kg (3 lb) carrots, peeled and diced
225 g (8 oz) golden syrup
¼ teaspoon white pepper
2 teaspoons sea salt
1 tablespoon cornflour
675 g (1½ lb) potatoes, peeled and cut in large dice
For the dumpling (optional)
75 g (3 oz) margarine
175 g (6 oz) plain flour
1½ teaspoons baking powder
½ teaspoon sea salt
4–5 tablespoons water

Trim most of the excess fat off the meat, leaving a thin edging.

Put the meat and carrots into a large pot and barely cover with hot water. Add 2 tablespoons of the golden syrup, the pepper and ½ teaspoon of the salt. Bring to the boil, reduce the heat and simmer for 2 hours. Skim, or if possible, chill overnight, so that most of the fat can be removed.

154

Preheat the oven to 150°C (300°F/Gas 2).

Four hours before you want to serve the *tsimmes*, make the dumpling by combining the flour, baking powder and salt, and rubbing in the margarine. Add the water and mix to a soft dough.

Put the dumpling in the middle of a large casserole. Lift the meat and carrots from their cooking liquid with a perforated spoon and arrange around it. (Without a dumpling, simply put the meat and carrots into the casserole.)

Mix the cornflour with enough water to make a smooth liquid, then stir into the reserved stock from the carrots and meat. Bring to the boil and pour over them.

Arrange the potatoes on top of the meat, adding extra boiling water if necessary so that they are just submerged. Sprinkle with the remaining 1½ teaspoons salt and the remaining syrup. Cover and bring to the boil on top of the cooker, then transfer to the oven for 3½ hours. Uncover and taste, adding a little more syrup if necessary. Allow to brown, uncovered, for a further half an hour, then serve. The potatoes and the dumpling should be slightly brown and the sauce slightly thickened.

Variation

Add 225 g (8 oz) tenderised prunes and/or 225 g (8 oz) tenderised apricots when the dish is cooked for the second time. You can also include 2 large sweet potatoes, peeled and cut in large dice, as well as the ordinary ones.

Serve as a main dish or as a side dish to accompany roast meat and poultry.

MOROCCAN BEEF CASSEROLE WITH HONEY-GLAZED APPLES

Tagine   *Judi*

MELTINGLY TENDER CUBES of beef in a sweet sauce, fragrant with
Middle Eastern spices, make this an exotic centrepiece to a Rosh Hashana feast.
Apples glazed with honey add the finishing touch. The casserole can be cooked
and served in an enamelled cast-iron pot or large casserole, but is most traditional
in a Moroccan terracotta lidded pot or *tagine*, available from speciality cookware
suppliers.

Makes 6–8 servings
Keeps 3 days under refrigeration.
Freezes up to 1 month.

1.4 kg (3 lb) lean braising steak,
    cut in 4 cm (1½ in) cubes
For the marinade
    25 g (1 oz) margarine, melted
    2 tablespoons sunflower or olive oil
    ¼ teaspoon turmeric or pinch of saffron
    1½ teaspoons sea salt
    40 grinds black pepper
    1 teaspoon ground ginger
    1 teaspoon cinnamon
    1 large onion, coarsely grated
    4 or 5 sprigs fresh coriander, tied together with kitchen twine
For cooking
    boiling water
    350 g (12 oz) ready-to-eat stoned prunes or dried apricots
    1½ teaspoons cinnamon
    3 tablespoons honey
    25 g (1 oz) ground almonds

156

For the garnish
  1 tablespoon honey
  ½ tablespoon margarine
  1 tart apple such as Granny Smith, peeled, cored
    and cut in 8 mm (⅓ in) slices
  1 tablespoon sesame seeds or 50 g (2 oz) slivered almonds, toasted

Trim the meat well to remove any fat and gristle. Combine the marinade ingredients in a large bowl. Add the beef and mix until thoroughly coated with the spicy mixture. At this point the mixture can be refrigerated for several hours before cooking.

Put the beef with any marinade into a large, lidded casserole or *tagine*. (If using a *tagine*, follow instructions for soaking before use.) Fry the meat, uncovered, over moderate heat, stirring once or twice until sealed on all sides and a wonderful aroma rises from the pan, about 6 minutes. Add enough boiling water to almost cover the meat, bring to the boil, then cover and simmer for 2 hours, or cook in the oven at 160°C (325°F/Gas 3) for the same amount of time until fork-tender.

Lift out the meat with a slotted spoon and put in a bowl or shallow dish.

Add the prunes or apricots to the pot, along with the cinnamon and honey. Bubble, uncovered, on the stove until about 300 ml (10 fl oz) of liquid remain in the pan, about 5 minutes, then stir in the almonds. Return the beef to this mixture and keep hot over a very low heat.

To prepare the garnish, heat the honey and margarine in a wide pan and fry the apple slices in this mixture over moderate heat until they are bathed in a golden glaze, about 5 minutes. Toss the sesame seeds or almonds in a heavy-based pan over moderate heat until they smell 'toasty', about 2 minutes.

Serve piping hot, garnished with the apple slices and scattered with the toasted sesame seeds or almonds.

157

TURKISH MEATBALLS
IN A SWEET-AND-SOUR SAUCE

Izmir Koefteh
Evelyn

THESE TENDER AND TASTY MEATBALLS are stewed in a smooth sweet-and-sour sauce. They can be found in most of the Sephardi cuisines that originated in the former Ottoman Empire.

Makes 6–8 servings
Keeps 4 days under refrigeration.
Freezes up to 2 months.

2 large slices white or brown bread
2 large eggs
½ large onion, peeled and cut in 2.5 cm (1 in) pieces
1 large sprig curly parsley
1 teaspoon sea salt
15 grinds black pepper
1 tablespoon soy sauce
900 g (2 lb) minced beef

For the sauce
2 tablespoons olive oil
1 medium onion, peeled and halved and thinly sliced
1 small can tomato purée mixed with water,
    to make 425 ml (15 fl oz) of liquid
juice of ½ large lemon
1 tablespoon light brown sugar
½ teaspoon sea salt and 10 grinds black pepper

For the garnish
2 tablespoons finely chopped curly parsley
2 heaped tablespoons pine kernels, toasted in a non-stick pan
    until golden brown

158

Soak the bread in water to cover for a minute or so, then squeeze dry. To prepare the beef mixture, put the eggs, soaked bread slices, onion, parsley and seasonings into a blender or food processor and process for 30 seconds, or until smooth.

With the hands or a large fork, gently mix the egg mixture with the minced beef until smoothly blended. Leave for 30 minutes to firm up.

While the meat is standing, start the sauce. Heat the oil in a deep frying pan or casserole, add the onion and cook over low heat until limp, about 5 minutes. Meanwhile, shape the meat into 'golf balls'. Add to the pan but do not crowd (in two batches if necessary) and cook gently until golden brown, about 7 minutes. Now add the remaining sauce ingredients and bring to the boil. (The meatballs should be barely covered; if not, add a little more water.)

Cover and simmer over very low heat on top of the cooker for 1 hour.

Sprinkle the meatballs with the chopped parsley and toasted pine kernels. Serve with rice or Bulgur and Vermicelli Pilaf (page 220).

♫ THE UBIQUITOUS MEATBALL has its place in every Jewish ⸫
ethnic cuisine, from the Roumanian-style *carnatzlich*, which are rolled in paprika then stewed with eggplant in a sweet-and-sour sauce or the German equivalent, *Koenigsburger klops*, cooked in thickened gravy, to the Sephardi-style *kofta keftedes eem tahini*, which are spiced with cumin, allspice or cinnamon and grilled under a covering of sesame seed paste.

Nearly all the Sephardi meatballs are stewed in some kind of tomato sauce, which is sometimes flavoured with honey, sometimes with lemon juice.

Whichever you choose, provided you use best-quality lean minced beef and lighten it with egg and a filler such as matzah meal, oatmeal, bread or ground rice, you are always in for a treat.

159

FLORENTINE MEATBALLS WITH RENAISSANCE SPICES

Judi

IN THESE UNUSUAL MEATBALLS, whose origins go back 500 years, the beef is bound with oatmeal and cooked aubergine, then seasoned with coriander, giving a fluffy texture and slightly nutty flavour. Grilling rather than frying the aubergine dramatically reduces the amount of oil it absorbs, avoiding the more conventional — and tedious — process of salting it before frying.

Makes 8 servings
Keeps 3 days under refrigeration.
Freezes raw or cooked up to 3 months.

675 g (1½ lb) aubergine, peeled and cut in 1 cm (½ in) slices
2–3 tablespoons sunflower oil
1 medium onion, peeled and finely chopped
2 tablespoons olive oil
450 g (1 lb) lean minced beef
2 teaspoons sea salt
20 grinds black pepper
1 teaspoon ground coriander
1 large egg, beaten
50 g (2 oz) oatmeal or matzah meal
2 teaspoons whole coriander seeds, or 1 teaspoon ground coriander
3 tablespoons plain white flour

Lightly brush each slice of aubergine with some of the sunflower oil, then lay oiled-side-down in a grill tin. Brush the upper surface with a little more oil, then grill, about 5 cm (2 in) beneath the heat, until golden, about 5 minutes. Turn the slices over with kitchen tongs and grill until the second side is golden and the aubergine feels soft when pierced with a pointed knife, about 4 minutes. Chop to a rough purée.

160

In a large pan, fry the onion in the olive oil over moderate heat until soft and golden, about 5 minutes. Put the meat in a large bowl, then add the cooked onion, the aubergine purée, 1½ teaspoons of the salt, the pepper, coriander, beaten egg and enough of the oatmeal or matzah meal to make a soft, tacky mixture that can be shaped into balls. Chill for 30 minutes (or up to 2 hours) to firm up.

Crush the whole coriander seeds in a small, strong bowl with the end of a rolling pin, or in a mortar and pestle, until almost powdery. Mix with the flour and the remaining ½ teaspoon salt on a plate or in a shallow soup dish. With wetted hands, take some of the meat mixture and form into 'golf balls' between the palms of the hands. Drop into the flour mixture to coat lightly.

Heat 2 tablespoons of the sunflower oil in a large nonstick pan over gentle heat for 2–3 minutes, then add the meatballs (they should sizzle) and fry, turning from time to time, until they are crisp on the outside and cooked right through, about 10 minutes.

Best served hot off the pan, but the meatballs can be reheated when needed by tossing in the pan until sizzling and heated through. They can also be reheated in the microwave, but the coating will be less crunchy. Delicious with Bulgur and Vermicelli Pilaf (page 220) and a juicy vegetable dish such as Fat-free Courgettes in a Herbed Tomato Sauce (page 181).

SOMETIMES THE BEST IDEAS are the oldest ones. We came across the inspiration for this exotic dish in a book of recipes from the Italian Renaissance. In sixteenth-century Italy, pungent spices were used to disguise the dubious flavour of meat stored without refrigeration. History does not record whether Leonardo da Vinci or Michelangelo ever feasted on these delicious meatballs with their meltingly tender interior and crunchy coriander coating, but they're certainly worthy of a latter-day renaissance in the culinary arts.

ROAST BONED LAMB STUFFED WITH A PINWHEEL OF FRESH HERBS

Evelyn

A BONED SHOULDER OF LAMB is 'stuffed' with a lavish layer of fresh herbs, then rolled before roasting so that as each slice is carved it reveals a fragrant pinwheel of green. This is equally good served hot or cold for a summer buffet.

Makes 6–8 servings

Leftovers will **keep** up to 3 days under refrigeration.

Freezes up to 2 months.

5 tablespoons finely snipped chives

2 tablespoons finely chopped parsley

2 tablespoons finely chopped fresh basil,
   or 2 teaspoons dried basil

2 teaspoons finely chopped fresh rosemary,
   or ½ teaspoon dried rosemary

1 teaspoon grated lemon zest

1 × 1.6 kg (3½ lb) (net weight) boned shoulder of lamb

½ teaspoon sea salt

10 grinds black pepper

1 tablespoon olive oil

1 teaspoon dry mustard

1 teaspoon plain flour

2 tablespoons Demerara or light brown sugar
   (see page 147)

1 onion, peeled and sliced

For the gravy

2 teaspoons fat from the roasting pan

2 teaspoons cornflour mixed with 300 ml (10 fl oz) cold water

1 beef stock cube, crumbled

1 teaspoon light or dark brown sugar

sea salt and freshly ground black pepper

162

About 3 hours before you intend to roast the meat, mix all the herbs and the lemon zest together in a small bowl.

Lay the meat, skin-side-down, on a board and cut out any lumps of fat. Cover with a piece of greaseproof paper and pound to a fairly even thickness with a meat mallet or the end of a rolling pin. Remove the paper. Lightly sprinkle the meat with salt and pepper, then spread the herb mixture over the surface. Roll the meat up tightly and secure it in 2 or 3 places with kitchen twine.

Leave the meat until you are ready to roast it, then place on a rack in a roasting tin. Brush all over with the oil. Then mix together the mustard and flour and coat the meat with the mixture.

Preheat the oven to 180°C (350°F/Gas 4).

Roast the meat for half an hour, then baste it well, sprinkle with the sugar and slip the onion slices under it to brown and flavour the juices. Roast for a further 1½ hours, basting once, until the meat is a rich brown.

Lift the meat on to a dish, cover loosely with aluminium foil and keep warm in a warming oven or in the regular oven turned down to its lowest setting.

To make the gravy, skim off all but 2 teaspoons of fat from the pan and remove the onion. Add the cornflour mixed to a smooth consistency with the water, the crumbled stock cube, the sugar and a pinch of sea salt and black pepper. Simmer on top of the cooker until thick and glossy, about 3 minutes.

Serve the gravy with the sliced meat and vegetables such as Swedish 'Fan' Potatoes (page 167) and Minted Peas and Cucumber with Shallots (page 176). It is also delicious cold served with an assortment of salads or in sandwiches.

163

ORANGE-SCENTED LAMB RAGOÛT

Judi

Apple CASSEROLE OF MELTINGLY TENDER CUBES of lamb in a smooth sauce is subtly infused with the tang and sweetness of fresh oranges. This is a marvellous party dish as it can be prepared well in advance and simply heated up before serving. You can also make it with chicken—use skinned joints and cook for half the time.

Makes 8 servings

Keeps 3 days under refrigeration. **Freezes** up to 2 months.

2 tablespoons sunflower oil

2.25 kg (5 lb) shoulder of lamb, trimmed of any fat and
   cut in 4 cm (1½ in) cubes

1 large onion, peeled and finely chopped

1 tablespoon dark brown sugar

225 ml (8 fl oz) dry white wine such as Sauvignon Blanc

225 ml (8 fl oz) hot chicken stock

1½ teaspoons sea salt

4 oranges, preferably navel

1 tablespoon cornflour mixed to a liquid with a little cold water

75 ml (3 fl oz) orange-flavoured liqueur such Cointreau or Curaçao
   (optional but delicious)

1 tablespoon chopped parsley

Preheat the oven to 160°C (325°F/Gas 3).

Heat 1 tablespoon of the oil in a large non-stick frying pan over moderate heat for 1 minute, then add the meat in three batches and fry until a rich brown on all sides, about 6 minutes per batch (do not crowd or the meat will steam rather than brown). Lift out with a slotted spoon and transfer to a large, ovenproof casserole.

Put the remaining tablespoon of oil in the pan, add the onion and brown sugar, and fry over low heat, stirring well, until the onion is golden brown, about 6 minutes. Add the wine, stirring vigorously to incorporate any tasty bits sticking to the bottom.

164

Simmer for 3 minutes to intensify the flavour, then add this mixture to the meat, together with the hot stock and the salt. The liquid should just cover the meat. If not, add a little extra hot stock or water.

Peel the oranges with a serrated knife, removing the pith as well, then cut between the sections to release the fruit. Add this to the casserole, together with any juice that can be squeezed out of the orange 'skeletons'.

Bring slowly to simmering point, then cover and transfer to the oven. Cook until the meat is absolutely tender, about 1¾ hours.

Transfer to the top of the stove and add the cornflour liquid, stirring well. Bubble for 3 minutes, then stir in the liqueur. Reduce the heat, cover and leave on the lowest setting until required, or allow to cool and refrigerate for up to 2 days.

Reheat over low heat until piping hot. Just before serving, sprinkle with the chopped parsley. The dish goes extremely well with mashed potatoes or Golden Persian Rice (page 207) to soak up the juices and a green vegetable such as peas or courgettes.

Fruit of the Earth:
Vegetable
Delights

"Better is a dinner of vegetables where love is"

—Proverbs 15:17

THE POTATO HAS ALWAYS BEEN THE MAINSTAY OF THE JEWISH vegetable basket—in the days of large families and low incomes it was nourishing and satisfying. And we don't propose to question that. But we have tried to be innovative even with roast potatoes and chips. Did you know that you can produce these formerly calorific dishes without any fat whatsoever? All you need is some strong chicken stock for one and aluminium foil for the other. Evelyn has a lovely way to make fluffy clouds of mashed potatoes, while Judi whirls butternut squash and apples into a sweet and spicy purée made in moments with a food processor.

Cabbage, carrots, onions and potatoes—that's about all our great-grandmothers had to cook for a vegetable accompaniment in the villages of Russia, Poland and Lithuania. So Evelyn visits Vienna for the wonderful sweet-and-sour red cabbage casserole, while Judi borrows from Spain a dish of Baby Spinach with Nuts and Raisins. Evelyn counters with a wonderfully light vegetable kugel (potatoes definitely the minority ingredient), while Judi contributes an elegant dish of Fragrant Green Beans from the south of France. We reckon the honours are pretty even in this category!

166

SWEDISH 'FAN' POTATOES

HASSELBACKS
Evelyn

T HE CURIOUS NAME DERIVES from that of a restaurant in Sweden which invented the method of part-slicing the potatoes in a fan shape before roasting. For extra flavour, strew some unpeeled garlic cloves in the roasting dish, which will perfume the oil with which the potatoes are basted. The garlic is roasted to a creamy purée which is scooped out of its skin on the plate. Cook the potatoes in an ovenproof dish which can go straight to the table.

Makes 8 servings
Serve immediately. **Do not refrigerate or freeze.**

8 large 225 g (8 oz) baking potatoes, peeled and cut across in half
2 teaspoons sea salt, approximately
12 unpeeled garlic cloves (optional)
50 ml (2 fl oz) olive oil
40 g (1½ oz) margarine

In a large saucepan, cover the halves of potato with cold water and 1 teaspoon of the sea salt and bring to the boil. Lower the heat and simmer, covered, for 5 minutes. Remove from the heat. Pour off the water, cover the pan with a cloth and leave for 2 minutes to absorb any surface moisture. When cool enough to handle, push a skewer lengthwise through the bottom third of each potato in turn, then slice down at 5 mm (¼ in) intervals at a slight angle just as far as the skewer. Remove the skewer.

Arrange the potatoes in one layer in an ovenproof dish or roasting tin surrounded by the cloves of garlic, if using.

Preheat the oven to 200°C (400°F)/Gas 6.

When ready to roast, heat the oil and margarine until steaming (1 minute in the microwave), then pour over the potatoes and sprinkle with more sea salt. Roast for 1 hour, basting three times in the last half hour.

The potatoes can be kept hot without going soggy at 110°C (225°F/Gas ¼) for up to 30 minutes.

Serve from the dish with roast meat or poultry.

167

OLIVE OIL ACTUALLY GIVES a better colour and flavour to roast potatoes than sunflower oil. However, you don't need to use the extra-virgin oil, which in any case has too fruity a flavour to marry with potatoes. Instead, use 'pure' olive oil — a blend of refined (tasteless) oil with extra-virgin, which is lighter in flavour and therefore excellent for use when roasting, frying or making mayonnaise, where you don't want the flavour to dominate. I've recently used this oil with great success for dinner party potatoes. As olive oil is the favoured dietary oil of the moment, I've even felt virtuous, since despite giving my guests a large, if tasty, dollop of calories, I was also boosting their intake of monounsaturates.

NO-FAT CRISPY ROAST POTATOES
AND FAT-FREE CHIPS

Judi

ALL THE TASTE OF CONVENTIONAL ROAST POTATOES with none of the fat. The technique is a new twist on the ancient cooking technique of roasting potatoes in a sealed earthenware or terracotta pot. The heat of the oven browns them while the sealed pot—or, in this case, an aluminium foil package—prevents them from drying out.

And believe it or not, it's perfectly possible to enjoy brown and crispy chips on a fat-free diet. The secret: dipping the raw chips in hot stock. As the potatoes cook, the stock evaporates, producing a crisp, golden brown finish.

Makes 4 servings
Serve freshly made. **Do not reheat or freeze.**

700–900 g (1½–2 lb) large baking potatoes, peeled
For roast potatoes
    2 teaspoons sea salt
For chips
    1 chicken or vegetable stock cube
    225 ml (8 fl oz) 1 cup boiling water

Preheat the oven to 220°C (425°F/Gas 7).

For the roast potatoes, cut the potatoes into wedges 4 cm (1½ in) thick. Put in a covered dish with 3 tablespoons water and microwave for 5 minutes on full power, or parboil in a large saucepan until almost tender, about 7 minutes.

Take a sheet of aluminium foil large enough to enclose the potatoes in a single layer. Drain them and dry well (most easily done by returning them to the pot off the heat and covering with paper towels or a cloth for 3–5 minutes). Lay the dry potatoes side by side on the aluminium foil, sprinkle lightly with some of the sea salt and make into an airtight but loose parcel.

Bake for 30 minutes, then turn the parcel over without opening it and cook for

169

a further 30 minutes. To serve, open the parcel and turn the golden brown potatoes into a warm dish and sprinkle lightly with more sea salt.

To make chips, cut the potatoes into sticks of whatever thickness you prefer. Dissolve the stock cube in the boiling water and put in a bowl. Dip the potato pieces so they are well coated with the stock. Arrange in one layer, 1 cm (½ in) apart, in a shallow roasting pan.

Bake for 30 minutes until golden brown and crisp, turning once or twice, then serve at once.

LAYERED POTATO BAKE
WITH GARLIC AND BLACK PEPPER

Evelyn

THE THINLY SLICED POTATOES ABSORB all the flavours of the stock as they cook, while the top layer crisps temptingly. Use butter and vegetable stock for a milk meal, margarine and chicken stock for a meat meal. To save cooking time, the dish can be started off in the microwave. Cook on full power for 5 minutes, then transfer to the oven.

Makes 6–8 servings. Leftovers **keep** 1 day under refrigeration.
Do not freeze.

1.1 kg (2½ lb) small potatoes, peeled and sliced 5 mm (¼ in) thick
50 g (2 oz) butter or margarine, melted
600 ml (1 pint) hot vegetable or chicken stock
1½ teaspoons sea salt
20 grinds black pepper
good pinch of ground nutmeg
1 clove garlic, crushed or finely chopped

Preheat the oven to 180°C (350°F/Gas 4). Choose an ovenproof dish about 28 cm (11 in) long but not more than 4 cm (1½ in) deep.

Turn the potato slices into a large bowl of cold water. Melt the butter or margarine. Generously grease the dish with some of the melted fat.

Heat the stock until it is steaming (3 minutes on full power in the microwave), then stir in the seasonings, fat and the garlic.

Meanwhile, drain the potato slices and return them to the bowl. Pour the steaming stock over, mixing them gently together.

Turn the potatoes and liquid into the prepared dish and press down with a spatula so that the top layer is almost submerged. If not, pour in a little boiling water.

Transfer to the oven and bake for 1¼–1½ hours, until the potatoes are absolutely tender when pierced with a slim knife and the top is crisp and brown. If the top layer seems to be drying out during the cooking period, add a little boiling water. Keep the potatoes hot in a low oven until required.

BABY POTATOES ROASTED IN HERBED OLIVE OIL

Judi

THESE CRISP MOUTHFULS have the added advantage of cooking in half the time of regular roast potatoes, albeit at a higher temperature. They also make an interesting alternative to plain roast or boiled potatoes. Rosemary, sea salt and olive oil form a delicious coating.

Makes 6–8 servings
Serve freshly cooked.

700–900 g (1½–2 lb) cleaned baby new potatoes
2 teaspoons sea salt
50 ml (2 fl oz) olive oil
1½ teaspoons finely chopped fresh rosemary or thyme,
    or 1 teaspoon dried
10 grinds black pepper
sprig of fresh rosemary, thyme or curly parsley

Cover the potatoes with cold water, add 1 teaspoon of the salt, bring to the boil and cook over low heat until almost tender, about 8 minutes. Drain and dry off well (most easily done by returning them to the pan off the heat with a cloth laid over them).

Preheat the oven to 220°C (425°F/Gas 7).

In a roasting tin just large enough to hold the potatoes in one layer, mix the oil and chopped herbs together. Add the potatoes and toss until well coated. Season with another ½ teaspoon sea salt and the pepper, then roast for 40 minutes or until crisp and golden brown.

To serve, sprinkle lightly with the remaining ½ teaspoon sea salt and a few grinds of black pepper, then garnish with a sprig of herb.

172

CREAMY PUFF PERFECT MASHED POTATOES

Evelyn

THE SECRET OF REALLY LIGHT and creamy mashed potatoes is to mix them with hot cream or milk, or chicken stock for a meat meal. The simplest way is to pour the liquid down the inside of the pan of cooked potatoes and wait until it is steaming hot before whisking it into them.

Makes 6–8 servings. **Serve** immediately or reheat, preferably in the microwave, on the same day. **Do not freeze.**

1.1 kg (2½ lb) starchy potatoes (weight when peeled), peeled and quartered
150 ml (5 fl oz) single cream, milk or chicken stock
1 teaspoon sea salt
25 g (1 oz) butter or margarine
½ teaspoon white pepper
10 grinds black pepper
½ teaspoon ground nutmeg

Cook the potatoes in a covered saucepan of boiling salted water until tender when pierced with a slim pointed knife, about 15 minutes. Drain the water off, then return the saucepan to the cooker and shake over gentle heat until all the surface moisture has evaporated from the potatoes.

Pour the cream, milk or stock down the inside of the pot and when it starts to steam, add the sea salt, butter or margarine, peppers and nutmeg. Beat over the lowest heat (most easily with a hand-held electric mixer) until the potatoes lighten in colour and look creamy in texture. Taste and add more sea salt if necessary.

Pile into an ovenproof dish, smooth level, dot with the butter or margarine and keep hot. For the lightest texture, serve within 15 minutes.

To reheat later, either reheat in the oven at 200°C (400°F/Gas 6) for 15 minutes or in the microwave until very hot to the touch, then brown under the grill.

Variation

Before serving, stir in 125 g (4 oz) cup of chopped spinach tossed with a little garlic, sea salt and melted butter or margarine.

173

BUTTERNUT SQUASH AND SPICED APPLE PURÉE

Judi

THIS LIGHTLY SPICED VEGETABLE AND FRUIT COMBINATION makes a perfect accompaniment to both poultry and meat. Topped with buttered crumbs and grated cheese, it becomes an unusual gratin that is satisfying enough to serve as a vegetarian entrée.

Makes 6–7 servings
Keeps 3 days under refrigeration.
Freezes up to 2 months.

1.4 kg (3 lb) butternut squash
25 g (1 oz) margarine or butter
6 rounded tablespoons apple sauce
1 teaspoon sea salt
pinch of ground nutmeg
20 grinds black pepper
1 teaspoon mixed sweet spice or cinnamon
For the topping (optional)
3 tablespoons fine dry breadcrumbs or matzah meal
50 g (2 oz) grated well-flavoured cheese, such as mature Cheddar
40g (1½ oz) butter or margarine, melted

Halve the squash and scoop out the seeds and any fibre. Cover with clingfilm and cook in the microwave on 100 per cent power for 16 minutes, or cover with aluminium foil and bake at 200°C (400°F/Gas 6) in a conventional oven for 45 minutes to 1 hour, until the flesh is tender.

Leave until cool enough to handle, then uncover, scoop out the flesh and purée in the food processor or mash with a fork. Add all the remaining ingredients, mix well and spoon into a casserole. The mixture can be refrigerated at this point until needed.

174

To reheat, cover with clingfilm and microwave on full power for 3 minutes, or cover with aluminium foil and bake in a preheated oven at 180°C (350°F/Gas 4) for 20–25 minutes.

To make into a gratin, mix the topping ingredients together and scatter on top of the hot purée. Grill until golden and bubbly, about 5 minutes, or bake in the oven at 200°C (400°F/Gas 6) for 20 minutes. Serve piping hot, straight from the dish.

175

MINTED PEAS AND CUCUMBER
WITH SHALLOTS

Evelyn

Aperfect 'specialty' vegetable dish, ideal to serve with any hot or cold entrée, particularly poached or grilled salmon. It is also delicious without the mint. Sliced spring onions can be substituted for the shallots.

Makes 6–8 servings
Keeps up to 1 day under refrigeration. **Do not freeze.**

1 large cucumber
25 g (1 oz) butter or margarine
2 teaspoons olive oil
6 shallots, peeled and finely chopped
450 g (1 lb) fresh or frozen peas
1 teaspoon sugar
1½ teaspoons sea salt
¼ teaspoon white pepper
large sprig of fresh mint, or 2 teaspoons dried

Cut the cucumber into 2.5 cm (1 in) thick slices, then cut each slice into 5 mm (¼ in) thick vertical slices, first one way and then the other, so that the cucumber is cut into julienne strips each 5 mm (¼ in) thick and 2.5 cm (1 in) long.

Heat the butter or margarine and olive oil in a heavy lidded frying pan and gently cook the shallots, stirring, until tender and golden, about 6 minutes.

Add the cucumber, then lower the heat and simmer for 5 minutes, until the cucumber becomes translucent. Add the peas, seasonings and mint. Stir well, cover again and cook gently until the peas are tender, about 5 minutes. Uncover the pan and lift the vegetables into a serving dish with a slotted spoon. Boil down the juices in the pan until about 2 tablespoons remain. Serve the vegetables with the juices spooned over them.

176

BABY SPINACH WITH NUTS AND RAISINS

Judi

THIS IS A TASTY AND ORIGINAL WAY TO PREPARE fresh spinach. The recipe can be made with packets of fresh pre-washed spinach (which can often be microwaved directly in the bag—check the instructions on the packet). The entire dish can be made up to 30 minutes before serving, then reheated, which actually improves the flavour. This version goes well with grilled fish, or as part of a vegetarian main course. The 'meaty' version with salami or wursht is delicious with grilled chops or to pep up cold meats.

Makes 6 servings
Leftovers **keep** 1 day under refrigeration. **Do not freeze.**

75 g (3 oz) seedless raisins
700 g (1½ lb) fresh baby spinach, well rinsed
1 tablespoon olive oil
125 g (4 oz) diced salami or wursht (optional)
50 g (2 oz) broken cashews or pine kernels
½ teaspoon sea salt
15 grinds black pepper

First plump the raisins. Put them in a small microwave-proof bowl with 1½ tablespoons water, cover and cook on full power for 1½ minutes. Or put in a bowl, cover with boiling water and leave for 10 minutes, then drain.

Lightly cook the spinach with a little water in a wok or frying pan over moderate heat, tossing, until limp, about 2 minutes. Drain. Turn on to a board and roughly chop.

Heat the oil in the same pan for 1 minute over high heat, add the wursht, if using and the nuts, then stir well. Reduce the heat and fry, stirring frequently, until the nuts are golden, about 2 minutes. Add the raisins and spinach, followed by the salt and pepper. Cook, stirring constantly, until everything is piping hot, about 1 minute. Serve at once.

Alternatively, cook 30 minutes in advance, then reheat in the same pan over moderate heat, stirring, until piping hot, about 2 minutes.

177

VIENNESE RED CABBAGE

Evelyn

IHAD FORGOTTEN HOW DELICIOUS BRAISED RED CABBAGE is until I was served it at a recent dinner party. It went superbly well with a main dish of roast duck, but it's equally good with pickled brisket or a meat casserole.

Makes 6–8 servings
Keeps up to 4 days under refrigeration. **Freezes** up to 2 months.

generous 900 g (2 lb) red cabbage, quartered
25 g (1 oz) margarine
1 large onion, peeled and finely chopped
2 tablespoons light brown sugar
2 generous tablespoons redcurrant jelly, cranberry jelly, or cranberry sauce
2 tablespoons wine vinegar
2 tablespoons cold water
2 teaspoons sea salt
¼ teaspoon white pepper
1 large bay leaf

Preheat the oven to 190°C (375°F/Gas 5).

Remove the cabbage stalk section and discard, then shred the leaves finely by hand or machine. Rinse in cold water and drain well.

Melt the margarine in a heavy saucepan large enough to hold the cabbage. Add the onion and cook over moderate heat for 5 minutes, until golden. Add the brown sugar and stir until it begins to caramelise, about 3 minutes. Now add the cabbage and all the remaining ingredients, stirring well to blend until bubbling. Transfer to a casserole dish—a covered roasting tin or enamelled cast-iron dish are both excellent.

Cook in the oven for 45 minutes, stirring twice in that time. Taste and add more sugar if necessary. The cabbage should have an equal balance of sweet and sour. It should also have a little 'bite' left when it is ready. If too tough, cook a further 15 minutes. It can then be kept hot at 140°C (275°F/Gas 1) for as long as required.

If the cabbage turns blue, add a squeeze of lemon juice or a few drops of vinegar. Serve as an accompaniment to hot or cold meat or poultry.

178

FRAGRANT GREEN BEANS
A LA CÔTE D'AZUR

Judi

I FIRST HAD THESE MARVELLOUS GARLICKY BEANS, succulent yet crunchy, at a tiny open-air bistro in the old quarter of Nice. The beans are braised with finely chopped shallots and garlic, to produce a rustic, richly flavoured side dish that goes particularly well with fish. The recipe is best made with the very thin French beans, but will work with ordinary green beans if those are not available.

Makes 6–8 servings
Serve the same day. **Do not freeze**.

675–900 g (1½–2 lb) fresh French beans
2 tablespoons extra-virgin olive oil
15 g (½ oz) butter or margarine
4 shallots, peeled and chopped
1 teaspoon sea salt
2 cloves garlic, peeled and finely chopped
225 ml (8 fl oz) hot water
10 grinds black pepper

Trim the beans and rinse with cold water.

In a non-stick frying pan or sauté pan, heat the oil and butter or margarine and add the chopped shallots, sprinkling with ½ teaspoon of the salt. Fry, stirring, over moderate heat until the shallots are soft, about 5 minutes. Add the garlic, followed by the beans, hot water and remaining ½ teaspoon salt. Reduce the heat, partially cover and cook gently until the beans are bite-tender, about 12 minutes.

Increase the heat and fry uncovered, stirring, until any remaining water has disappeared and the shallots are a rich golden brown, about 5 minutes. The beans should be limp but still bite-tender. Add the freshly ground black pepper and mix well.

Serve hot off the pan or reheat in the microwave when needed. The beans are particularly good with Miraculous Fish (page 104) and roasts such as Roast Boned Lamb Stuffed with a Pinwheel of Fresh Herbs (page 162).

179

ISRAELI-STYLE COURGETTES

Kishuim Rehovot

Evelyn

THIS DELICIOUS TASTY VEGETABLE RAGOÛT is one of the many Israeli vegetable dishes that have been developed during the last 60 years. It can be served hot with roasts and grills, at room temperature as a side dish with cold meats and poultry, or as a starter with warm pita bread.

Makes 6–8 servings

Keeps up to 4 days under refrigeration.

Do not freeze.

2 tablespoons olive oil
1 large onion, peeled and finely chopped
1 fat clove garlic, finely chopped
2 red peppers, seeds and pith removed, cut in 1 cm (½ in) cubes
900 g (2 lb) courgettes, unpeeled but trimmed and cut in 1 cm (½ in) slices
1½ teaspoons sea salt
10 grinds black pepper
1 teaspoon light brown sugar
good pinch of cayenne pepper
2 rounded tablespoons tomato purée
150 ml (5 fl oz) water
1 tablespoon chopped parsley

Heat the oil in a deep frying pan and cook the onion and garlic, stirring, until softened and golden, about 5 minutes.

Add the peppers and cook for a further 5 minutes, until they are beginning to colour. Add the courgette slices, salt, pepper, brown sugar and cayenne, and cook, covered, for a further 10 minutes.

Add the tomato purée diluted with the water and simmer uncovered for about 5 minutes, until thick and juicy, like ratatouille. Stir in the parsley. Serve hot or cold. May be reheated.

FAT-FREE COURGETTES
IN A HERBED TOMATO SAUCE

Judi

THIS IS A LOW-CAL COUSIN of its rich and famous French relative, rata-touille. Slices of zucchini are simmered in an intensely flavoured sauce with absolutely no fat and the entire dish is cooked is a single pot, making it easy as well as healthy. The dish takes advantage of the very low calorie content of zucchini, while adding the kick of tomato and herbs.

Makes 4–6 servings

Keeps 3 days under refrigeration. **Do not freeze.**

450–675 g (1–1½ lb) **shiny-skinned courgettes**

For the sauce

    1 × 400 g (14 oz) can chopped tomatoes

    1 tablespoon finely chopped dried onion

    1 teaspoon finely chopped garlic

    1 teaspoon dried Italian herbs

    ½ teaspoon paprika

    1 bay leaf

    1 teaspoon sea salt

    15 grinds black pepper

    1 teaspoon light brown sugar

    1 tablespoon fresh chopped basil or parsley

Trim the courgettes, then cut into 2.5 cm (1 in) slices.

Put all the sauce ingredients into a medium saucepan and bring to the boil over moderate heat. Add the sliced courgettes, cover and simmer gently until just tender when pierced with a slim sharp knife, about 6 minutes (don't overcook or they will go mushy). The sauce should be almost as thick as ketchup. If not, simmer uncovered for 2–3 more minutes.

Serve hot as a side dish with chicken or fish, or at room temperature as an accompaniment to cold meats. Reheats well.

181

VIKKI'S LIGHT VEGETABLE KUGEL

Evelyn

IN THE OLD DAYS kugel was served as a meatless main dish; nowadays it makes an excellent accompaniment to chicken or meat. Alternatively, it could be the star of a vegetarian main course for six. For the smaller family, halve all the ingredients but bake just as long in a smaller dish.

Makes 8–10 servings

Keeps up to 3 days under refrigeration. **Freezes** up to 2 months.

3 large courgettes, about 450 g (1 lb), topped and tailed
3 large carrots, about 250–300 g (9–10 oz), peeled
2 baking potatoes, about 450 g (1 lb), peeled
1 large onion, about 200–225 g (7–8 oz), peeled
4 large eggs, whisked together
1½ teaspoons sea salt
25 grinds black pepper
150 ml (5 fl oz) sunflower oil
125 g (4 oz) matzah meal
50 g (2 oz) dried breadcrumbs

Select an oven-to-table dish measuring approximately 25 × 20 × 5 cm (10 × 8 × 2 in) deep, or use an oval gratin dish 28–30 cm (11–12 in) long.

Preheat the oven to 180°C (350°F/Gas 4).

Grate all the vegetables on the finest blade of the food processor (or by hand) and mix together in a bowl. In a very large bowl, whisk the eggs and seasonings until fluffy, then stir in the oil, matzah meal and breadcrumbs followed by the vegetables. Mix very thoroughly, then pour into the baking dish and smooth level.

Bake for 1–1¼ hours or until a rich golden brown.

To serve, cut into squares. The kugel reheats well either in a moderate oven or in the microwave.

TO COUNT AS 'comfort food' a generation or three ago, a dish had to stick to the ribs and keep hunger at bay for the foreseeable future. This meant, alas, that its calories had to come mainly from fat and carbohydrates—not the most popular words in today's healthy-eating canon. Kugels are a prime example.

So I was surprised—and curious—when I was served a dish that had faint echoes of that most delicious but calorie-packed of all the kugels, potato kugel. It was at the table of a go-ahead young niece who I knew had the nutritional needs of her six young children very much in mind.

This new-style kugel was light and spongy with a mouthwatering selection of vegetables—of which the potato content was fairly low on the list. It wasn't her invention, Vikki confessed, but a friend had got it from a friend—like all the best recipes.

Looking into my own files, I found what could have been its first manifestation in a savoury carrot ring I tasted in the United States many years ago. This recipe must have emigrated to the UK and gradually metamorphosed—rather like the game of Chinese Whispers—into this wonderful vegetable kugel.

ROASTED TOMATOES
WITH A HERB CRUNCH TOPPING

Tomates à la Languedocienne

Judi

From the languedoc region in south-west France comes this easy and delicious way to prepare tomatoes. They're best made with very ripe, juicy beefsteak or vine-ripened fruit and fresh herbs, but out of season they can give even the blandest tomatoes a new lease on life. The dish can be assembled, uncooked, up to 2 hours ahead.

Makes 6–8 servings
Serve freshly cooked. **Do not freeze.**

6–8 vine-ripened tomatoes, about 8 cm (3 in) in diameter
2 teaspoons sea salt
For the topping
2 large slices slightly stale white or wholemeal bread,
    cut or torn into 2.5 cm (1 in) pieces
2 sprigs fresh parsley
2–3 cloves garlic
½ teaspoon sea salt
2 tablespoons extra virgin olive oil
10 grinds black pepper
1 teaspoon chopped fresh thyme or marjoram,
    or large pinch of dried

Cut the tomatoes in half around the 'equator'. Using a teaspoon, scoop out the pulp and seeds, then sprinkle with the sea salt. Invert each tomato half on to a paper towel and leave for 30 minutes (and up to 3 hours) to drain.

Put the bread, parsley and garlic in the food processor and process until fine crumbs are formed, about 1 minute. Add all the remaining topping ingredients and process until evenly mixed, about 30 seconds.

184

Gently squeeze the tomatoes to remove any excess juice, then gently press the breadcrumb mixture into the centre and mound it up slightly on the top. At this stage, the tomatoes can be refrigerated for up to 2 hours.

To cook, arrange the tomatoes in a lightly oiled ovenproof dish or grill pan. Grill about 15 cm (6 in) from the heat for 12 minutes, then move to about 7.5 cm (3 in) from the heat and grill for a further 3–5 minutes, until the topping is rich golden brown and crisp to the touch. Alternatively, bake in a preheated oven at 190°C (375°F/Gas 5 for 20 minutes, then brown under the grill as above.

Serve within 15 minutes as an accompaniment to barbecued or grilled fish or chicken, or as part of a vegetable platter.

Leaves for all Seasons:
Splendid Salads

"Behold, I have given you every herb bearing seed"

—Genesis 1:29

WHEN EVELYN AND HER HUSBAND WERE INVITED TO A KOSHER luncheon in the Jewish Town Hall in Prague, they were served a salad of spring onions, potatoes and cucumber. This was before the Berlin Wall came down and food was still scarce, yet it was all an earlier generation ever had to offer to their families.

Now we are blessed with a cornucopia of glorious salad ingredients—oranges and endives (which Judi sprinkles with chrysanthemum petals), mouth-watering marinated peppers of every colour, Florence fennel, here partnered with salted roasted almonds and black grapes. There will always be room on the menu, however, for a perfect potato salad or a delicious German cucumber salad perfumed with fresh dill. While not strictly a salad, we both agree that Grandpa Rose's Pickles, a recipe passed down through the Rose family for generations, has to be preserved as a national treasure!

186

MARINATED ROAST PEPPERS

Escalivada   *Evelyn*

THIS WONDERFUL SALAD FROM the Sephardi cuisine is best made the day before to allow the dressing to be absorbed by the vegetables. *Escalivada* is its Catalan name. You can turn this dish into an interesting starter by adding 50 g (2oz) of roughly chopped anchovy fillets and a sprinkling of chopped fresh oregano.

Makes 6–8 servings
Keeps up to 4 days under refrigeration.
Do not freeze.

2 each large red, yellow and green peppers,
    halved and with pith and seeds removed
olive oil for brushing
175 g (6 oz) fat black olives, pitted
For the dressing
    50 ml (2 fl oz) extra-virgin olive oil
    1 tablespoon fresh lemon juice
    2 large cloves garlic, crushed
    1 teaspoon sea salt
    10 grinds black pepper

Brush the pepper halves with olive oil and arrange side by side on a grill pan. Cook under a preheated, very hot grill until the skin has blackened. Leave covered with paper towels—the trapped steam will soften the skin and make it easy to peel off.

Peel all the peppers and cut into 1 cm (½ in) strips. Arrange in a shallow dish with the black olives.

Shake the dressing ingredients together in a large screw-top jar until thickened, then spoon over the peppers. Cover and refrigerate.

continued

187

Leave at room temperature for 1 hour before serving as a starter with good brown bread, or as a salad to accompany cold meat and chicken dishes.

TO SEPHARDI JEWS who fled from Spain's Inquisition to Gibraltar and Morocco, this colourful dish is known as *Ensalada de Pimiento*. To Egyptian Jews it is known as *Salade de Poivrons Grillés* and to Ladino 'Spanish Yiddish' speakers as *Ensalada de Pimientos Rojos*.

188

SHADES OF GREEN TOSSED SALAD

Judi

Slices of avocado and green pepper marinated in a garlic and honey dressing add a delicious touch to a mixture of crisp green leaves, each with a different texture and tone. The mix of salad greens can be varied according to what's available.

Makes 6–8 servings

Keeps up to 24 hours under refrigeration without avocado or dressing.
Once dressed, **use** within 1 hour.

about 225 g (8 oz) mixed salad leaves such as chicory, rocket,
    watercress and cos lettuces

For the dressing
    2 tablespoons sunflower oil
    1 tablespoon olive oil
    1 teaspoon fresh lemon juice
    1 tablespoon white wine vinegar
    1 teaspoon Dijon mustard
    1 clove garlic, halved
    1 tablespoon finely cut fresh chives (optional)
    1 teaspoon sea salt
    1 teaspoon honey
    10 grinds black pepper

To marinate
    1 small green pepper, seeds and pith removed and thinly sliced
    1 medium-sized ripe avocado, peeled and thinly sliced

Several hours before serving, shake all the dressing ingredients together in a lidded jar until thickened, 1–2 minutes.

Put the sliced pepper and avocado in a small bowl and pour on the dressing. Cover and leave to marinate in the refrigerator until ready to serve.

Wash and dry the salad leaves and arrange in the salad bowl. Remove the garlic

189

from the dressing, then add the pepper, avocado and dressing to the leaves, tossing together gently until evenly coated.

Serve immediately. The salad goes particularly well with salmon dishes such Juicy Grilled Kebabs with a Sesame Crunch Coating (page 102) or Fresh Salmon Strudel Perfumed with Dill (page 94).

RIPENING AVOCADOS

AS THE RIPE FRUIT BRUISES easily on its way to market, avocados are often sold rock-hard. Using unripe avocado in this salad, however, undermines the whole dish—you may as well substitute turnip!

The nobbly, dark-skinned Haas variety of avocado is almost black when ripe and yields slightly to the touch. The smooth, bottle-green Fuerte should be free of large black patches (which may indicate bruising) and give easily when gently pressed at the base of the stalk. If you cannot find ripe avocados, however, don't despair. At least 2 days before you need them, place the fruit in a paper bag with a ripe banana, fold the top over and leave in a warm place. The banana releases compounds which ripen its bag-mate. By the way, burying an avocado pit in a bowl of guacamole will not, alas, prevent it from discoloring.

190

ISRAELI MINTED TOMATO AND CUCUMBER SALAD

Evelyn

Anyone who's ever done breakfast duty in a kibbutz kitchen will gladly regale you with stories of slicing cucumbers, peppers and tomatoes for hours on end. Now elaborated on in every hotel in Israel, this sophisticated version, with its tiny jewels of red and green vegetables, is well worth the preparation time—it's positively bursting with flavour.

Makes 6–8 servings
Serve the same day.

4 large firm but ripe tomatoes, diced
1 each red and green pepper, halved, seeds and white pith removed,
    cut in 8 mm (³⁄₈ in) dice
1 large cucumber, unpeeled (unless the skin is coarse),
    cut in 8 mm (³⁄₈ in) dice
2 teaspoons sea salt

For the dressing
75 ml (3 fl oz) extra-virgin olive oil
1 tablespoon each wine vinegar and lemon juice
1 fat clove garlic, crushed
1 teaspoon sea salt
10 grinds black pepper
1 teaspoon sugar
1 tablespoon finely snipped fresh mint, or 1 teaspoon dried
2 tablespoons chopped parsley

Put the tomatoes and peppers into separate bowls, cover and refrigerate.

Put the cucumber into a salad spinner or colander, sprinkle with the sea salt and leave for 30 minutes, then spin or drain and refrigerate.

In a screw-top jar, shake together all the dressing ingredients except the fresh

191

mint and parsley until thickened. Add the dried mint if using, then leave for several hours to mature in flavour.

To assemble the salad, put the cucumber, pepper and tomato dice into a large bowl. Stir in the chopped fresh mint and parsley together with the dressing and mix well, using two spoons.

Arrange the salad in a fairly shallow dish—it looks particularly effective against black or white. Serve cool but not chilled.

WHICH OLIVE OIL?

USE EXTRA-VIRGIN OLIVE OIL for dishes where its fruity taste and low acidity are of paramount importance, such as salad dressings, vegetable ragoûts and dressed grilled vegetables Italian-style. Use pure olive oil or light olive oil where its qualities as a frying agent (a higher smoke point and slower breakdown than other oils) are top of the list, with flavour and texture well down.

Once your taste buds have become accustomed to the nuances of flavour—using a medium-priced extra-virgin oil as a benchmark—it's worth experimenting with the more expensive premium or single-estate, unblended, first-cold-pressed oils, some as expensive as vintage wines and requiring an equally discerning palate to enjoy. To taste one oil against another, sprinkle a few drops on a piece of country style bread . . . and savour the flavour.

192

FENNEL, ALMOND
AND GRAPE SALAD

Judi

BULB FENNEL ADDS A SEDUCTIVE LIQUORICE TASTE to the salad bowl. In this recipe its assertive flavour is mellowed by macerating it in a little lemon juice, which later becomes part of the dressing. Add a few fresh orange segments or crumble a little blue cheese on top and you can turn this into an unusual starter.

Makes 6–8 servings
Keeps 24 hours under refrigeration without dressing.
Once dressed, **use** within 1 hour.

3 small to medium fennel bulbs
2 tablespoons fresh lemon juice
50 g (2 oz) split almonds, with or without skin
sea salt
1 medium head iceberg lettuce
225 g (8 oz) seedless red grapes
1–2 tablespoons mildly flavoured extra virgin olive oil

The night before, cut out and discard the core of the fennel, then shred the bulbs as finely as possible. Put into a container, toss well with the lemon juice, cover and refrigerate overnight.

Toast the almonds on a baking tray either under the grill for 3 minutes or in the oven at 180°C (350°F/Gas 4) for 12–15 minutes, until they turn a pale brown. Sprinkle lightly with sea salt and put aside.

To assemble the salad, shred the lettuce, halve the grapes, then put in a salad bowl with the fennel, lemon juice and toasted, salted almonds. Toss gently to mix.

Add just enough olive oil to make the leaves glisten. Serve within 1 hour.

193

PERFECT POTATO SALAD

Evelyn

I COULD NEVER REPRODUCE the potato salad I used to have as a child, which was bought from the local deli in Manchester, until I met a Jewish woman 30 years ago while flying to Switzerland. She told me her secret—always add the vinaigrette to the warm potatoes and add the mayonnaise just before serving.

Makes 6–8 servings
Keeps up to 2 days under refrigeration.
Do not freeze.

675 g (1½ lb) waxy or new potatoes
For the dressing
    50 ml (2 fl oz) vinaigrette dressing
      (pages 195 and 196)
    1 tablespoon finely chopped red onion
    1 tablespoon finely chopped chives
    1 tablespoon finely chopped parsley
    4 rounded tablespoons mayonnaise
    1 teaspoon Dijon mustard
    1 tablespoon boiling water
    1 tablespoon fresh lemon juice
    1 tablespoon chopped parsley

Boil the potatoes in their skins until almost tender, 15–20 minutes. Drain. Return to the same pot over the lowest heat, covered with a cloth, then steam gently for a further 3–4 minutes, until tender and absolutely dry (they will still be firm). Spread the potatoes on a cloth and leave until cool enough to handle. Skin the potatoes if desired, then cut or slice into a bowl.

Make the dressing of your choice. Stir the vinaigrette mixture gently through the potatoes. Blend together the mayonnaise, mustard, boiling water and lemon juice. Spoon on top of the potatoes. Leave in a cool place for at least 1 hour.

Just before serving, gently mix the mayonnaise through the potato salad. Heap into a shallow bowl and scatter with the chopped parsley.

Serve the salad at room temperature rather than chilled.

Here's an easy recipe to make your own vinaigrette.

3 tablespoons sunflower oil
1 tablespoon vinegar
½ teaspoon sea salt
10 grinds black pepper
pinch of sugar, or 1 teaspoon honey
pinch of powdered mustard
1 tablespoon finely chopped onion or spring onion
1 tablespoon finely snipped chives (optional)
1 tablespoon finely chopped parsley (optional)

Put all the ingredients in a screw-top jar. With the lid on tightly, shake for 1 minute or until thickened.

SPRING GARLAND SALAD
WITH A WALNUT OIL DRESSING

Judi

AN INTENSELY FLAVOURED combination of sun-dried tomatoes, Cape gooseberries, toasted nuts and crisp salad leaves, offset by a nutty vinaigrette dressing.

Makes 6–8 servings

Keeps 24 hours under refrigeration without dressing.

Once dressed, **use** within 1 hour. Dressing **keeps** 1 week under refrigeration.

Do not freeze.

For the nut oil vinaigrette
> 50 ml (2 fl oz) white wine or cider vinegar
> 2 tablespoons lemon juice
> 50 ml (2 fl oz) sunflower oil
> 2 tablespoons best-quality walnut or hazelnut oil
> 1 fat clove garlic, crushed
> 2 teaspoons sugar
> 1 teaspoon Dijon mustard
> 1 teaspoon sea salt
> 20 grinds black pepper

For the salad
> 2 rounded tablespoons pecans, walnuts or pine kernels
> 1 *lollo rosso* or 1 oakleaf lettuce
> 1 small head chicory
> 1 medium yellow pepper, seeded and finely diced
> 25–50 g (1–2 oz) oil-packed sun-dried tomatoes, finely diced
> 8 yellow Cape gooseberries (*Physalis*), papery skins removed,
>> halved if larger than 1 cm (½ in) in diameter
> 6–8 brown bread rolls

196

Put all the vinaigrette ingredients into a large screw-top jar and shake together until thoroughly blended and thickened, about 1 minute. Leave at room temperature until required.

Toss the nuts in a small, heavy-based frying pan over medium heat, shaking all the time, until they smell 'toasty', about 2 minutes. Wash and dry the salad leaves, then tear the leaves with your fingers into bite-sized shreds. Put in a salad bowl with the diced pepper, sun-dried tomato, nuts and Cape gooseberries. Toss with just enough dressing to coat the leaves lightly.

Arrange the leaves on individual serving plates. Place a warm roll or a crispy hot starter such as Provençal Sun-Dried Tomato, Olive and Basil Tarte (page 61) in the centre. If using rolls, cut a small cross in the top of each roll, brush with a little vinaigrette and crisp in a hot oven for 5 minutes.

NUT OILS

THE OILS OF THE WALNUT, hazelnut and sesame seed can add variety to a salad dressing. However, as their flavour is generally more insistent than even olive oil, use them cautiously and in partnership with a milder, flavourless oil such as sunflower, safflower or grapeseed.

If the salad already contains nuts or sesame seeds, a little of a matching oil in the dressing will help to bring out their flavour. Walnut and hazelnut oils, in the proportion of one part to three of a vegetable oil, work well in the dressing for any mixed green salad.

Ninety-five per cent of nut oils are produced in France. For my money, the best walnut and hazelnut oils come from local French producers, so if while on holiday you come across any in a French market, buy some!

Nut oils are less stable than the more refined vegetable oils and quickly become rancid if stored incorrectly. When buying imported oils, check to see if there is a 'best before' date on the bottle and buy only from a shop with a rapid turnover of these relatively esoteric products. Like olive oil, nut oil should be stored away from light. However, unlike olive oil, which crystallises when cold, it should be kept in the door of the refrigerator once opened. Taste before adding to a dressing to be sure it hasn't gone rancid since last used.

197

MOROCCAN-STYLE CARROT, RAISIN AND TOASTED NUT SALAD

Evelyn

ANOTHER 'NATURALISED' ISRAELI SALAD. The fruit juices make it especially refreshing, with the cumin adding a final little kick.

Makes 6–8 servings
Keeps up to 2 days under refrigeration.
Do not freeze.

50 g (2 oz) hazelnuts, in their skins
675 g (1½ lb) young carrots, peeled and coarsely grated
6 tablespoons raisins
For the dressing
    4 rounded tablespoons reduced-fat mayonnaise
    4 rounded tablespoons or 1 × 125 g (4 oz) carton natural yoghurt
    1 tablespoon fresh lemon juice
    1 tablespoon orange juice
    1 tablespoon light brown sugar
    pinch of sea salt
    15 grinds black pepper
    ½ teaspoon ground cumin

To toast the hazelnuts, preheat the oven to 180°C (350°F/Gas 4). Place the nuts on a baking tray and leave in the oven for 15–20 minutes, until they are golden brown and bursting out of the papery skins. Wrap in a tea towel, leave for 5 minutes, then rub vigorously to remove the skins. Chop the nuts coarsely and store in an airtight container until required (they will stay crisp for several weeks).

Put the dressing ingredients into a bowl and stir well to blend, then mix in the grated carrots and the raisins. Cover and leave for several hours.

To serve, pile the carrot mixture lightly into a bowl and scatter with the nuts.

198

ORANGE AND ENDIVE SALAD WITH CHRYSANTHEMUM PETALS

Judi

Edible flower petals add a romantic touch to this pretty salad, an enticing combination of mint, citrus and chicory, mellowed by lightly toasted pine kernels. Nasturtiums or tiny pansies can also be used in place of the chrysanthemum petals.

Makes 6–8 servings

Keeps covered under refrigeration without dressing for up to 24 hours. Once dressed, **serve** the same day.

4–5 heads Belgian chicory
4 large, thin-skinned oranges (seedless navels if possible)

For the dressing

2 tablespoons walnut or sunflower oil
1 tablespoon fresh lemon juice
2 teaspoons chopped fresh mint
1 teaspoon sugar or clear honey
½ teaspoon sea salt
speck of white pepper

For the garnish

2 tablespoons pine kernels
petals from 1 large, non-dyed chrysanthemum flower or other edible flower

Cut the ends off the chicory and separate the leaves. Peel the oranges as you would an apple, removing the white pith as well and divide into segments. Reserve any free orange juice and add to the dressing ingredients. Shake the dressing ingredients together in a jar to form a slightly thickened emulsion, about 1 minute.

Toss the pine kernels in a heavy-based frying pan over moderate heat until they smell 'toasty', about 2 minutes.

Arrange the leaves and orange segments in a salad bowl. To serve, coat with the dressing, then scatter the top with the nuts and petals.

199

DORIS'S GERMAN CUCUMBER SALAD

Evelyn

My FRIEND DORIS came to the UK in the late thirties and studied home economics, so she has an enviable collection of German and Anglo-Jewish recipes in her repertoire. This is typically simple but beautifully seasoned. It's excellent served well-chilled with grilled or poached salmon.

Makes 6–8 servings
Keeps up to 3 days under refrigeration.
Do not freeze.

1 large or 2 medium cucumbers
For the dressing
  50 ml (2 fl oz) sunflower oil
  1½ tablespoons white wine vinegar
  2 teaspoons fresh lemon juice
  1 teaspoon sea salt
  10 grinds black pepper
  1 teaspoon Dijon mustard
  1 teaspoon caster sugar
  1 tablespoon single cream, soured cream or natural yogurt
  1 tablespoon snipped fresh dill or chives
  1 teaspoon caraway seeds

Slice the unpeeled cucumber wafer-thin with a mandoline or in a food processor and put into a bowl. Put all the dressing ingredients into a screw-top jar and shake for 1–2 minutes, until thickened. Pour over the cucumbers.

Leave at least 1 hour before serving, arranging the salad in a shallow dish such as a gratin dish.

MELON, CUCUMBER AND STRAWBERRY SALAD WITH A FAT-FREE DRESSING

Judi

APERFECT SALAD to accompany poached salmon or fried fish. The melon and cucumber are drained of their excess liquid, ensuring an intense flavour. Unlike many salads, much of the preparation can be done the day before without compromising taste or texture. It's equally good served as a light summer starter.

Makes 6–8 servings
Serve the same day.

½ long cucumber
sea salt
1 large or 2 medium very ripe cantaloupe,
    Charentais, or similar sweet-fleshed melon
450 g (1 lb) ripe strawberries

For the dressing
    2 tablespoons sugar
    50 ml (2 fl oz) warm water
    2 tablespoons raspberry or red wine vinegar
    3 tablespoons coarsely chopped fresh mint

For the garnish
    6–8 tiny sprigs of fresh mint

Thinly slice the cucumber (most easily done in a food processor). Cut each slice in half and put in a salad spinner or colander, sprinkle lightly with salt and leave for 30 minutes to draw out the liquid. Spin, or pat dry with paper towels.

Halve and seed the melon. Scoop the flesh into balls (best done with a melon ball cutter), then put in a colander and leave to drain for at least 30 minutes. The cucumber and melon can now be covered, refrigerated and left overnight, if desired.

To make the dressing, put the sugar in a bowl and stir in the warm water. Add the vinegar and chopped mint, stirring well.

201

continued

On the day of serving, hull the strawberries and set aside. Thirty minutes before the meal, slice the strawberries and mix gently with the dressing, together with the melon balls and cucumber. Chill until needed.

To serve, arrange the chilled salad in a shallow dish. As a starter, divide between individual glass dishes or wine glasses. Garnish with sprigs of mint.

GRANDPA ROSE'S PICKLES

Evelyn

EVERY JEWISH HUSBAND makes the best pickled cucumbers and mine is no exception. The only time we've ever found anything comparable was in the *Nasch* (food) Market in Vienna. So enjoy!

Makes 2.8 kg (6 lb)

Keeps up to 4–6 weeks under refrigeration.

3.5 litres (6 pints) water
175 g (6 oz) sea salt
2 dried red chilli peppers
4 cloves garlic, peeled
1 tablespoon mixed pickling spice
4 bay leaves
1 teaspoon dill seed
4 tablespoons white vinegar
2.8 kg (6 lb) firm, green pickling cucumbers or gherkins,
    about 10–15 cm (4–6 in) long

To make the pickling solution, put the water in a large saucepan, add the salt and stir until dissolved. Add all the remaining ingredients except the cucumbers.

Scrub the cucumbers thoroughly with a small, soft-bristle brush (kept especially for the purpose), discarding any that have soft or diseased parts. Rinse the cucumbers in cold water, then put them in a large plastic or enamel bucket to within 7.5 cm (3 in) of the top.

Slowly pour the cold pickling solution into the bucket until the cucumbers are covered to a depth of 2.5 cm (1 in). Place a large upturned plate on top of the cucumbers, then weigh them down with a heavy weight such as a clean brick sealed in a plastic bag, or a large glass jar filled with water.

Cover with a thin tea towel or other cloth and leave in a cool place for 5 days.

After this time, skim off any froth that may have appeared on the surface. Cover again and skim every 2–3 days as before.

203

After 7 or 8 days, test by slicing into a cucumber. It should be translucent, with a spicy, sour flavour and a firm, crisp texture. If the taste is not right, leave them for a further week, skimming as before, or until ready (the speed of the pickling depends on the air temperature).

When the cucumbers are ready, skim again, pack into large plastic or glass containers and fill up with the pickling liquid until the cucumbers are completely submerged. Store in the refrigerator.

To serve, cut in spears or fans and arrange on a flat dish.

ON HIS WEDDING DAY, my husband was given a handwritten recipe by his father as part of his dowry. It was the Rose family recipe for these very special pickles, passed down through the male members of the family from one generation to the next.

The women of the family were not permitted to read the recipe, let alone make the pickles as, according to old wives' tales, they might sour them! So we had been married ten years before I was allowed to look at it. I felt that such a masterpiece should have a wider public.

What I read then astounded me. For in the age-old recipe, developed long before the scientific basis of pickling had been established, every step was correct according to current knowledge. Thus, my husband spent time scrubbing the cucumbers with a special soft brush. We now know because we've got microscopes, but they only knew from folk knowledge, that this would remove most of the yeasts on the skins that, if left, would spoil the pickle.

The only concession my husband makes to the twenty-first century is to store the bottled cucumbers in the refrigerator to keep them at peak condition.

One problem: The salt content was originally always measured by the handful—not exactly scientific. So though my husband protested that you could only tell if it was 'salty enough' by tasting, I took his salt-filled hand to the scale and tipped the contents out on to it!

204

JEWELLED THREE-BEAN SALAD

Judi

A GLEAMING DISH of jewel-like legumes and crisp vegetables in a tasty dressing. The dash of tomato ketchup is the magic ingredient here. You can substitute sweetcorn for the *borlotti* beans if you prefer.

Makes 6–8 servings

Keeps 3 days under refrigeration. **Do not freeze**.

For the dressing
50 ml (2 fl oz) extra-virgin olive oil
2 tablespoons red wine vinegar
1 fat clove garlic, peeled and finely chopped
1 rounded tablespoon ketchup
generous teaspoon sea salt
15 grinds black pepper

For the salad
1 × 400 g (14 oz) can kidney beans
1 × 400 g (14 oz) can haricot beans
1 × 400 g (14 oz) can *borlotti* or white haricot beans, or sweetcorn
½ red pepper, seeds and pith removed, finely diced
½ orange or yellow pepper, finely diced
2 spring onions, whites plus 10 cm (4 in) of green, finely sliced

For the garnish
1 tablespoon finely chopped parsley or fresh chives

Put all the ingredients for the dressing into a large, tightly closed screw-top jar and shake vigorously for 1 minute until thickened, then turn into a mixing bowl.

Rinse the beans in a sieve under running water, drain well and turn into the bowl with the dressing, together with the peppers and spring onions. Stir gently with two forks to coat the beans and vegetables with the dressing, then cover and refrigerate for several hours or overnight. To serve, pile into a pottery dish or gratin dish and sprinkle with the parsley or chives. Serve slightly chilled.

205

Naturally Nutritious:
Rice and Grains

'Man does not live by bread alone'

—Deuteronomy 8:3

ONE AREA IN WHICH THE TRADITIONAL JEWISH DIET IS particularly nutritious is rice and grains. Think of kasha (buckwheat), bulgur (cracked wheat), couscous (semolina) and *hobene gropen* (cracked oats) and you're talking about foods rich in the B vitamins as well as dietary fibre. But you're also talking wonderful, satisfying flavours and textures.

Rice was not generally available to Ashkenazi Jews, with the exception of so-called pudding rice, imported from North Carolina and made into a heavy, rib-sticking kugel, a dish which has not stood the test of time.

For pilafs and risottos we have raided the repertoire of Persian, Italian and Indian Jews. Evelyn has to be honest and say that her favourite recipe in this section is actually Judi's Bulgur and Vermicelli Pilaf, so good to eat, so easy to prepare, so convenient to freeze and reheat as though freshly cooked. But here you will also find more unusual dishes such as Quinoa Pilaf with Raisins and Paella with Chicken, every bit as tasty as the real thing and not a shrimp in sight!

GOLDEN PERSIAN RICE

Evelyn

THIS UNUSUAL RICE DISH, fragrant with turmeric and lightly caramelised carrots, makes a delicious accompaniment to casseroles and grills. Basmati rice (the word translates as 'Queen of Fragrance') has been grown in the foothills of the Himalayas for thousands of years. The nuts can be omitted.

Makes 4–6 servings
Keeps up to 3 days under refrigeration.
Freezes up to 2 months.

250 g (9 oz) basmati or other long-grain rice
1 large onion, peeled and finely chopped
1 clove garlic, peeled and finely chopped
3 tablespoons sunflower oil
700 ml (1¼ pints) chicken or vegetable stock
½ teaspoon ground turmeric
125 g (4 oz) sultanas
125 g (4 oz) cashew nuts (optional)
225 g (8 oz) carrots, peeled and grated or finely chopped
2 teaspoons light brown sugar
For the garnish
1 lemon
1 orange

Rinse the rice carefully in a sieve under the cold tap until the water runs clear. Drain well.

In a large lidded saucepan over moderate heat, cook the onion and garlic in 2 tablespoons of the oil until softened and golden, 5–6 minutes. Stir in the rice and cook for 2–3 minutes. Add the hot stock, turmeric and sultanas and bring to the boil. Stir well, reduce the heat and simmer, covered, for 20 minutes, until the liquid has been absorbed and the rice is tender. Fluff with a fork.

207

Meanwhile, if using cashew nuts, heat the remaining tablespoon of oil in a small pan over moderate heat and fry them until golden brown, about 5 minutes, stirring all the time as they burn easily. Drain on paper towels.

Add the carrots to the pan, sprinkle with the sugar, cover and cook over gentle heat, stirring once or twice, until beginning to caramelise, about 10 minutes. Using a fork, gently mix the nuts and carrots into the cooked rice.

Turn into a serving dish. Cut the unpeeled lemon and orange into wedges and use as a garnish.

208

BOTANISTS HAVE COUNTED 7000 varieties of rice grown throughout the world, but for most of us it's just a question of picking a packet off the supermarket shelf, knowing that every grain is clean and completely free from the dust and stones that the old-style sacks of rice contained. Because this pre-packed rice is so uniform in quality, you really can't cook it badly. However, you do need to take rather more care when bringing frozen rice back to life, or when reheating freshly cooked rice.

To defrost rice in a covered container: Either defrost overnight in the refrigerator or in the microwave for 3 minutes, then check and stir with a fork.

To reheat either defrosted or freshly cooked rice in a covered container: first sprinkle the surface lightly with water (to create steam). Next, either heat, covered, in the microwave on 100 per cent power for 4 minutes until steaming, or reheat, covered, in the oven preheated to 180°C (350°F/Gas 4) for 15 minutes or until steaming.

Always fluff up rice with a fork; never stir it with a spoon, which crushes the grains together.

209

FRESH ASPARAGUS AND SAFFRON RISOTTO

Judi

ALTHOUGH PURISTS ARGUE that risotto must be cooked from start to finish in one go, I have had excellent results cooking it in two stages, with several hours in between. The main advantage is that you avoid being trapped in the kitchen for half an hour right before the meal.

Makes 3–4 servings
Serve at once.
Leftovers keep 2 days under refrigeration.
Do not freeze.

225–300 g (8–10 oz) fresh asparagus (about ½ bunch)
1 tablespoon olive oil
20 g (¾ oz) butter
4 spring onions, white part only, sliced
1 teaspoon sea salt
175 g (6 oz) risotto rice, such as Arborio or Carnaroli
125 ml (4 fl oz) white wine or vermouth
1.2 litres (2 pints) hot vegetable stock, preferably home-made
small pinch of saffron threads mixed with
    2 teaspoons boiling water
10 grinds black pepper
100 g (3½ oz) freshly grated Parmesan cheese

With a vegetable peeler, strip the bottom third of the asparagus stalks till you see the tender white core, so that the entire stalk is an even thickness from top to bottom. Cut into 2.5 cm (1 in) long diagonal slices, leaving the tips intact. Keep the tips and stalks separate.

In a large non-stick frying pan at least 5 cm (2 in) deep, heat the oil and 15 g (½ oz) of the butter over moderate heat for 1 minute. Add the spring onions and sprinkle with the sea salt. Cook gently, stirring, until the spring onions are softened

210

but not brown, about 3 minutes. Turn up the heat and add the rice, stirring to coat it with the butter mixture. Add the wine or vermouth and sizzle, stirring, until no liquid is visible, about 1 minute.

Add half the hot stock and the saffron infusion, then bubble, stirring constantly, over moderate heat, until most of the liquid has disappeared, about 10 minutes. At this point, the risotto may be removed from the heat and left for up to 3 hours before the meal.

Fifteen minutes before serving, add 125 ml (4 fl oz) of hot stock, stirring well, followed by the asparagus stalks. Bubble gently over moderate heat, stirring constantly, until the liquid has been absorbed but the mixture is still very moist, about 2 minutes. Repeat this process, adding 125 ml (4 fl oz) hot stock at a time and stirring constantly, until only about 235 ml (8 fl oz) of stock remains, about 10 minutes.

Add the asparagus tips and 125 ml (4 fl oz) of stock, stirring gently. Cook over low heat for a further 5 minutes, then turn off the heat. Add the remaining stock, then stir in the remaining butter, the pepper and half the Parmesan cheese. Check the seasoning and add more salt or pepper if necessary.

Serve at once, offering plenty of freshly grated Parmesan and black pepper. Left-over risotto will thicken on standing, so for second helpings stir in a little more hot water or stock before serving. Refrigerated left-overs are delicious formed into patties and fried.

211

A SUCCESSFUL RISOTTO takes time and patience, but your efforts will be rewarded by a wondrous concoction, bursting with flavour. The texture in this version is creamy but very moist, somewhere between the loose 'soupy' style of risotto favoured in Italy's Veneto region and the drier, clumpier texture of its Milanese cousin.

A few strands of saffron impart a subtle and unusual undertone to the palate of flavours, as well as a delicate golden colour, although the dish is also delicious without it. What is crucial, though, is to use short-grained risotto rice such as Arborio or Carnaroli — if you make this dish with ordinary long-grain rice you'll end up with something at best strange, at worst, quite inedible!

212

ROASTED BUCKWHEAT WITH NOODLES

Kasha Varnishkes

Evelyn

ROASTED BUCKWHEAT GROATS, or kasha as it was known to immigrants from Eastern Europe, has a delicious nutty flavour and makes a great companion to both meat and chicken dishes.

Makes 6 servings

Keeps up to 3 days under refrigeration.

Freezes up to 2 months.

225 g (8 oz) kasha (groats), ready roasted
1 large egg, beaten
450 ml (16 fl oz) boiling chicken stock
2 teaspoons paprika
½ teaspoon sea salt
10 grinds black pepper
225 g (8 oz) bow tie pasta (farfalle)
1 large onion, peeled and finely chopped
1½ tablespoons sunflower oil
125 ml (4 fl oz) good chicken or beef gravy or strong stock

Put the kasha into a large non-stick frying pan and add the beaten egg. Mix well, then cook over medium heat for 5 minutes, stirring occasionally, until the kasha looks puffy and dry. Add the boiling stock and the seasonings. Cover and simmer for 15 minutes, until the liquid is absorbed.

Meanwhile, cook the pasta according to the packet directions. Also gently cook the onion in the oil in a covered pan until soft and golden, about 6 minutes. Add the onion and the cooked pasta to the cooked kasha, stirring well. Stir in the gravy or stock.

This is a delicious alternative to potatoes to team up with chicken or meat casseroles. May be reheated.

213

PAELLA WITH CHICKEN

Evelyn

THIS VERSION OF Spain's national dish comes from Valencia on the east coast. Instead of the traditional shellfish, I have substituted whole stuffed olives, which add a delightful piquancy.

Makes 4 servings
Keeps up to 2 days under refrigeration.
Freezes up to 2 months.

5 tablespoons olive oil
4 chicken breasts about 900 g (2 lb) with the bone, skinned and patted dry
1 medium red pepper, seeded and finely diced
2 cloves garlic, crushed
1 beefsteak tomato (or 2 large canned tomatoes), peeled and diced
1 litre (1¾ pints) chicken stock
½ teaspoon turmeric or powdered saffron
350 g (12 oz) long-grain rice (preferably Spanish paella rice)
225 g (8 oz) frozen peas
125 g (4 oz) pimiento-stuffed olives
1 teaspoon sea salt
15 grinds black pepper

Heat the oil in a 28–30 cm (11–12 in) paella pan or 25 cm (10 in) frying pan over moderate heat, then add the well-dried chicken breasts and cook for 5 minutes, turning so that they cook to an even gold.

Add the pepper and garlic and cook for a further 5 minutes, until they take on a little colour. Add the tomato and cook, stirring, for a further 3 minutes.

Pour in the stock with the turmeric or saffron and simmer for 15 minutes, turning the chicken once or twice.

Add the rice to the pan and mix gently with the contents. Turn up the heat a little and cook more quickly for 10–12 minutes, stirring occasionally. Add the peas and cook for a further 5 minutes.

Just before serving, stir in the whole stuffed olives and add the seasonings, adjusting the seasoning to taste. The dish can be kept hot in a preheated 160°C (325°F/Gas 3) oven for up to 20 minutes.

~ THE FIRST PAELLA was created by rice farmers in the wetlands of Valencia. They would cook it on open fires for their midday meal, throwing in whatever came to hand—frogs, snails, eels or rabbit. Definitely *not* kosher!

The texture of the rice in a paella should be creamy rather than dry, with every grain separate. If you cannot find any Spanish rice from Valencia, use an Italian risotto rice. Failing that, use long-grain rice.

The traditional paella pan is usually made from steel with twin handles—I have seen them in Spain measuring 90 cm (36 in) across! However, a large frying pan approximately 5 cm (2 in) deep will do very well instead.

215

QUINOA PILAF WITH RAISINS

Judi

AN ANCIENT SOUTH AMERICAN grain, quinoa (pronounced 'kin-wa') has a nutty taste and slightly chewy texture. The tiny spherical grains, rich in protein and minerals, make a delicious alternative to rice. This pilaf works equally well served hot as a side dish or cold as a salad.

Quinoa is available at many supermarkets and health-food stores.

Makes 6 servings
Keeps 1 week under refrigeration.
Freezes up to 3 months.

1 large onion, peeled and finely chopped
2 tablespoons sunflower oil
250 g (9 oz) uncooked quinoa
1 teaspoon finely grated orange zest
75 g (3 oz) currants or raisins
600 ml (1 pint) chicken or vegetable stock
1 tablespoon finely chopped parsley
2 tablespoons thinly sliced spring onions, white and green part

In a large, heavy saucepan or lidded frying pan, cook the onion in the oil over moderate heat, stirring, until softened and golden, about 3 minutes. Stir in the quinoa and the orange zest, mixing well with the onion, then add the currants or raisins and stock. Bring to the boil, cover and simmer over low heat until the liquid has been absorbed, about 10 minutes.

Fluff up the grains with a fork, then stir in the parsley and spring onions.

Serve hot as a side dish in place of rice, or at room temperature as a salad with cold meat, poultry or fish.

216

SEVEN SPICE INDIAN PILAU RICE

Judi

GOLDEN, FLUFFY GRAINS of rice are made fragrant with roasted spices. This recipe uses the Asian rice-cooking technique: the rice is rinsed well in several changes of water to remove the excess starch, then simmered, uncovered, to boil off most of the liquid, before being covered and steamed. It is a surefire way to produce a perfect pilau—a light, fluffy texture with nicely separated grains.

Makes 6–8 servings
Keeps 3 days under refrigeration.
Do not freeze.

350 g (12 oz) long-grain rice, such as basmati or Thai fragrant jasmine
    (fragrant)
2 tablespoons sunflower oil
1 teaspoon whole cumin seeds
6 cardamom pods
1 small stick cinnamon
1 bay leaf
1 medium onion, finely chopped
700 ml (1½ pints) hot vegetable stock or water
1 tablespoon sultanas (optional)
½ teaspoon ground turmeric
1½ teaspoons sea salt
75 g (3 oz) frozen peas (optional)
For the garnish
    sprig of fresh coriander, chopped
    1 teaspoon paprika

Rinse the rice in a sieve under running water until the liquid runs clear. Leave to drain.

In a large frying pan with a well-fitting lid, heat the oil over moderate heat for 1 minute. Add the cumin seeds and toss for 30 seconds, then add the cardamom pods,

217

cinnamon stick and bay leaf, tossing in the hot oil for another 30 seconds until the spices smell fragrant. Add the onion and cook, stirring, until softened, about 2 minutes. Add the drained rice and mix well, followed by the hot stock or water, the sultanas if using, turmeric and salt. Stir gently.

Simmer over low heat, uncovered, until the liquid is no longer visible and small steam holes appear on the surface of the rice, then cover and turn the heat as low as possible. (If you have a gas cooker with no 'simmer' setting, move the pan partly off the burner to ensure very low heat without the flame going out.) Leave for at least 15 minutes, without lifting the lid, then gently stir in the frozen peas, cover and turn off the heat. The rice will now stay hot with the lid on for up to 30 minutes, or it can be microwaved to reheat when required in a covered microwave-proof dish at full power for 3 minutes.

To serve, fluff with a fork. Transfer to a warm serving dish if desired and garnish with a little chopped coriander and a sprinkling of paprika. Don't eat the cardamom pods!

QUICK COUSCOUS

Evelyn

THIS MAKES A delicious bed for any kind of casserole or stew.

Makes 4–6 servings
Keeps up to 2 days under refrigeration.
Freezes up to 2 months.

350 g (12 oz) easy-cook couscous
2–3 tablespoons sunflower oil
1 teaspoon sea salt
400 ml (14 fl oz) warm water or stock

Put the couscous in a bowl, add the oil, sea salt and warm liquid and stir well. Transfer to a large sieve or colander lined with a disposable kitchen cloth and steam, covered, over a pot of boiling water for 10 minutes, until the grains are fluffy and separate. For an especially well-flavoured couscous, cover and steam over the stew or casserole with which you plan to serve it.

To serve, turn on to a large platter and top with casseroled meat, vegetables or poultry. Moroccan Beef Casserole with Honey-Glazed Apples (page 156) is a perfect partner.

~ COUSCOUS, MUCH USED in North African and Israeli cuisines, ∾ is actually semolina. A precooked form is widely available in large supermarkets. The name also refers to an early kind of one-pot meal, very similar to the 'cauldron' meals of medieval Britain. The grain is steamed in the top of a two-tiered pot called a *couscoussière*, while in the lower part, chicken or meat is gently stewed with vegetables and chickpeas.

BULGUR AND VERMICELLI PILAF

Judi

A MOUTHWATERING COMBINATION of fluffy grains and pan-fried vermicelli steamed in a tasty broth, this is easy to prepare and makes an unusual and delicious alternative to rice. The pilaf reheats well, particularly in the microwave.

Makes 6–8 servings
Keeps 3 days under refrigeration.
Freezes up to 3 months.

1 large onion, peeled and finely chopped
3 tablespoons olive or sunflower oil
75 g (3 oz) vermicelli pasta or fine egg noodles,
    broken into short lengths
250 g (9 oz) bulgur (cracked wheat)
½ teaspoon paprika
½ teaspoon sea salt
15 grinds black pepper
675 ml (1¼ pints) hot chicken or vegetable stock

In a large frying pan with a well-fitting lid, cook the onion in the oil over moderate heat until soft and golden, about 3 minutes. Add the pasta, then stir around in the onion for a further 3 minutes. Add the bulgur and seasonings and continue to cook for a further 3–4 minutes. Finally add enough of the hot stock barely to cover the mixture, reduce the heat, cover and simmer until the stock has almost been absorbed, about 10 minutes. Taste to ensure the bulgur is tender; if not, add the remaining stock, cover and simmer for a further 2–3 minutes.

Remove from the heat, cover the pan with a cloth under the lid and let stand for 10 minutes.

Fluff with a fork and serve immediately.

220

Divine Inspiration:
Show-stopping
Desserts

'sweeter also than honey and the honeycomb'

TODAY FEW OF US MAKE DESSERTS FOR EVERYDAY MEALS. Refrigerated air and sea transport have given us access to a positive cornucopia of exotic fresh fruit, which provides the perfect light and refreshing end to any meal at any season. But for special occasions, we have gathered together a variety of old-style and new-style finales that we're sure will become traditions in your home.

Each generation has its own favourites. Evelyn offers a cinnamon-scented two-crust Apple Pie and a luscious family-style open Country Peach and Nectarine Pie glazed with apricot preserves. Judi strikes a more contemporary note with a Caramel Glazed Upside-down Pear Tarte and an exquisite bowl of Perfumed Peaches with Muscatel and Blossoms.

Soufflés do not figure in traditional Jewish cooking. In earlier times, few people except the most prosperous had ovens and those had no temperature control as we know it today. Judi celebrates the hi-tech oven of today with no less than two hot soufflés: a superb

Orange Liqueur Soufflé that locks in the flavours by concentrating them in a layer of soaked sponge cake; and individual chocolate and coffee mini-soufflés that can be prepared earlier in the day and baked between courses. (Yes, you do have to be a little brave the first time, but it really does work!)

Traditional in many Russian Jewish families was the *kissel*. A purée made with a glorious medley of summer fruits, *kissel* is just as delicious made with dried fruit, as in *khoshab*, an Armenian apricot mousse, lightened with cream and decorated with pistachios.

More than 30 years ago Evelyn introduced her Jewish readers to the Pavlova, that amazing concoction of fruit and cream sandwiched between layers of meringue. It has now become a Jewish classic among several generations and we guarantee that our wicked Sticky Toffee Pavlova will become a long-term fixture in your entertaining menus that will delight your guests, as it has ours, for years to come. From our family treasury of recipes for cakes and biscuits, we have made a mouth-watering selection of those we believe best represent the Jewish philosophy of home baking—taste, texture and simplicity.

Almost more than any other kind of cooking, baking reflects the ingredients and skills of the different countries where Jews have made their homes. But there are delights gleaned from other culinary heritages—Evelyn's irresistible classic Fluffy Scottish Scones are a delicious addition to the repertoire.

As the years have gone by, many recipes have been modified to encompass new ingredients and more especially new mixing techniques and appliances. The wonderful Wine and Chocolate Gâteau, for instance, would once have needed a tedious half hour of hand-beating to ensure its moist, delicate texture. Now, using a food processor, one can count the time it takes to achieve a similar result in seconds.

A whole category of kuchens that were originally raised with yeast, such as the moist Old-fashioned Chocolate Swirl Cake, can be modernised using baking powder instead. The Feather-light Cake with Banana Crunch Topping *(Streusel Kuchen)* takes on a totally different texture when made with today's ultra-fine cake flour.

222

Contemporary recipes such as the Healthy Somerset Apple Cake or the Banana and Pecan Loaf still reflect the spirit of the traditional ones, but use ingredients such as brown sugar, pecans and, yes, bananas, which were just not available to earlier *heimishe* bakers.

The word *kichel*—Yiddish for biscuit—encompasses a whole world of wonderful biscuits, always ready in days gone by to hand out to hungry children or to offer with a glass of schnapps to casual callers. Biscuit making used to be a labour of love, with rolling and cutting out—not for clock-watchers! But Evelyn has modified the method for making her Great-grandma's Feather-light Lemon Biscuits so that the batter is actually dropped from a teaspoon, then flattened into the traditional shape with nothing more complicated than an empty glass with its base dipped in oil and sugar. Enjoy!

A Note on Baking Ingredients

The ingredients in each recipe—the type of flour, sugar and shortening—are those that we have found give the finest results. In the same way, the method of mixing—by hand, electric mixer or food processor—has proved its worth for each particular cake or biscuit.

Sugar. In certain cakes and biscuits, we have found that caster sugar gives the very best texture. However, these recipes will also work with granulated sugar.

Brown, unrefined sugars contain significant amounts of important minerals and trace elements. However, they must be the genuine artcle and not white sugar which has had colouring and flavouring added without the nutrients. Many supermarkets now sell unrefined sugars with a special recognition symbol.

Moderate amounts of the right variety of unrefined sugar also make good culinary sense.

Golden granulated can be substituted for ordinary granulated.

Demerara is excellent in fruit crumbles and sprinkled on breakfast cereals, porridge and muesli.

Light muscovado has a soft texture and mild flavour, making it interchangeable with caster sugar.

Dark muscovado has a mild, toffee-like flavour which makes it ideal for ginger and fruit cakes.

Molasses tastes just like treacle toffee and is best when used in already highly flavoured dishes such as barbecue sauce, chutney and pickles.

224

One-stage method. This is quick and uncomplicated for family-type baking, but doesn't produce such a good texture or volume for rich cakes. In this method, which relies on soft butter or margarine and usually extra baking powder, all the ingredients are beaten by electric mixer, food processor or hand, until the mixture is smooth and creamy.

Creaming method. This produces the finest texture and largest volume. It is the classic method employed before the days of electric mixers and food processors. It gives a very fine result but is time-consuming, even with a mixer. The fat is creamed until it resembles mayonnaise, then the sugar is beaten in, one tablespoon at a time, so that it dissolves in the fat and is then followed by the eggs, beaten to blend and any flavourings. Lastly the flour is folded or gently mixed in, alternately with the liquid.

Food processor method. This produces the same texture and volume as the creaming method, but the standard work bowl is only big enough for moderate quantities of ingredients. The unbeaten eggs and the sugar are processed together for two minutes, then the fat and flavourings are pulsed in until the mixture resembles thick mayonnaise. Finally the flour and any liquid are gently pulsed in and the mixture is ready.

STICKY TOFFEE PAVLOVA

Evelyn

A DESSERT TO DIE FOR! The combination of the butterscotch-flavoured cream and the crisp meringue layers enfolding it is quite irresistible.

Makes 8–10 servings
Keeps up to 3 days under refrigeration.
Freezes up to 2 months.

For the Pavlova layers
   2 teaspoons cornflour
   300 g (10 oz) sugar
   5 large egg whites
   ¼ teaspoon cream of tartar
For the toffee filling and topping
   75 g (3 oz) unsalted butter
   125 g (4 oz) dark brown sugar
   3 tablespoons golden syrup or maple syrup
   425 ml (15 fl oz) double cream
For the garnish
   15 g (½ oz) chopped walnuts, almonds or hazelnuts

To make the Pavlova, use the base of a 20–22 cm (8–8½ in) round cake tin to draw two circles on baking parchment, then lay on two flat baking trays. Preheat the oven to 150°C (350°F/Gas 2).

Toss the nuts in a small, heavy-based frying pan over medium heat until they smell 'toasty', about 2 minutes. Allow to cool, then roughly chop.

Mix the cornflour and the sugar in a bowl. Separate the egg yolks from the whites. Put the yolks into an airtight container and refrigerate at once for another use within 24 hours.

Put the whites into a large mixing bowl and add the cream of tartar. Using an electric mixer, start whisking at low speed until the mixture is frothy. Increase the speed and whisk until the mixture stands in floppy peaks.

226

Now start adding the cornflour-sugar mixture 1 rounded tablespoon at a time, whisking until very stiff again after each addition. Be patient: if you add the sugar mixture too quickly, the meringue will flop.

Pipe or spoon the meringue mixture on to the two paper circles, making sure that the round to be used on top is neat and even. If preferred, pipe the top layer using a 1 cm (½ in) fluted piping nozzle.

Put the two meringue rounds in the oven, turn it down to 140°C (275°F/Gas 1) and bake for 1–1¼ hours. Change the position of the layers at half-time. They are ready when the top feels really firm and crisp to the touch and the layers can be lifted easily off the paper when a spatula is slipped underneath. If in doubt, leave to go cold in the turned-off oven.

To make the sticky toffee filling, melt the butter in a small saucepan, then add the sugar and syrup. Bring to the boil, stirring constantly, then lower the heat and simmer for 1 minute. Leave to cool for 10 minutes, then stir in 3 tablespoons of the cream — the mixture should be thick but pourable. If too thick, stir in 1 more table-spoon of cream and heat very gently until pourable. Allow to cool slightly.

To complete the Pavlova, whip the remaining cream until it stands in peaks, then gently fold in three-quarters of the cooled filling to achieve a marbled effect. Put the bottom layer of meringue on a serving plate and spoon on the filling. Put on the top layer, then drizzle the remaining filling on top in a random pattern. Finally, sprinkle with the chopped nuts. Chill or freeze as convenient.

The Pavlova has the finest flavour if refrigerated overnight (before freezing) to allow the layers to soften a little.

If frozen, defrost at room temperature 1–2 hours, or until the filling is the consistency of soft ice cream, then refrigerate until served. If preferred, take out and keep in the refrigerator to defrost overnight. Check just before the meal and if still too firm, leave at room temperature. Serve in slices with a tangy fruit compôte or sliced oranges.

227

THIS LUSCIOUS COMBINATION of soft-centred meringue with a flavoured whipped cream filling was originally created in Australia in honour of a visit there in the 1920s by the legendary prima ballerina, Anna Pavlova. My own version is derived from a recipe that once appeared in the food pages of *The New York Times* from the wife of the Australian ambassador to the United States. Give or take a few minor variations in technique, it has stood the test of time remarkably well.

Unlike the typical snow-white classic meringue, which is dried out for several hours in a very low oven, the Pavlova is baked more quickly so that the outside becomes crisp and pale gold while the centre develops a marshmallow-like texture.

The secret of the successful Pavlova lies in the way the sugar is added to the egg whites. They are first whisked by themselves until they form floppy peaks when the whisk is withdrawn. Only then is the sugar added slowly, with the meringue whisked until the stiff-peak stage after each addition. Add the sugar too quickly and the meringue will never stiffen to the right texture.

Pavlovas freeze superbly well, which makes them the perfect dessert for entertaining. Although it's possible to keep the unfilled layers in an airtight container for several weeks, I think it's better to freeze the complete dessert, as the filling then seems to marry better with the meringue than when it is inserted at the last moment.

INDIVIDUAL MOCHA SOUFFLÉS

Judi

WONDROUS MINI-SOUFFLÉS that wait patiently for several hours to be baked! The secret ingredient is bread flour, which has a higher protein content than plain flour, ensuring that the soufflés will rise perfectly every time. The mixture can be prepared and portioned 1–2 hours ahead, then left at room temperature (preferably cool) to pop into the oven as the main-course dishes are cleared away. Each guest is then presented with his or her own baby soufflé, whose crisp shell conceals a moist and intensely chocolatey centre.

Makes 8 soufflés
Serve immediately.

15 g (½ oz) melted butter
20 g (¾ oz) firm butter
75 g (3 oz) sugar
50 g (2 oz) bread flour
25 g (1 oz) unsweetened cocoa powder
300 ml (10 fl oz) milk
1 tablespoon instant coffee granules
2 teaspoons pure vanilla extract
5 large eggs, separated, at room temperature
1 tablespoon icing sugar
Irish cream liqueur, or vanilla ice cream

You will need 8 individual soufflé dishes (ramekins), about 9 cm (3½ in) wide and 4 cm (1½ in) deep. Paint the inside of each with the melted butter, then coat generously with sugar. Chill.

Combine the firm butter, 75 g (3 oz) of the sugar, the flour and the cocoa powder in a food processor or mixer. Process to form a crumbly mixture.

In a medium saucepan, bring the milk and coffee granules to the boil over gentle heat, stirring (do not leave unattended as the mixture easily boils over). Whisk in the

229

cocoa mixture, then return to the boil, stirring until there are no lumps, about 1 minute. Remove from the heat.

Stir in the vanilla, then whisk in the egg yolks one at a time, stirring well between each addition.

In a mixing bowl, whisk the egg whites until soft peaks form, about 2 minutes using an electric mixer. Whisk in the remaining 2 tablespoons sugar and whisk again until stiff. Stir about a quarter of the meringue into the warm cocoa mixture to lighten it, then gently fold in the remainder. Divide the mixture between the ramekins, almost filling them.

Line the bottom of a large roasting tin with a few paper towels. Set the ramekins on top. The unbaked soufflés may be left at room temperature for up to 2 hours at this point.

To bake, preheat the oven to 200°C (400°F/Gas 6). About 25 minutes before the soufflés are to be served, pour enough boiling water in the lined roasting tin to reach halfway up the sides of the ramekins.

Put in the centre of the oven and bake for 17–20 minutes, without opening the oven door. When ready, the top will be firm and the centre still slightly liquid.

Dust each soufflé with sifted icing sugar and serve at once. Each guest can make a slit in the top and spoon a little liqueur or ice cream into the centre.

230

COUNTRY PEACH AND NECTARINE PIE

Evelyn

Besides adding a touch of the exotic, the marzipan helps to protect the bottom pastry from the fruit juices of this luscious country-style pie.

Makes 6–8 servings
Best **eaten** on the day made. Leftovers **keep** up to 2 days under refrigeration.
Freezes up to 6 weeks.

4 ripe peaches
4 ripe nectarines
1 sheet, about 225 g (8 oz), puff pastry, thawed but still very cold
125 g (4 oz) white marzipan, chilled
1 large egg, beaten
3 tablespoons apricot jam
juice of 1 lemon

Preheat the oven to 220°C (425°F/Gas 7).

Blanch the fruit by plunging it into boiling water for 3 minutes, then into a bowl of very cold water for 2 minutes. The skins will then be easy to lift off. Carefully cut in half and remove the stones. If the fruit is difficult to halve, cut away from the stone in thick slices.

Roll out the pastry as thinly as possible, then lay in a round oven-to-table pie dish 23–25 cm (9–10 in) in diameter or an oval gratin-type dish 35 × 23 × 4 cm (14 × 9 × 1½ in). There will be a large overhang of pastry at the edges. Coarsely grate the chilled marzipan evenly over the pastry base, then arrange the halved or sliced fruit decoratively on top.

Bunch up the additional pastry around the edge to form a rough rim, very slightly overlapping the fruit at the edge. Glaze the pastry with the beaten egg.

Bake for 30 minutes or until the pastry is a rich golden brown and crisp to the touch. Place on a cooling rack.

Melt the apricot jam, then stir in the lemon juice. With a pastry brush, thickly glaze both the fruit and the pastry with the jam mixture.

Cut in wedges and serve, slightly warm, plain or with sour cream or ice cream. The pie reheats well on the day of serving.

231

CARAMEL GLAZED
UPSIDE-DOWN PEAR TARTE

Tarte Tatin aux Poires   *Judi*

A MOUTHWATERING VARIATION of the classic French apple pastry invented by the Sisters Tatin in the Loire Valley. This version uses ready-made puff pastry for the base, making the dish much simpler to prepare without compromising the finished result—tender golden pears bathed in rich caramel on a crisp pastry disk. Kitchen tongs are useful to turn over the pears as they caramelise.

Makes 6–8 servings
Reheats well up to 24 hours after baking.
Freezes up to 2 weeks.

1 sheet, about 225 g (8 oz), puff pastry,
   thawed but still very cold
5 large ripe but firm pears such as Comice or William,
   about 1.4 kg (3 lb)
65 g (2½ oz) butter or margarine
175 g (6 oz) granulated sugar
75 g (3 oz) light brown sugar
finely grated zest and juice of 1 large lemon

Preheat the oven to 220°C (425°F/Gas 7). Have ready a lightly greased 23–25 cm (9–10 in) cake tin at least 4 cm (1½ in) deep, or a copper *tarte Tatin* tin.

Roll out the pastry into a disc 28–30 cm (11–12 in) in diameter (depending on the size of your cake tin) and 3 mm (⅛ in) thick. Put on a plate, cover with clingfilm and chill while you cook the pears (chilling the pastry helps to prevent it shrinking in the oven).

Peel the pears, cut into quarters and core. Melt the fat in a large frying pan, then add the sugars, stirring with a wooden spoon over moderate heat until the mixture bubbles and turns golden, about 4 minutes. Add the fruit in an even layer, sprinkling

232

with the lemon zest and juice. Cook over gentle heat for 20 minutes, shaking the pan from time to time and basting the pears with the caramel that forms around the edges.

Increase the heat and continue to cook for another 15 minutes, basting the pears as before and turning them so that they colour evenly, until the small amount of caramel now left is a rich golden brown. Keep your eye on it so it doesn't burn! Turn off the heat, then lift out the pears and arrange neatly in the cake tin in concentric circles, spooning the caramel over them.

Lay the chilled pastry on top of the pears, tucking it in between the sides of the pan and the fruit. Slash the top in 4 places for the steam to escape and bake for 30–35 minutes, until the pastry is a rich golden brown.

Once baked, leave in the pan until ready to unmould with the pastry uppermost so it does not go soggy. (It will keep warm enough in the pan for a good hour after baking. If left longer, reheat it in a moderate oven 190°C (375°F/Gas 5) for 10 minutes.)

Unmould by placing a serving plate slightly wider than the tin on top of the tart, hold the edges of the tin and the plate firmly together, turn them both over, giving the tin a gentle tap and allow the tarte to slide on to the serving dish. You will find that the pears have become permeated with the caramel and are a deep golden brown right through.

Serve warm on its own, with vanilla ice cream or with crème fraîche laced with a little fruit brandy or orange liqueur.

233

RASPBERRY AND REDCURRANT COMPÔTE

Kissel

Evelyn

A LIGHT AND FRUITY DESSERT to serve after a hearty main course and a great favourite with Jews of Russian origin. It is made with an interesting combination of fruits, some of which are puréed and some left whole. If redcurrants are not available, black currants can be substituted. It can also be made with frozen fruit. *Kissel* comes from the Russian *kislyi*, meaning sour.

Makes 8 servings
Keeps up to 3 days under refrigeration. **Freezes** up to 2 months.

175–225 g (6–8 oz) each redcurrants, blueberries and raspberries
425 ml (15 fl oz) water
125–175 g (4–6 oz) sugar (according to the tartness of the fruit)
    plus more for sprinkling
50 g (2 oz) cornflour
75 ml (3 fl oz) fruity white wine such as Riesling,
    or orange juice plus a squeeze of lemon
2 tablespoons fruit liqueur such as framboise (optional)
225 g (8 oz) sweet cherries, stoned
tiny sprigs of mint
crisp biscuits, such as Great-grandma's Feather-light Lemon
    Biscuits (page 262)

Put the currants, blueberries and half of the raspberries into a pan with the water and bring to the boil. Bubble uncovered until the fruit is tender, about 5 minutes. Push the contents of the pan through a fine sieve.

Return the purée to the pan with the sugar. Bring to the boil, stirring to dissolve the sugar. Mix the cornflour with the wine or juice and add to the pan, stirring constantly. Cook until the mixture thickens and looks quite clear, about 3 minutes.

234

Cool until it stops steaming. Stir in the liqueur, if using. Pour into a bowl and leave until it begins to set, about 30 minutes, then fold in the remaining raspberries and the cherries.

Spoon into a glass bowl or individual glasses, then sprinkle the surface with a little sugar to prevent a skin forming. Chill for several hours, preferably overnight.

Just before serving, decorate with tiny sprigs of mint and serve with a light, crisp biscuit.

꙳ TODAY MY KITCHEN IS FILLED with a very subtle fragrance — ꙳ that of freshly picked soft fruit. What then is to be done with this luscious harvest?

Like most people nowadays, I don't indulge anymore in a preserve-making marathon, so most of the fruit (except for the strawberries) is open-frozen on trays till as hard as bullets to prevent crushing, then bagged and stored in the freezer.

The strawberries are best stored as purée. This is a simple matter of whirling each 450g (1 lb) of fruit in the food processor for 2 minutes together with 75 g (3 oz) sugar and 2 teaspoons lemon juice. If you substitute 3 rounded tablespoons granulated non-sugar sweetener for the sugar, diabetic friends will bless you.

This makes a wonderful sauce for ice cream, to spoon through a fresh fruit salad, or to accompany a cheesecake.

The purée freezes well in small containers for up to 6 months — longer and it loses its colour.

235

BERRIES AND CHERRIES IN WINE

Judi

THIS IS A DIRECT DESCENDANT of *kissel,* the traditional East European purée of fresh summer fruits (page 234). This dish, however, can also be made in winter by using frozen berries and canned cherries. And unlike *kissel,* the fruit is left whole and served in a slightly thickened sauce. It's also a marvellous way to use up slightly bruised or over-ripe berries (but be sure there is absolutely no mould on them or the flavour will be spoiled).

Makes 6–8 servings
Keeps 1 week under refrigeration. **Freezes** up to 2 months.

1½ tablespoons cornflour
1 × 675 g (1½ lb) jar stoned Morello cherries in syrup, bottled or canned
125 ml (4 fl oz) fruity red wine
3 tablespoons light brown sugar
1 tablespoon fresh lemon juice
450 g (1 lb) mixed berries such as raspberries, strawberries
    or blackberries, fresh or frozen
2 tablespoons cherry brandy, framboise or cassis (optional)
icing sugar

Put the cornflour into a medium saucepan. Drain the cherries and reserve the syrup (there should be about 300 ml (10 fl oz). With a wooden spoon, gradually stir the cherry syrup into the cornflour, mixing to a smooth liquid. Stir in the wine and brown sugar. Bring to the boil over gentle heat, stirring, and simmer until the mixture has lost is cloudiness and has thickened slightly, about 3 minutes. Remove from the heat and stir in the lemon juice.

Put the berries (no need to defrost if frozen) and cherries in a serving bowl, then pour on the hot syrup. When the fruit has defrosted, stir together carefully, then add the liqueur if using. Chill well.

236

Lightly dust with icing sugar and serve on its own or with ice cream, frozen yogurt, crème fraîche or reduced-fat soured cream.

LEMON DAINTY WITH
STRAWBERRY SAUCE

Evelyn

THIS LUSCIOUS LEMONY PUDDING has stood the test of four generations of good Jewish cooks. With its superb balance of sweet and tart, creamy and spongy, it can still surprise and charm. Call it a food tradition in the making, but since I developed a non-dairy version using 225 ml (8 fl oz) of coconut milk and 125 ml (4 fl oz) of water in place of the milk, it's become too useful to miss out.

The pudding can be served either at room temperature an hour or two after baking, or well chilled. As it separates into a creamy sauce topped with a light sponge, it's essential to use dishes of the right size—too wide or shallow will result in a dry pudding. It is delicious served with a sweetened fruit purée such as strawberry, apple or tinned apricots.

Makes 4–6 servings
Keeps up to 2 days under refrigeration. **Do not freeze.**

25 g (1 oz) soft butter or margarine
175 g (6 oz) caster sugar
grated zest and juice of 2 lemons
3 large eggs, separated
6 tablespoons plain flour
½ teaspoon baking powder
350 ml (12 fl oz) milk

For the strawberry sauce
450 g (1 lb) ripe strawberries
75 g (3 oz) sugar
2 tablespoons fresh lemon juice

Grease an oven-to-table casserole dish at least 5 cm (2 in) deep and of 2 litres (3 pints) capacity. Half-fill a roasting tin with boiling water, put it in the oven and preheat to 180°C (350°F/Gas 4).

continued

Put the butter, 125 g (4 oz) of the sugar, the lemon zest and juice, egg yolks, flour and baking powder into a food processor or blender and process until creamy. With the motor running, add the milk through the feed tube and process until evenly mixed.

In a large bowl, whisk the egg whites until they hold soft peaks. Whisk in the remaining sugar, 1 teaspoon at a time. Gradually pour the yolk mixture on to the meringue, folding the two together with a rubber spatula until evenly blended. Gently pour into the prepared dish and place in the pan of hot water.

Bake for 35–40 minutes, until golden brown and firm to a gentle touch.

To make the sauce, put the fruit, sugar and lemon juice into a food processor or blender and process for 3 minutes or until the sauce has thickened and no sugar crystals can be felt.

Serve at room temperature or well chilled. Spoon from the baking dish into individual bowls or plates and pass the sauce around the table.

238

PERFUMED PEACHES WITH MUSCATEL AND FLOWER PETALS

Judi

FRESH PEACHES are macerated in a light syrup perfumed with sweet muscatel wine and orange-flower water. Bananas and pistachios provide a delightful contrast in texture. If ripe peaches are not available, substitute 675 g (1½ lb) ripe strawberries. An orange liqueur cream gives a delicious contrast, but the peaches are also wonderful on their own.

Makes 6–8 servings
Serve the same day. **Do not freeze**.

125 g (4 oz) sugar
125 ml (4 fl oz) muscatel or similar white dessert wine
1 tablespoon fresh lemon juice
2 tablespoons orange-flower water
450 g (1 lb) fresh ripe peaches
175 g (6 oz) fresh kumquats
2 ripe bananas
50 g (2 oz) shelled pistachio nuts
For the orange liqueur cream
zest and juice of ½ lemon
zest and juice of ½ orange
2 tablespoons Cointreau or other orange-flavoured liqueur
350 ml (12 fl oz) double cream
For the garnish
few teaspoons of mildly flavoured, edible flower petals such as
rose, pansy or scented geranium

First make the syrup. In a medium saucepan, dissolve the sugar in the wine, stirring over moderate heat for about 2 minutes, then boil rapidly for 1 minute. Remove from the heat, then stir in the lemon juice and orange-flower water. Chill while you prepare the fruit.

239

continued

Wash, halve and stone the peaches. Cut the kumquats in quarters. Put both fruits in a decorative glass bowl and pour over the chilled syrup. Refrigerate until 1 hour before serving, then add the sliced bananas and pistachios and leave at room temperature.

To make the orange liqueur cream, put all the ingredients in a bowl and whisk with an electric beater until the cream stands in stiff peaks. Pile into a serving dish or sauceboat and chill well. If more convenient, freeze then defrost in the refrigerator for 1 hour.

Serve the fruit at room temperature sprinkled with the flower petals and pass around the chilled liqueur cream.

CLASSIC APPLE PIE

Evelyn

APPLE PIE, Jewish style, comes in many guises. I think this is one of the very best. The crisp, melt-in-the-mouth pastry partners the juicy apple filling to perfection.

Makes 6 servings
Keeps up to 3 days under refrigeration.
Freezes up to 2 months.

For the filling
- 4–5 large apples such as Bramleys, about 675 g (1½ lb), peeled and sliced 3 mm (⅛ in) thick
- 75 g (3 oz) granulated or light brown sugar
- 2 teaspoons cornflour
- 1 teaspoon ground cinnamon
- pinch of grated nutmeg
- 3 tablespoons raisins (optional)

For the pastry
- 225 g (8 oz) plain flour
- pinch of sea salt
- 2 tablespoons icing sugar
- 125 g (4 oz) butter or margarine
- 25 g (1 oz) vegetable shortening
- 1 large egg yolk
- juice of ½ lemon (about 2 tablespoons)
- 2 tablespoons iced water

For the glaze
- 1 large egg white, whisked until frothy
- 2 tablespoons Demerara or granulated sugar (page 147)

Put the apple slices in a bowl and mix well with all the remaining filling ingredients.

241

continued

To make the pastry by hand or mixer, combine the flour, salt and sugar. Add the butter and shortening and rub in until the mixture resembles coarse, floury crumbs. Mix together the egg yolk, lemon juice and water, then sprinkle on to the mixture, using a fork to ensure that it is evenly moistened, and gather into a ball.

To make the pastry by food processor, put the dry ingredients and the firm butter and shortening, cut into 2.5 cm (1 in) cubes into the bowl. Mix the liquid ingredients (including the egg yolk) together, then turn on the machine and pour them down the feed tube, pulsing only until the mixture looks like a moist crumble. Tip it into a bowl and gather into a ball.

Turn the pastry on to a lightly floured board or work surface, divide into two discs each 2.5 cm (1 in) thick and chill for at least half an hour.

Preheat the oven to 200°C (400°F/Gas 6).

Choose a pie dish 20 cm (8 in) in diameter and 2.5 cm (1 in) deep. Roll out 1 pastry disc into a circle about 28 cm (11 in) in diameter to fit the base and sides of the dish. Carefully ease the pastry circle on to the back of the rolling pin, then lay it gently into position in the pie dish. Spoon in the filling. Use a sharp knife to cut off the overhanging pastry all the way round. Knead these remains into the second portion of pastry and roll out in exactly the same way, to fit the top of the pie.

With a pastry brush, dampen the edge of the bottom crust all the way round and then gently transfer the remaining pastry circle via the rolling pin to fit the top. With the side of the index finger, press the two crusts together. Use a blunt-edged knife to join them together all the way round, making nicks every 3 mm (⅛ in) or crimp the edges together by pinching with the fingers and thumb. Brush the top of the pie with the egg white and sprinkle with the sugar, then make 4 slashes in the top with a very sharp knife, to allow the steam to escape.

Bake for 10 minutes, then reduce the heat to 180°C (350°F/Gas 4) and bake for a further 40 minutes or until the apple feels tender when the pie is pierced with a slim pointed knife and the pastry is a rich golden brown.

Serve just warm, cut in portions, plain or with ice cream or single cream.

VIENNESE APPLE SQUARES WITH CINNAMON-SCENTED CREAM

Apfelschnitten   Judi

This is an elegant variation of apple pie, a scrumptious combination of melt-in-the-mouth almond pastry and cinnamon-perfumed apples. What makes this particularly delectable, however, is the crunchy upper crust, which is grated rather than rolled, giving an unusual 'woven' appearance. The pastry is grated while frozen, making the handling of the fragile dough as easy as pie!

Makes 6–8 servings as a dessert, or 20–24 little squares to serve with coffee
Raw pastry keeps 24 hours under refrigeration.
Freezes raw up to 1 month. Do not freeze once cooked.

For the almond pastry
    250 g (9 oz) plain flour
    pinch of sea salt
    25 g (1 oz) ground almonds or hazelnuts
    75 g (3 oz) sugar
    grated zest of ½ lemon
    175 g (6 oz) butter or firm margarine,
        cut in 2.5 cm (1 in) cubes
    1 large egg yolk
    2 tablespoons evaporated milk or single cream
For the filling
    900 g (2 lb) cooking apples such as Bramleys
    50 g (2 oz) dark brown sugar
    1 teaspoon ground cinnamon
    3 tablespoons raisins or sultanas
    50 g (2 oz) walnuts, coarsely chopped (optional)
    2 tablespoons fresh lemon juice
For sprinkling on top
    demerara or granulated sugar (page 147)

243

continued

For the cinnamon cream
    125 g (4 oz) soured cream or strained Greek yoghurt
    2 teaspoons sugar
    2 teaspoons ground cinnamon

To make the pastry, put the flour, salt, ground nuts, sugar and lemon zest into a bowl. Add the butter and rub in gently until the mixture resembles dry bread crumbs. Mix the egg yolk and the evaporated milk or cream, then sprinkle on the dry ingredients and mix with the fingers to form a soft dough. If it seems dry, add a little more milk.

Divide the dough in half and knead each piece gently on a floured board until smooth. Flatten each piece into a 2.5 cm (1 in) thick disc. Wrap each disc in aluminium foil, then refrigerate one and freeze the other for 1 hour.

Preheat the oven to 190°C (375°F/Gas 5). Have ready a Swiss roll tin approximately 30 × 20 × 2 cm (12 × 8 × ¾ in).

On a floured board, roll the refrigerated piece of pastry to fit the base of the tin, then gently ease it into place and trim the edges level. If the pastry breaks, simply patch the pieces together.

Do not combine the filling and pastry until just before baking, or the juicy apple mixture will make the pastry soggy. Peel and core the apples, then coarsely grate or finely slice them and mix with all the other filling ingredients. Immediately spread in an even layer over the pastry. Coarsely grate the frozen pastry over the top. Sprinkle with the sugar and bake for 45 minutes, until golden brown.

To make the cinnamon-scented cream, combine the soured cream or yoghurt, sugar and cinnamon in a bowl and chill.

Serve warm or at room temperature, accompanied by the chilled cream or yoghurt.

244

ARMENIAN APRICOT MOUSSE WITH PISTACHIOS

Koshab

Evelyn

ALTHOUGH IT CONTAINS neither gelatine nor cornflour, this fruit- and liqueur-flavoured cream sets overnight to a mousse-like consistency. It can be served either in glasses like a syllabub or used as a filling for a Pavlova (page 226).

Makes 6–8 servings
Keeps up to 2 days under refrigeration. **Freezes** up to 3 weeks.

50 g (2 oz) sugar
225 ml (8 fl oz) water
225–250 g (8–9 oz) ready-to-eat dried apricots
1 tablespoon fresh lemon juice
½ teaspoon vanilla extract
3 tablespoons apricot liqueur or orange juice
275 ml (10 fl oz) double or non-dairy cream
50 g (2 oz) shelled pistachios, chopped
sprigs of fresh mint

Bring the sugar and water to the boil in a medium saucepan, add the apricots, then lower the heat, cover and simmer for 15 minutes, until tender but not mushy.

Take off the heat and stir in the lemon juice, vanilla and liqueur or juice. Refrigerate for 40 minutes, then strain, reserving the apricots. Finely dice the apricots.

Put the cream into a bowl with the syrup drained from the apricots. Whip with an electric whisk until it stands in stiff peaks, then fold in the apricots, reserving a few for garnish. Fold in almost all the pistachios.

Divide the flavoured cream between individual flutes or glass bowls and decorate with the remaining fruit and nuts. Chill until required.

Just before serving, garnish with sprigs of fresh mint.

245

ORANGE LIQUEUR SOUFFLÉ

Judi

THIS SOUFFLÉ IS SO MEMORABLE it just has to be the star of the meal. So make something very good but simple beforehand, perhaps half a perfect cantaloupe or Galia melon filled with a few raspberries, followed by grilled salmon with the best new potatoes you can buy and a lovely green salad scattered with toasted pine kernels. The soufflé can be prepared in stages, reducing the workload right before dinner. The sauce base can be made earlier in the day. Once the egg whites have been added, the oven-ready soufflé can be left for up to 1 hour before baking.

Makes 6–7 servings
Serve immediately.

For the sauce

50 g (2 oz) plain flour

125 g (4 oz) sugar

350 ml (12 fl oz) semi-skimmed milk or 150 ml (5 fl oz) each full cream
    milk and single cream

finely grated zest of 1 large orange

5 large egg yolks

25 g (1 oz) soft butter

3 tablespoons fresh orange juice

For the base

20 sponge fingers

125 ml (4 fl oz) orange-flavoured liqueur such as Cointreau
    or Curaçao, mixed with 50 ml (2 fl oz) cold water

To continue

15 g (½ oz) butter

2–3 tablespoons sugar

6 large egg whites

pinch of sea salt

2 rounded teaspoons sugar

orange liqueur

246

To make the sauce, mix the flour and sugar in a heavy saucepan. Gradually stir in the milk or milk and cream, together with the grated orange zest. Whisk constantly over moderate heat until it starts to boil, then stir with a wooden spoon for 3–4 minutes to cook the flour.

Stir the egg yolks into the warm sauce. When all the yolks have been added, stir in the butter and orange juice, mixing until smooth. If the sauce is to be left during the day, dot the top with a little butter to stop a skin from forming (this is not necessary if the egg whites are to be added within 1 hour).

Cut the sponge fingers into 2.5 cm (1 in) pieces, place in a small bowl and pour the liqueur and water mixture on top.

Select an oval ovenproof dish measuring about 38×23 cm (15×9 in) rim-to-rim and about 5 cm (2 in) deep. Butter the dish, then dust with the sugar. Arrange the soaked sponge finger mixture evenly on the bottom.

If the sauce was prepared earlier in the day, warm it gently on the cooker just until it feels tepid when touched with a finger.

To prepare the meringue, with an electric beater whisk the egg whites in a large bowl with a pinch of salt just until they hold soft peaks, then whisk in the 2 teaspoons of sugar until stiff peaks are formed. Stir 2 large spoonfuls of the meringue into the sauce to lighten it, then gently fold in the remainder with a rubber spatula. Turn into the prepared dish and smooth the top level. At this point the uncooked soufflé may be left at room temperature for up to 1 hour.

Before the meal starts, preheat the oven to 220°C (425°F/Gas 7).

Half an hour before you intend to serve the soufflé, put it into the oven, reduce the heat to 200°C (400°F/Gas 6) and bake for 30 minutes without opening the oven door. When ready it will be golden brown on top and will wobble when gently shaken.

If the soufflé is accidentally left in the oven for more then 30 minutes, the sides will stick to the edge of the dish (although the centre will still be fine). If you are worried about timing, fill a baking tin with enough very hot water to reach halfway up the side of the dish (best done right next to the oven) and bake as before.

Serve at once. Pass the bottle of liqueur around for each guest to pour a little over their soufflé.

TWO STREETS AWAY FROM the Paris Ritz in the rue Tabor there's a restaurant called Le Soufflé where they make a divine Soufflé au Cointreau. What's more, it comes with a bottle of Cointreau, so you can pour the libation into its creamy heart.

I couldn't wait to make one myself—at a hopefully slimmer price—so I bought a bottle of the liqueur in the airport in anticipation. Le Soufflé's soufflé for one came in the traditional round dish, but I couldn't see myself juggling six of them at a time. So I cooked mine in one very large gratin dish, which meant it held up well because the mixture was less deep. Best of all, I found the uncooked soufflé could wait for up to 1 hour before baking, which makes it a practical proposition for entertaining.

There's far too much mystique about making a soufflé, so let's divide its preparation into its separate parts: the thick custard that forms the base, the cunningly concealed flavouring and the meringue that gives it lift-off. Once that's clear in your mind, it's easy all the way!

248

WINE AND CHOCOLATE GÂTEAU
WITH CAPPUCCINO ICING

Evelyn

A FLUFFY, TENDER-TEXTURED CAKE with a beguiling flavour, complemented by the rich coffee icing. One for a special occasion!

Makes 10–12 servings

Keeps up to 1 week at room temperature in an airtight container.

Freezes up to 2 months.

4 large eggs
225 g (8 oz) sugar
240 g (8½ oz) soft butter or margarine
1 teaspoon vanilla extract
1 teaspoon ground cinnamon
1 teaspoon cocoa powder
250 g (9 oz) super-sifted self-raising flour
10 g (3½ oz) plain chocolate, coarsely grated
125 ml (4 fl oz) any red wine

For the icing
350 g (12 oz) sifted icing sugar
2 teaspoons instant coffee
50 ml (2 fl oz) boiling water

For the garnish (optional)
a little grated chocolate

Preheat the oven to 160°C (325°F/Gas 3). Grease then bottom-line a 25 cm (10 in) springform cake pan with greaseproof paper or baking parchment.

In a large-capacity food processor, process the eggs and sugar for 2 minutes. Add spoonfuls of butter or margarine down the feed tube, processing constantly. (Don't worry if it begins to curdle.) Add the vanilla, cinnamon and cocoa, then take off the lid and add the flour, baking powder, chocolate and wine. Pulse about 5 times, until the consistency is even, scraping down the sides of the bowl once if necessary.

249

Turn the cake mixture into the tin, smooth level, then bake for 55 minutes, until firm to a gentle touch and a skewer comes out clean from the centre. Cool on a wire rack, then gently remove from the tin.

To make the icing, sieve the sugar into a small saucepan and add the coffee dissolved in 2 tablespoons of the water. Heat very gently for 3–4 minutes, stirring constantly, to remove the raw sugar taste, adding the remaining water if necessary. The icing should be of a coating consistency that will flow off the spoon.

Put a plate beneath the wire rack, then pour the icing over the cake, coaxing it down the sides with a knife dipped in hot water. Leave plain, or decorate with grated chocolate.

Serve with tea or coffee, plain or with ice cream or frozen yogurt.

LUSCIOUS LEMON DRIZZLE CAKE

Judi

AN INTENSE LEMON FLAVOUR permeates this light and exquisitely tart cake. The magic touch is a lemon syrup drizzled on top while the cake is still warm, which soaks through the top layers as it cools. It's at its best served freshly made. For a Purim version, stir a tablespoon of poppy seeds into the cake mixture before baking.

Makes 8–10 servings. Best eaten freshly baked.
Keeps 1 week under refrigeration in an airtight container.
Freezes up to 3 months.

2 large eggs
175 g (6 oz) sugar
150 g (5 oz) soft butter or margarine
grated zest of 1 lemon
175 g (6 oz) super-sifted self-raising flour
125 ml (4 fl oz) milk
pinch of sea salt
For the lemon syrup
150 g (5 oz) icing sugar
50 ml (2 fl oz) fresh lemon juice (about 1½ large lemons)

Preheat the oven to 180°C (350°F/Gas 4). Line the bottom of a well-oiled 23 × 13 × 7.5 cm (9 × 5 × 3 in) loaf tin with baking parchment.

Put the eggs and sugar in the bowl of the food processor and process for 2 minutes, scraping the sides down once with a rubber spatula. Take off the lid and drop spoonfuls of the soft butter or margarine on top of this mixture, together with the lemon zest, then pulse just until it disappears. The mixture should now resemble mayonnaise.

Add the flour, milk and salt, cover and pulse just until the mixture is smooth in texture and even in colour, scraping the sides down with a rubber spatula if necessary. Do not over-beat or the cake will be tough.

251

continued

Spoon the cake mixture into the prepared tin and bake for 45 minutes, until golden brown on top and firm to the touch. Remove from the oven and stand the tin on a cooling rack.

To make the syrup, gently heat the sugar and lemon juice in a small saucepan, stirring until a clear syrup is formed, about 3 minutes. Do not boil.

Prick the warm cake all over with a fork, then gently pour the syrup over it, until it has been completely absorbed.

Leave until cool, then carefully ease the cake from the baking tin and remove the baking parchment.

Just before serving, sift a little more icing sugar on the top. Serve in generous slices.

OLD-FASHIONED CHOCOLATE SWIRL CAKE

Evelyn

THIS CAKE HAS AN IRRESISTIBLE FLAVOUR and a moist texture. A luscious chocolate and cinnamon mixture is swirled through the sponge.

Makes 8–10 servings

Keeps 1 week at room temperature in an airtight container.

Freezes for up to 3 months.

1 tablespoon white vinegar

1 × 150 g (5 oz) can evaporated milk

For the chocolate swirl

130 g (4½ oz) good-quality plain chocolate,
    broken into 2.5 cm (1 in) chunks

2 tablespoons sugar

½ teaspoon ground cinnamon

For the cake mixture

125 g (4 oz) dark brown sugar, firmly packed

225 g (8 oz) granulated sugar

125 g (4 oz) butter

125 g (4 oz) margarine

1 teaspoon pure vanilla extract

2 large eggs

225 g (8 oz) self-raising flour

½ teaspoon bicarbonate of soda

¼ teaspoon sea salt

To sprinkle on the cake

sifted icing sugar

Preheat the oven to 180° C (350°F/Gas 4). Butter and flour a 23 cm (9 in) ring tin.

In a glass or plastic measuring cup, add the vinegar to the evaporated milk and allow to curdle until needed.

253

continued

Put the chocolate, the 2 tablespoons sugar and the cinnamon into the bowl of the food processor. Process until the texture of coarse meal, about 15 seconds. Do not over-process or the chocolate will melt. Transfer the mixture to a bowl.

To make the cake mixture, in the food processor (no need to wash it), cream the sugars with the butter and margarine until fluffy and the texture of mayonnaise, about 1 minute. Add the vanilla, followed by the eggs one at a time, pulsing twice after each addition. Add the curdled evaporated milk and process until evenly mixed, about 5–10 seconds.

In a bowl, mix the flour, bicarbonate of soda and salt. Add them to the mixture in the food processor bowl one-third at a time, pulsing a couple of times and cleaning down the sides of the bowl with a rubber spatula between additions. When combined, the mixture will be soft.

Starting and ending with cake mixture, fill the tin with three layers of cake mixture and two layers of evenly sprinkled chocolate mixture.

Smooth the top layer level, then put in the oven and bake for 50–60 minutes until slightly shrunken from the sides and a skewer inserted into the centre of the cake comes out dry. Turn upside down on to a wire rack, leave to cool for 10–15 minutes, then carefully ease out of the tin.

Leave until quite cold, then dust with sifted icing sugar and serve in slices.

THIS WONDERFUL AND ORIGINAL CAKE comes from a Litvak household, but it owes a great deal to the tradition of German-Jewish cuisine, in particular the *kugelhopf* or *bundkuchen*, a high cake baked in a fluted or plain ring tin.

Originally this type of cake was raised with yeast, but Jewish immigrants to Britain and the United States were quick to adapt the recipe to the far simpler baking powder as the raising agent, which was invented in the middle of the nineteenth century, just about the time of a large wave of German-Jewish immigration. Jews from Eastern Europe who arrived later adopted this new method with enthusiasm, but added chocolate or cocoa—popular ingredients in their traditional *kuchen*—to the original German recipe.

Now here's a further twist to the tale. They then added sour cream to the mixture which, when combined with a little bicarbonate of soda, gave the cake a wonderfully soft texture. And to bring the story right up to date, the latest cholesterol-conscious generation of cooks now substitute the lower-fat evaporated milk and sour it with vinegar!

255

HEALTHY SOMERSET
APPLE CAKE

Judi

A DELICIOUS, MOIST SPONGE CAKE, chock-full of healthy ingredients. Dried fruit and apples add fibre and sweetness, low-fat milk and margarine keep the calorie and cholesterol count down, while wholemeal flour provides fibre and vitamins as well as a delicious nutty flavour. The cake is named after the county of Somerset, renowned for its apple orchards.

Makes 8 servings
Keeps 4 days at room temperature in an airtight container;
1 week in the refrigerator.
Freezes up to 1 month.

50 g (2 oz) margarine
50 g (2 oz) light brown sugar
2 large eggs, lightly whisked
225 g (8 oz) brown or white self-raising flour
1½ teaspoons ground cinnamon
pinch of ground ginger
125 ml (4 fl oz) milk
225–250 g (8–9 oz) tart apples, such as Granny Smiths,
   peeled, cored and finely chopped
75 g (3 oz) raisins or sultanas
40 g (1½ oz) coarsely chopped walnuts (optional)

Preheat the oven to 160°C (325°F/Gas 3). Lightly oil a 17–18 cm (6½–7-in) round cake tin at least 5 cm (2 in) deep and line the base with a circle of baking parchment or greaseproof paper.

By hand or machine, cream the margarine and sugar together until they lighten in colour. Add the whisked eggs, 1 tablespoonful at a time, adding a little of the flour if necessary to prevent curdling.

256

Mix the rest of the flour with the spices, then add to the cake mixture 1 spoonful at a time, alternating with the milk. Stir in the apples, raisins and walnuts if using. Spoon into the prepared pan and smooth level.

Bake for 1¼ hours, until well risen and firm to the touch. Remove from the oven and leave the tin on a wire rack to cool for 20 minutes, before carefully easing the cake out.

257

FEATHERLIGHT COFFEE CAKE WITH BANANA CRUNCH TOPPING

Streusel Kuchen

Evelyn

THIS HAS A CRUNCHY CINNAMON TOPPING which contrasts well with the creamy baked bananas and the spongy cake below.

Makes about 12 servings
Keeps 3 days under refrigeration if tightly wrapped in aluminum foil.
Do not freeze.

For the cake mixture
- 225 g (8 oz) self-raising flour
- 1 level teaspoon baking powder
- 75 g (3 oz) soft butter or margarine
- 75 g (3 oz) sugar
- 1 large egg
- 1 teaspoon pure vanilla extract
- 150 ml (5 fl oz) natural yoghurt or soured cream
- 125 ml (4 fl oz) milk

For the topping
- 3 large bananas
- 2 tablespoons fresh lemon juice
- 50 g (2 oz) plain or self-raising flour
- 2 teaspoons ground cinnamon
- 50 g (2 oz) soft butter or margarine, cut in pieces
- 125 g (4 oz) light brown sugar

Preheat the oven to 190°C (375°F/Gas 5). Have ready a well-oiled 23–25 cm (9–10 in) springform tin, or a rectangular cake tin measuring 30 × 23 × 5 cm (12 × 9 × 2 in).

258

Put all the cake ingredients into a bowl and mix by hand or machine until a thick, smooth batter is formed (15 seconds with a food processor, 2–3 minutes by hand or mixer). Spoon the cake mixture into the chosen tin and smooth level.

Peel and slice the bananas about 8 mm (⅜ in) thick. Arrange them in rows on top of the batter and sprinkle evenly with the lemon juice.

Rub the flour, cinnamon, butter or margarine and sugar together until they form a crumble. Sprinkle this evenly over the bananas. Bake for 40–45 minutes or until golden brown.

Serve freshly baked, plain or with ice cream.

259

BANANA AND PECAN LOAF

Judi

 THE BANANA GIVES THIS DELICIOUS 'cakey' quick bread a wonderfully moist texture, with nuggets of crunchy pecans scattered throughout. Optional slivers of dried banana are a wonderful addition, enhancing both taste and texture.

Makes 10 servings

Keeps 1 week under refrigeration. **Do not freeze** as it goes heavy.

675 g (1½ lb) bananas (about 4 medium)
2 large eggs
175 g (6 oz) dark brown sugar
1 teaspoon pure vanilla extract
grated zest of ½ lemon
½ teaspoon ground ginger
50 g (2 oz) soft margarine
225 g (8 oz) self-raising flour
pinch of sea salt
2 teaspoons baking powder
½ teaspoon bicarbonate of soda
50 g (2 oz) shelled pecans
1 tablespoon coarsely broken dried banana chips (optional)

For the garnish

1 tablespoon whole shelled pecans
2 teaspoons coarsely broken dried banana chips (optional)

Preheat the oven to 180°C (350°F/Gas 4). Lightly oil a 23 × 13 × 7.5 cm (9 × 5 × 3 in) loaf tin and line the bottom and both short ends with a strip of baking parchment or greaseproof paper.

Peel the bananas and cut in roughly 2.5 cm (1 in) chunks. Chop in the food processor until puréed, about 1 minute. Add the eggs and sugar, then process for 2 minutes. Take off the lid and add the vanilla, lemon zest, ginger and heaped teaspoons of the margarine. Process for 10 seconds or until the mixture looks like mayonnaise (don't worry if it curdles a little). Remove the lid and add the flour, salt, baking powder and bicarbonate of soda. Cover and pulse until the flour has almost disappeared, about 3 seconds. Scrape down the sides with a rubber spatula, then pulse in the pecans until coarsely chopped, about 3 seconds, followed by the 1 tablespoon of banana chips if using.

Spoon the cake mixture into the prepared tin, level the top with a rubber spatula and scatter the whole pecans and banana chips (if using) on top.

Bake for 50 minutes. When ready, the loaf will have shrunk slightly from the edges of the tin, a skewer will come out clean from the centre and the top will spring back when gently pressed. Place the tin on a wire rack, leave for 15 minutes, then ease the loaf out of the tin.

Leave to cool completely, then wrap in aluminium foil and leave overnight to allow the flavour and texture to develop.

Serve in generous slices plain, buttered or spread with cream cheese.

THE BANANA WAS ONE of the main food casualties of World War II in Europe. Not a single one was imported to Britain for six years and when shipments were finally resumed in 1945, children were so suspicious of this unfamiliar fruit that the government of the day had to stage a 'National Banana Day', when millions of volunteers ensured that everyone under 18 was given a free one and taught how to peel it.

No one now needs to be persuaded to unzip a banana. With its creamy texture and satisfying sweetness, it's one food that is acceptable from infancy to old age.

Quite apart from its high potassium content, which can help reduce levels of stress, bananas are an ideal between-meals snack. They contain fructose, sucrose and glucose, three naturally occurring sugars which, combined with the banana's high fibre content, provide a sustained energy boost. When baked, bananas take on an exotic, tropical flavour.

261

GREAT-GRANDMA'S FEATHER-LIGHT LEMON BISCUITS

Kichlach   Evelyn

DELICATE LITTLE BISCUITS, very different from the typical *heimishe* rolled *kichlach*, though both have their devotees. To mix them, you require nothing more hi-tech than a large fork, which must have been a godsend when you had a large family like my great-grandma's.

Makes 36 biscuits
Keep up to 2 weeks in an airtight container.
Freezes up to 2 months.

2 large eggs
150 ml (5 fl oz) sunflower oil
1 teaspoon vanilla extract
1 teaspoon grated lemon zest
150 g (2 oz) sugar
225 g (8 oz) self-raising flour
2 teaspoons baking powder
pinch of sea salt
2 teaspoons finely chopped almonds

Preheat the oven to 200°C (400°F/Gas 6).

Beat the eggs with a fork until well blended. Stir in the oil, vanilla and lemon zest. Blend in the sugar until the mixture thickens, then add the flour, baking powder and salt (the dough will be soft, like a very thick batter).

Drop rounded teaspoonfuls on to an ungreased baking tray, 5 cm (2 in) apart. Using the bottom of a glass which has been dipped in oil and then in sugar, gently flatten each biscuit into a round, then scatter the top with the chopped almonds.

Bake the biscuits for 8–10 minutes, or until golden. When cooked, carefully lift off the baking tray with a spatula and leave to cool on a wire rack.

Offer with after-dinner coffee or with coffee or tea anytime.

FLUFFY SCOTTISH SCONES

Judi

LIGHT, TENDER SCONES STUDDED with sultanas, with a crunchy topping. Ideal to serve spread with fruit preserves.

Makes 10 scones
Serve freshly baked, or **freeze** unbaked for up to 6 weeks
and defrost 1 hour before baking.
Do not freeze once cooked.

225 (8oz) plain flour
3 teaspoons baking powder
50 g (2 oz) sugar
½ teaspoon sea salt
40 g (1½ oz) butter
40 g (1½ oz) sultanas
75 ml (3 fl oz) milk
75 ml (3 fl oz) natural yoghurt
For the glaze
milk
demerara or granulated sugar (page 147)

Preheat the oven to 220°C (425°F/Gas 7). Line a large baking tray with baking parchment.

In a bowl, mix together the flour, baking powder, sugar and salt, then by hand rub in the butter until the mixture resembles fine crumbs. If using a food processor, process the dry ingredients and the butter to the fine-crumb stage, then transfer to a bowl.

Add the sultanas. Make a well in the centre, pour in the milk and yoghurt all at once and mix to a soft but non-sticky dough with a round-ended knife, cutting through and through the dry ingredients to moisten them evenly. Turn out on to a lightly floured board and knead for 30 seconds or until no cracks remain on the underside.

263

continued

Roll out the dough 1 cm (½ in) thick. Cut into circles 5 cm (2 in) in diameter and place on the prepared baking tray. To glaze, brush with milk then sprinkle each scone generously with sugar.

Bake for 12 minutes or until golden brown. Remove from the oven and put on a wire rack.

When cool, split, butter and serve plain, or with preserves and unsweetened whipped cream. Best eaten freshly made.

~   **SECRETS OF THE SCONE**   ⁖

SCONES WERE ONE of the first 'English' recipes that the children of Jewish immigrants to Britain were taught at school before World War I to 'Anglicise' them.

Invented by the wives of Scottish Highlanders, using milk that had soured in an age before the invention of the refrigerator, scones were originally patted rather than rolled out to keep them tender.

You can rub in the fat with the food processor, but don't attempt to mix to a dough using it. It doesn't work.

Spread with a little butter and a luscious fruit preserve or cream cheese, scones are one of the delights of home baking.

AUNTIE ANNIE'S CINNAMON BALLS

Evelyn

SOFT AND MOIST INSIDE, crisp on the outside, these delicious little spheres of ground almonds and cinnamon have become a Passover favourite in Anglo-Jewish families. They're simple and fun for kids to make, if you lend a hand with beating the egg whites.

Makes about 22 balls
Keep 1 week at room temperature in an airtight container.
Freezes up to 3 months.

2 large egg whites
125 g (4 oz) sugar
225 g (8 oz) ground almonds
1 tablespoon ground cinnamon
For the coating
small bowl of icing sugar

Preheat the oven to 160°C (325°F/Gas 3). Lightly grease 2 baking trays.

In a bowl, beat the egg whites until they form stiff peaks. Stir in the remaining ingredients, mixing until even in colour.

With wetted hands, form into 4 cm (1½ in) balls. The mixture should be the consistency of a soft paste (if it seems too soft, add a little more cinnamon).

Arrange the balls at least 1 cm (½ in) apart on the prepared trays and bake for 20 minutes or until just firm to the touch. Do not over-bake or they may dry out.

Remove from the trays, roll in the icing sugar while still warm and then again when cool.

Serve anytime with coffee or tea, or as an after-dinner treat with coffee.

NUTTY BUTTER CRISPS

Evelyn

D ELECTABLE LITTLE BISCUITS that literally melt in the mouth. Ideal to serve with after-dinner coffee.

Makes 30 biscuits
Keep up to 2 weeks at room temperature in an airtight container.
Do not freeze.

75 g (3 oz) butter
75 g (3 oz) plus 1 tablespoon sugar
1 tablespoon double cream
1 cup slivered almonds

Preheat the oven to 180°C (350°F/Gas 4). Line with baking parchment as many baking trays as you can fit into the oven at one time.

In a saucepan, slowly bring the butter, sugar and cream to boiling point, stirring constantly, about 4 minutes. Add the nuts and cook at a fast boil, stirring, until slightly caramelised (pale gold in colour), about 1 minute. Immediately take off the heat and leave to firm up for 10 minutes.

Using 2 teaspoons to shape the biscuits, scoop up a small amount of the mixture with one spoon and push it off with the other in a little mound on to the prepared baking tray, leaving 7.5 cm (3 in) between to allow them room to spread. Bake for 12 minutes until golden brown. Cool for 2–3 minutes, then use a spatula to lift them off the paper and on to a wire rack. Repeat, using the same parchment paper, until all the mixture has been baked.

Arrange decoratively on a small platter and offer with coffee or tea, or as an after-dinner treat.

266

OLD-STYLE APPLE AND ALMOND PUDDING

Evelyn

ONE FOR THE NUT-LOVER. A refreshing apple compôte is topped with an almond (or hazelnut) sponge. Simple and delicious, it's an ideal Passover dessert.

Makes 8 servings
Keeps up to 3 days under refrigeration. **Freeze** leftovers up to 2 months.

900 g (2 lb) tart apples such as Granny Smiths or Bramleys, peeled,
   cored, and cut in 1 cm (½ in) thick slices
50 g (2 oz) sugar
1 rounded tablespoon apricot jam
1 tablespoon fresh lemon juice
3 tablespoons orange juice
For the topping
   225 g (8 oz) soft butter or margarine
   225 g (8 oz) sugar
   225 g (8 oz) ground almonds or hazelnuts
   4 large eggs
   grated zest of 1 lemon

Preheat the oven to 180°C (350°F/Gas 4).

Put the sliced apples in a large saucepan with the sugar, apricot jam and lemon and orange juices. Simmer over low heat on top of the cooker until barely tender, about 15 minutes. Alternatively, cook on 100 per cent power in the microwave for 7 minutes, stirring once.

Arrange the fruit mixture in a greased gratin or other oven-to-table dish 25–28 cm (10–11 in) long and 5 cm (2 in) deep.

Beat all the topping ingredients together in a bowl until they form a smooth mixture, then spread on top of the apple mixture.

Bake for 40 minutes, or until golden and firm to a gentle touch. Serve plain or with frozen yoghurt or ice cream.

267

THE 'BIG APPLE' LAYERED GÂTEAU

Judi

Aᴄɪɴɴᴀᴍᴏɴ-ꜱᴄᴇɴᴛᴇᴅ ᴀᴘᴘʟᴇ ᴘᴜʀᴇ́ᴇ is sandwiched between layers of vanilla sponge. The mixture of potato flour and cake matzah meal gives the sponge a delicate, fluffy texture, making this a light but satisfying end to a filling Passover meal, but delicious any time of the year!

Makes 12 generous portions
Keeps 3 days under refrigeration.
Freezes up to 2 months.

For the filling
700 g (1½ lb) tart apples, such as Granny Smiths or Bramleys
3 tablespoons light or dark brown sugar mixed with
   1 teaspoon ground cinnamon
1 tablespoon fresh lemon juice

For the sponge
3 large eggs
225 g (8 oz) sugar
175 ml (6 fl oz) sunflower oil
1 teaspoon pure vanilla extract
75 g (3 oz) potato flour
75 g (3 oz) cake matzah meal
1½ teaspoons baking powder

To sprinkle on top
1–2 tablespoons sugar

Preheat the oven to 180°C (350°F/Gas 4). Grease a 23–24 cm (9–9½ in) round springform or loose-bottomed tin at least 4 cm (1½ in) deep.

To prepare the filling, peel and core the apples, then grate them coarsely into a mixing bowl. Add the sugar-cinnamon mixture and lemon juice, then mix well together.

Next make the sponge. By food processor, cream the eggs and sugar for 2 minutes. Pour in the oil and process until it disappears, then pulse in the vanilla and the dry ingredients until the mixture is smooth and even, about 3 seconds. If using an electric mixer, whisk the eggs and sugar until thick and lemon-coloured, then whisk in the oil, followed by the vanilla and the dry ingredients.

Pour half the sponge mixture into the prepared tin, smoothing it level. Spoon the apple filling on top, patting it into an even layer, then cover with the remainder of the sponge mixture. Sprinkle the top of the mixture with the sugar.

Bake for 55 minutes, or until well risen and firm to a gentle touch in the centre.

Serve warm or at room temperature, plain or with ice cream or frozen yoghurt.

QUEEN OF SHEBA FLOURLESS CHOCOLATE GATEAU WITH A BRANDY ICING

Evelyn

WONDERFULLY MOIST AND TENDER. Many people consider this the best chocolate cake ever! For a Passover version, use Passover brandy and baking powder.

Makes 10–12 servings

Keeps up to 1 week in an airtight container.

Freezes up to 2 months.

175 g (6 oz) butter or margarine

175 g(6 oz) sugar

250 g (9 oz) plain chocolate, broken into pieces

6 large eggs, separated

3 tablespoons brandy

75g (3 oz) potato flour plus 1 teaspoon baking powder

pinch of sea salt

icing sugar (optional)

For the brandy icing (optional)

50 g (2 oz) unsalted butter or margarine

125 g (4 oz) plain chocolate, broken into pieces

1 tablespoon brandy

Preheat the oven to 180°C (350°F/Gas 4). Grease the inner sides of a 24 cm (9½ in) round loose-bottomed or springform cake tin and line the base with a circle of baking parchment.

In a sturdy 20 cm (8 in) saucepan, melt the butter or margarine, then add the sugar and broken-up chocolate. Continue to heat over low heat, stirring constantly, until the mixture is smooth, about 3 minutes. Immediately take off the heat and stir in the egg yolks, brandy, potato flour and baking powder.

270

Whisk the egg whites with the pinch of salt until they hold floppy peaks, then stir a quarter of it into the chocolate mixture to lighten it. Finally, spoon the remaining egg white on top and fold the two mixtures together, using a rubber spatula.

Pour into the cake tin and bake for 45–50 minutes, until the top is firm to gentle pressure and a skewer comes out clean from the centre. Leave on a rack for 30 minutes, then carefully remove from the tin. (If the top cracks, serve the cake bottom side up.) Dust with icing sugar or cover with the icing (see below) when quite cold.

To make the icing, melt the butter or margarine and broken chocolate with the brandy, either in a small saucepan on top of the cooker or in the microwave (1½ minutes on 100 per cent power), then stir well together until smooth. Chill for 10 minutes until of coating consistency. Pour over the top and sides of the cake and allow to set.

Serve in small portions, as it is very rich and satisfying.

SUPER-LIGHT CITRUS CHIFFON CAKE

Judi

A FAMILY-SIZED FINE-TEXTURED Passover sponge with a delicate orange and lemon flavour that stays moist for several days.

The cake's moist, delicate texture really needs no embellishment, but for a more dramatic presentation it can be split into two layers and filled with jam or sweetened whipped cream.

Makes 10–12 servings
Keeps 1 week in an airtight container.
Freezes up to 2 months.

75 g (3 oz) potato flour
65 g (2½ oz) matzah cake meal
225 g (8 oz) caster sugar
5 large eggs
50 ml (2 fl oz) sunflower oil
50 ml (2 fl oz) orange juice, freshly squeezed if possible
1 rounded teaspoon finely grated lemon zest
1 rounded teaspoon finely grated orange zest
pinch of sea salt

Preheat the oven to 160°C (325°F/Gas 3). Grease and dust lightly with a little cake matzah meal a 23–25 cm (9–10 in) ring tin, about 7.5 cm (3 in) deep.

Sift the potato flour, cake meal and 150 g (5 oz) of the sugar into a large bowl and mix well.

Separate the eggs, putting the yolks in a small bowl and the whites in a large one. Add the oil, orange juice and lemon and orange zest to the yolks. Make a well in the middle of the dry ingredients and pour in the egg yolk mixture, stirring with a wooden spoon until smooth and evenly mixed.

Whisk the egg whites with a pinch of salt until they hold stiff, glossy peaks, then whisk in the remaining sugar, 1 tablespoon at a time, whisking after each addition.

Spoon this meringue on top of the yolk mixture, then fold the two together gently but thoroughly with a rubber spatula. Spoon into the prepared tin, smooth level, then bake for 1¼ hours until firm to a gentle touch.

Put the cake, still in its tin, on a wire rack and leave until it feels cool to the touch. Loosen from the edges of the pan with the tip of a knife and gently ease out.

CHIFFON CAKES — so-named because of their delicate texture — are made with oil rather than butter or margarine, resulting in a really moist, tender sponge (as well as cutting down on the cholesterol). The eggs are separated and the whites beaten to a meringue before being folded into the cake mixture, which produces a feather-light texture. Be sure to use caster, not granulated sugar or the cake will lack the refined texture that makes it so irresistible.

273

GINGERED HONEY CAKE

Lekach

Evelyn

THIS IS A PARTICULARLY MOIST *lekach*, whose flavour is enhanced with ginger preserve as well as the usual powdered spices. The cake rises at least 2.5 cm (1 in) in the oven, so to prevent the mixture bubbling over the sides, it is important to use the specified size of cake tin.

Makes 10 servings
Keeps up to 1 month in an airtight container.
Freezes up to 2 months.

250 g (9 oz) white self-raising flour
2 teaspoons ground ginger
1 teaspoon ground cinnamon
225 g (8 oz) honey
125 ml (4 fl oz) sunflower oil
75 g (3 oz) dark brown sugar
1 large egg
125 g (4 oz) ginger marmalade
¼ teaspoon bicarbonate of soda mixed with 175 ml (6 fl oz) hot water

Preheat the oven to 150°C (300°F/Gas 2).

Grease a loaf tin measuring approximately 23 × 13 × 7.5 cm (9 × 5 × 3 inches and line the bottom and both short ends with a long strip of baking parchment.

Sift the flour and spices into a bowl. Put the honey into another bowl, then add to it the oil, sugar, egg, ginger marmalade and half the flour mixture. Stir until smooth, then add the remaining flour mixture and the bicarbonate of soda mixed with the hot water, stirring until the batter is thoroughly blended—it will be thin. Pour carefully into the tin.

Bake for 1½ hours, or until the top is springy to a gentle touch and a skewer

274

comes out clean from the centre. Place on a wire rack and leave until cool to the touch.

Cut the cake into slices 1 cm (½ in) thick and then into fingers.

IT'S ONLY IN THE TWENTIETH CENTURY that the name *lekach* has been given to a cake made with honey for Rosh Hashanah. In fact, any special cake, particularly if made for a festival, can be called by that name.

As it does not need maturing for more than a day, you can make this *lekach* at any time up to the eve of a festival, storing it well wrapped in aluminium foil. It can easily be mixed by hand, but the ingredients can also be combined in an electric mixer or a large-capacity food processor. You can substitute the ginger marmalade for 2 tablespoons crystallised ginger mixed with 125 g (4 oz) apricot jam.

275

MOIST WINE AND SPICE CAKE

Judi

THIS IS A MOST UNUSUAL CAKE, light as a feather yet with a lovely moistness. The spicing is delicate—add a little more if you prefer a more intense flavour. A key ingredient is golden syrup, which imparts a wonderful flavour and texture. At Rosh Hashanah, however, honey is more traditional, so take your pick! The cake can be eaten fresh, but the flavour is best when allowed to mature for a couple of days wrapped in aluminium foil or in an airtight bag.

Makes 24– 36 servings
Keeps 2 weeks wrapped in aluminum foil in an airtight container.
Freezes up to 1 month.

450 g (1 lb) **honey or golden syrup**
300 ml (10 fl oz) **cold water**
225 g (8 oz) **sugar**
225 ml (8 fl oz) **sunflower oil**
3 **large eggs**
450 g (1 lb) **white self-raising flour**
1 teaspoon **baking powder**
1½ teaspoons **each ground ginger and cinnamon**
1 teaspoon **bicarbonate of soda**
2 tablespoons plus 2 teaspoons **port-type or sweet red wine**
    such as kiddush wine

Preheat the oven to 200°C (400°F/Gas 6).

Lightly oil a baking tin measuring 30 × 23 × 5 cm (12 × 9 × 2 in), then line the base and short sides with a strip of baking parchment.

Heat the honey or syrup, water, sugar and oil in a small saucepan over gentle heat, stirring until the mixture is smooth and the sugar has dissolved, about 3 minutes. In a large bowl, whisk the eggs until frothy, then very gradually add the syrup mixture, beating with a wooden spoon or balloon whisk all the time. (Do not add the hot mixture too quickly or the eggs will curdle.)

276

Sift together the flour, baking powder and spices, and stir into the mixture. Dissolve the bicarbonate of soda in the wine, then stir into the cake mixture. Make sure the cake mixture is smooth and even in colour, then pour into the prepared tin and put in the oven.

Immediately turn the heat down to 150°C (300°F/Gas 2) and bake for 1¼–1½ hours, or until firm to the touch and a rich brown.

Leave the cake in the tin until cool to the touch, then turn it out on to a wire rack and immediately invert it on to a second rack. When quite cold, wrap in aluminium foil or place in an airtight bag and leave to mature for at least 2 days.

Memories are Made of These:
Festival Menus

To everything there is a season

Ecclesiastes 3:1

THE TAPESTRY OF FESTIVALS THAT IS WOVEN THROUGH THE
Jewish year is one of the strongest links we have with our heritage.

Festivals are mainly about families and only partly about food.
But it is the food that we eat as a family that gives them their special,
unforgettable flavour. It is the images stamped on our minds from
early childhood, of the preparations that surround the different festivals and their special foods that we most vividly recall when far from
home: of our mother testing the Passover sponge with an anxious eye;
of our father mixing the *charoset* (apple and walnut 'mortar') for the
Seder with the ceremony of a master chef. We can conjure up the
musky smell of melon and the perfume of the chrysanthemums that
always filled the house at the New Year. And we can taste, as if we'd
eaten it yesterday, that first sweet-sour mouthful of *holishkes* at Sukkot
and that first, moist bite of honey cake at Rosh Hashanah.

278

THE JEWISH FESTIVAL YEAR

Pesach (Passover), 15 Nisan (March/April)

Shavuot (Pentecost), 6 Sivan (May/June)

Rosh Hashanah (New Year), 1 and 2 Tishri (September/October)

Yom Kippur (Day of Atonement), 10 Tishri (September/October)

Sukkot (Tabernacles), 15 Tishri (September/October)

Simchat Torah (Rejoicing of the Law), 23 Tishri (September/October)

Hanukkah (Feast of Lights), 25 Kislev (December)

Purim (Feast of Lots), 14 Adar (February/March)

Passover

WE CELEBRATE THE FREEING OF THE ISRAELITES FROM EGYPT-
ian slavery with matzah (unleavened bread). So no yeast, no ordinary
flour, no foods that can ferment. Instead, Super-light Citrus Chiffon
Cake made with matzah meal and potato flour, and Auntie Annie's
moist, once-a-year Cinnamon Balls based on ground almonds. And
then there's the best of all chocolate cakes, the divine Queen of Sheba
cake, a super-moist chocolate gâteau held together, oh, so lightly, with
chocolate and eggs.

Comes the start of Passover and the cakes and biscuits are stored,
ready to tempt our family and friends. For the Seder, Evelyn proffers
an exquisite dish of tender halibut in a delicate sweet-and-sour lemon
sauce, while combining the past and present, Judi suggests the memorable gefilte fish in an herb-scented Provençal sauce. And for the
finale, the luscious, fruity 'Big Apple' Layered Gâteau served with
Passover ice cream.

For those families to whom the Seder meal means chicken, there's
a simple but savoury Slow-cooked Chicken on a Bed of Potatoes, or
the more exotic contemporary version, *Poulet Grande Dame* (French-
style Chicken with a Rich Red Wine Sauce). For dessert, there's a
fruity Old-style Apple and Almond Pudding to get your spoon into, or
the light and luscious Berries and Cherries in Wine.

MENU 1: FISH-BASED

Courgette Paté with Buttered Matzah (page 39)
Halibut in a Velvet Lemon Sauce (page 105)
Minted Peas and Cucumber with Shallots (page 176)
New potatoes
Queen of Sheba Flourless Chocolate Gâteau with a
Brandy Icing (page 270)
Fresh strawberries tossed in lemon juice and sugar

MENU 2: FISH-BASED

Smoked Salmon Roulade with a Crushed Pecan Coating
(page 42)
Gefilte Fish Provençal (page 93)
Shades of Green Tossed Salad (page 189)
Perfect Potato Salad (page 194)
Super-light Citrus Chiffon Cake (page 272)
Perfumed Peaches with Muscatel and Flower Petals (page 239)
With coffee: Nutty Butter Crisps (page 266)

MENU 3: CHICKEN-BASED

Best of Both Worlds Chicken Soup with Matzah Balls
(pages 8–11)
Slow-Cooked Chicken on a Bed of Potatoes
(*Gedaemte Chicken*) (page 114)
A green vegetable and a purée of carrots
Old-style Apple and Almond Pudding (page 267)
Fresh pineapple sprinkled with Passover orange liqueur

MENU 4: CHICKEN-BASED

California Salad with Raspberries and Glazed Pecans
(page 52)
French-style Chicken with a Rich Red Wine Sauce
(*Poulet Grande Dame*) (page 120)
New potatoes and a green vegetable
The 'Big Apple' Layered Gâteau (page 268)
Berries and Cherries in Wine
(page 236; substitute potato flour for cornflour
in this recipe when making for Passover)
With coffee: Auntie Annie's Cinnamon Balls (page 265)

281

shavuot

ALL THINGS WHITE AND WONDERFUL FOR THIS HARVEST FESTI-
val that celebrates the giving of the Law to Moses on Mount Sinai.

The 'white' is usually cream cheese, as in those tender stuffed
crêpes, cheese blintzes. We introduce you to a sophisticated dish of
sole arranged on a bed of new potatoes and enveloped in a creamy
sauce made without flour—just seasoned cream, topped with cheese.
Rather more adventurous but well worth the effort are Judi's little
choux pastry Gruyère puffs (*Petites Gougères*) and a memorable Normandy-style fish in cider, garnished with lightly caramelised apples.

Menu 1

Grandma's *Milchike* Soup with Springtime Vegetables
(page 20)
Sole Gratin in a Light Cream Sauce (page 87)
Orange and Endive Salad with Chrysanthemum Petals
(page 199)
Lemon Dainty with Strawberry Sauce (page 237)

Menu 2

Light Cheese Blintzes (page 66)
Normandy-Style Fish with Cider and Apples (page 88)
Fennel, Almond and Grape Salad (page 193)
Armenian Apricot Mousse with Pistachios (page 245)
Fresh fruit platter

Rosh Hashanah

OUR HOPES ARE FOR A YEAR AHEAD THAT IS AS ROUND AND FULL of good things as the melons that we enjoy and as sweet as the apples and the other more exotic fruits such as the pomegranates that are on the menu at this season.

Fish is a traditional dish for New Year—the eggs in its roe symbolic of fertility and prosperity. So from the western Mediterranean come succulent fillets of salmon baked under an unusual sun-dried tomato crust.

The dish that says 'Rosh Hashanah' because it's the only time it is served in our house is *Tsimmes mit Halkes*, that classic sweet carrot and meat casserole with dumpling, which can only be cooked in traditional style since it has a 5-hour cooking time! Evelyn conjures up the unforgettable Biblical Chicken in an Orange, Honey and Raisin Sauce made with chicken breasts.

Honey, the symbolic sweetener of this festival, figures in *lekach*— a marvellous honey cake that stays moist for as long as the family will let it—one version from Evelyn mixed with ginger and another from Judi made with wine.

MENU 1: FISH-BASED

Cream of Watercress Soup with a Toasted Walnut
Garnish (page 18)
Délices of Salmon under a Sun-dried Tomato Crust with
a Basil Cream Sauce (page 107)
Doris's German Cucumber Salad (page 200)
Shades of Green Tossed Salad (page 189)
New potatoes
Healthy Somerset Apple Cake (page 256)

283

MENU 2: MEAT-BASED

Chopped Egg and Onion (page 38)
Beef and Sweet Carrot Casserole with Dumpling
(*Tsimmes mit Halke*) (page 154)
Raspberry and Redcurrant Compôte (*Kissel*) (page 234)
Great-Grandma's Featherlight Lemon Biscuits (page 262)

MENU 3: CHICKEN-BASED

Tuscan Bean Soup with a Parsley Pesto (page 30)
Biblical Chicken in an Orange, Honey and Raisin Sauce
(page 132)
Golden Persian Rice (page 207)
Viennese Apple Squares with Cinnamon-scented Cream
(page 243)

Succot

THIS IS YET ANOTHER HARVEST FESTIVAL, ONE OF THREE IN THE Jewish year. The theme is stuffed foods, using vegetables such as aubergine, vine leaves or cabbage leaves, full to bursting with savoury mixtures. Then there are the strudels, some using ready-rolled pastry such as Evelyn's Savoury Beef Strudel studded with pine kernels.

MENU 1: FISH-BASED

With drinks: French Cheese Puffs (page 48)
Fresh Salmon Strudel Perfumed with Dill (page 94)
Baby Spinach with Nuts and Raisins (page 177)
Layered Potato Bake with Garlic and Black Pepper
(page 171)
Sticky Toffee Pavlova (page 226)

MENU 2: MEAT-BASED

Fresh Figs and Melon with a Mint and Citrus Dressing
(page 45)
Beef-filled Cabbage Leaves in a Sweet-and-sour Sauce
(*Holishkes*) (page 142)
Creamy Puff Perfect Mashed Potatoes (page 173)
Classic Apple Pie (page 241)

MENU 3: MEAT-BASED

Spanish Slim-line Red Pepper Soup (page 26)
Savory Beef Strudel with Pine Kernels (page 138)
Quinoa Pilaf with Raisins (page 216)
Israeli-Style Courgettes (page 180)
Country Peach and Nectarine Pie (page 231)

285

Hanukkah

SWEET DISHES SUCH AS OLD-FASHIONED CHOCOLATE SWIRL
Cake are among the goodies of this happy festival, celebrating the
defeat of the Greeks by Judas Maccabeus and his troops. There's a
miracle, also, to celebrate—the tiny vial of sacred oil that lasted for
eight days instead of one, so that the everlasting lamp in the Temple
never went out. So oil is a main theme of the festival—hence fried
foods like potato latkes and the more unusual Israeli Cream Cheese
Pancakes (*Chremslach*) (page 63) for those who want something a little lighter.

Purim

A WONDERFUL STORY OF A KING AND HIS BEAUTIFUL JEWISH queen, Esther, and of her uncle Mordecai, who discovered a plot to murder the Jews of Persia, thought up by the wicked vizier Haman who planned to line his pockets with Jewish gold. The story ends happily (though not for Haman).

For centuries at this festival all kinds of sweet things have been baked or fried in Jewish homes, using chickpeas, poppy or sesame seeds (to represent coins of gold) and triangular pastries ('Haman's pockets') in celebration of his overthrow. So Evelyn suggests Sephardi Cheese Puffs (page 47), crescents of fragile puff pastry coated with sesame seeds enclosing a tangy cheese filling, while Judi recommends Luscious Lemon Drizzle Cake (page 251), spiked with poppy seeds.

GLOSSARY OF YIDDISH
AND HEBREW TERMS

Blintzes. Crêpes

Challah. (Pronounced hall-ah.) Traditional bread, enriched with egg, usually in a plait or spiral

Eingemacht. Home-made (referring to a sweet preserve)

Forspeise. Tasty appetisers

Gedaempte. Braised slowly

Gefilte. Filled or stuffed (referring to a raw fish mixture which was originally 'stuffed' back in the skin of the fish—originally carp)

Gribenes. 'Crackling' made with the fatty skin of chicken

Hackbrattle. Wooden board with sides

Hackmesser. Wooden- or metal-handled chopping knife

Der heim. Former home of immigrant Jews, usually in Eastern Europe

Heimishe. Traditional, home-made

Kaes. Cream cheese made from naturally soured milk

Kichel. Traditional biscuit, often made with oil

Kichlach. Plural of kichel—see above

Kuchen. Cake, usually referring to those made with yeast or (as a substitute) baking powder

Kugel. Baked pudding usually made with eggs and fat, together with noodles, vegetables, grains or fruit

Lekach. Special cake, usually honey cake, baked at New Year

Litvak. Jew whose family originally came from Lithuania

Lokshen. Egg noodles

Matzah. Unleavened bread

Matzah meal. Meal made from crushed matzah. Used as coating (for fish, for example), as a 'binder' for fish and meat balls and as a substitute for flour in Passover baking

Milchik(e). Dairy

Parev. Neither milk nor meat

Rebeizen. Hand grater

Roumanische. Originating in Romania—usually referring to style of cooking

288

Schmaltz. Fat—usually referring to chicken fat or herring, such
as *schmalz (matjes)* herring

Shtetl. Village in Pale of Settlement where Jews were confined by
Russian authorities before the 1918 Revolution

Smetana. The soured cream skimmed off the top of the soured
milk used to make cream cheese

Strudel. Sweet or savoury dish using pastry of some kind to roll
around a filling such as ground meat or apple

INDEX

in Grandma's *lokshen* kugel,
72–73
with Parmesan and walnuts,
Austrian, 80
roasted buckwheat with, 213
in tahini sauce, Hong Kong
style, 78–79
wheat-free, 73
see also pasta
nut(s), 103
baby spinach with raisins and,
177
toasted, carrot and raisin salad,
Moroccan-style, 198
see also specific nuts
nut oils, 197
nutty butter crisps, 266

olive, sun-dried tomato and basil
torte, Provençal, 61–62
olive oil, 168, 192
herbed, baby potatoes roasted
in, 172
omelette, Tunisian baked, with
tomatoes and aubergine,
56–57
onion(s), 31, 60
and egg, chopped, 38
tarte from Alsace, 59–60
orange:
and endive salad with
chrysanthemum petals,
199
honey and raisin sauce, biblical
chicken in, 132–33
liqueur soufflé, 246–48
-scented lamb ragoût, 164–65

paella, with chicken, 214–15
pancakes, Israeli cream cheese,
63
Parmesan, Austrian noodles with
walnuts and, 80
Passover menus, 280–81
pasta, 70–85
bow tie, with cream cheese and
walnuts, 81
bulgur and vermicelli pilaf,
220
shells with a mushroom and
mozzarella filling, baked,
74–75
see also noodles

pâté:
chopped egg and onion, 38
courgette, 39
see also liver, chopped
Pavlova, sticky toffee, 226–28
peach(es):
and nectarine pie, country, 231
perfumed with muscatel and
flower petals, 239–40
pear(s):
chicken liver pâté with a citrus
and redcurrant sauce and,
36–37
tarte, caramel glazed upside-
down, 232–33
peas and cucumber with shallots,
minted, 176
pecan(s):
and banana loaf, 260–61
coating, crushed, smoked
salmon roulade with,
42–43
glazed, California salad with
raspberries and, 52–53
peppers:
marinated roast, 188–89
red, soup, Spanish slim-line,
26–27
skinning of, 27
pickles, Grandpa Rose's, 203–4
pie:
classic apple, 241–42
country peach and nectarine,
231
immigrant's fish, 98–99
pilaf:
bulgur and vermicelli, 220
quinoa with raisins, 216
pineapple and coriander salsa,
grilled chicken in a lime
and chicken marinade
with, 130–31
pine nuts, savoury beef strudel
with, 138–39
pistachios, Armenian apricot
mousse with, 245
potato(es):
baby, roasted in herbed olive
oil, 172
bake, layered, with garlic and
black pepper, 171
creamy puff perfect mashed,
173

no-fat crispy roast, and fat-free
chips, 169–70
salad, perfect, 194–95
slow-cooked chicken on a bed
of, 114–15
Swedish 'fan', 168–69
pudding, old-style apple and
almond, 267
Purim menu, 287

quinoa pilaf with raisins, 216

raisin(s):
baby spinach with nuts and,
177
carrot and toasted nut salad,
Moroccan-style, 198
orange and honey sauce,
biblical chicken in, 132–33
quinoa pilaf with, 216
raspberry(ies):
California salad with glazed
pecans and, 52–53
and redcurrant compote,
234–35
redcurrant:
and citrus sauce, chicken liver
pâté with pears and,
36–37
and raspberry compôte,
234–35
rice, 206, 209
golden Persian, 207–9
paella with chicken, 214–15
seven spice Indian pilau,
217–18
risotto, fresh asparagus and
saffron, 210–12
Rosh Hashanah menus, 283–84

salad, 186–205
California, with raspberries and
glazed pecans, 52–53
Doris's German cucumber, 200
fennel, almond, and grape, 193
Israeli minted tomato and
cucumber, 191–92
jewelled three-bean, 205
melon, cucumber and
strawberry, with a fat-free
dressing, 201–2
Moroccan-style carrot, raisin,
and toasted nut, 198

293